THE MOST REQUESTED ALABAMA RESTAURANT RECIPES
PAST & PRESENT

THE MOST REQUESTED ALABAMA RESTAURANT RECIPES PAST & PRESENT

MARTIE DUNCAN

FUELED BY ALABAMA NATURAL GAS

On the Cover:
Top row: Coconut Shrimp at King Neptune's (158), Alabama Bushwacker at Flora-Bama (36). Middle row: Tomato Salad at Hot And Hot Fish Club (119), Lucy Buffet's Famous Seafood Gumbo at LuLu's Gulf Shores (124), Pimento Cheese Biscuits at Buzzcatz Bakery & Sweets (78). Last row: Big Bob Gibson BBQ Original White Sauce (76), Freight House Strawberry Cake (194).

Disclaimer:
Recipes are submitted by the restaurants and chefs indicated and may not be reproduced or reprinted without written permission. Images may not be used without written permission.

Published By:
Advance Local

Copyright © 2018 Advance Local. All rights reserved.

Reviewers and writers of magazine and newspaper articles may quote from this book, with attribution, as needed for their work. Otherwise, no part of this book may be reproduced in any form or by any means, electronic or mechanical, including photocopying, recording, or by any information storage and retrieval system, without written permission of the publisher and author.

Library of Congress Control Number: Applied for.

ISBN: 9781575710013

To order copies of this book, please contact:
Advance Local
Carl Bates
1731 1st Avenue North
Birmingham, Alabama 35203
cbates@advancelocal.com
205-325-2237

For appearances or book signings with the author: info@alabamacravings.com

To the Alabama Natural Gas Association, thank you for making my dream a reality and for helping me shine a light on Alabama's restaurants and our vast food heritage.

Dedicated to all the people who make Alabama's restaurants so amazing: the front of the house, the back of the house, the owners, and the families who sacrifice, toil, sweat, and bleed in their relentless pursuit of perfection. You greet us with kindness, patiently serve us with grace under pressure, and make the whole thing seem effortless—all while keeping our tea glasses filled. Thank you for your hospitality and for sharing your cherished recipes.

Since y'all asked...

We did it! Fans of *Magic City Cravings*, my previous cookbook about Birmingham's best food, asked for an Alabama version featuring recipes from restaurants around the state. It was a huge and delicious undertaking.

As I look over the numbers, I am astonished—4 months on the road, 4,232 miles driven, 92 restaurants visited, and over 460 dishes, drinks, and desserts sampled along the way. I am also astonished that I only gained 6 pounds. I ate Alabama. Literally. Using your requests and suggestions as a guide, I traveled the state with photographer Mo Davis in search of the recipes you asked me to track down. And I got almost everything on the list.

Food is everything in Alabama. We celebrate with it. We mourn with it. We talk about it, almost non-stop. On vacation, you are not from Alabama if you don't start talking about where you're going for lunch while you're still eating breakfast.

I'm certain that few of us consider the labor of love behind the food that shows up on our plates when we order at a restaurant. Acre's David Bancroft might have two smokers going at dawn for a special that day. JoAnn Gunner, the head pie maker at Big Bob Gibson's in Decatur, makes hundreds of pies in a single day...and over a thousand during the week of Thanksgiving. SpringHouse's Rob McDaniel and his staff will often have a full restaurant and serve dinner for 300 wedding guests at the same time. Mrs. Betty Kennedy still hand-cuts the steaks she serves at Gaines Ridge Dinner Club. And Dolester Miles, the country's top pastry chef according to the James Beard Foundation, and her pastry team arrive before daylight to make her famous coconut cakes (recipe on page 191) for Birmingham's four Stitt restaurants. These amazing folks and their peers across the state—the chefs, the bakers, butchers, line cooks, bartenders, dish washers, hosts, and servers—are the true heroes of Alabama food.

It requires an all-consuming passion to create, craft, cook, bake, smoke, fry, and grill the very best food they can for their customers. It isn't a job. It's a way of life, and I am so privileged to be able to share the recipes and tell some of their stories, too. Even if you never cook any of the recipes in the book, I hope you will make a reservation at one the many wonderful restaurants featured within these pages. And please tell them I sent you.

xo
Martie

4,232 miles

63 counties

92 restaurants

468 dishes

3,868 photos

6 pounds gained

1,000+ songs

100+ wrong turns

1 Million memories

Priceless...

VOYAGERS RESTAURANT AT PERDIDO BEACH RESORT | Orange Beach
45-Day Aged Ribeye with Root Vegetable Gratin | Chef Brody Olive

TABLE *of* CONTENTS

James Beard Winners & Nominees 7

Restaurants by City & Map 10

Famous Folks Crave 12

Martie's Alabama Playlist 26

Cocktails 30

Appetizers & Snacks 50

Sauces, Sides & Breads 74

Soups, Salads, Sandwiches & Stews 98

Main Courses 140

Desserts 186

Gone But Not Forgotten 222

Index 230

Contributors 236

You bring the passion. We bring the energy.

We're proud to play a part in inspiring moments of connection and creativity in homes throughout Alabama.

JAMES BEARD FOUNDATION AWARDS

The James Beard Foundation, a culinary organization dedicated to excellence in the culinary arts, presents their "Oscars" each year honoring elite restaurants and chefs who have reached the pinnacle of their profession. In 2018, Birmingham's Highlands Bar and Grill was awarded the organization's highest honor when it was named the most outstanding restaurant in America. Highlands' Dolester Miles was also recognized as the country's Best Pastry Chef.

Alabama's list of winners, nominees, and semi-finalists include:

2018

David Bancroft | Acre
Best Chef: South
Semi-finalist
Auburn, Alabama

Bill Briand | Fisher's Upstairs at Orange Beach Marina
Best Chef: South
Semi-finalist
Orange Beach, Alabama

Highlands Bar and Grill
Outstanding Restaurant
Winner
Birmingham, Alabama

Dolester Miles | Highlands Bar and Grill
Outstanding Pastry Chef
Winner
Birmingham, Alabama

Southern National
Best New Restaurant
Semi-finalist
Mobile, Alabama

The Atomic Bar and Lounge
Outstanding Bar Program
Semi-finalist
Birmingham, Alabama

2017

David Bancroft | Acre
Best Chef: South
Semi-finalist
Auburn, Alabama

Bill Briand | Fisher's Upstairs at Orange Beach Marina
Best Chef: South
Semi-finalist
Orange Beach, Alabama

Highlands Bar and Grill
Outstanding Restaurant
Nominee
Birmingham, Alabama

Rob McDaniel | SpringHouse
Best Chef: South
Semi-finalist
Alexander City, Alabama

Dolester Miles | Highlands Bar and Grill
Outstanding Pastry Chef
Nominee
Birmingham, Alabama

2016

David Bancroft | Acre
Best Chef: South
Semi-finalist
Auburn, Alabama

Bill Briand | Fisher's Upstairs at Orange Beach Marina
Best Chef: South
Semi-finalist
Orange Beach, Alabama

Highlands Bar and Grill
Outstanding Restaurant
Nominee
Birmingham, Alabama

Rob McDaniel | SpringHouse
Best Chef: South
Semi-finalist
Alexander City, Alabama

Dolester Miles | Highlands Bar and Grill
Outstanding Pastry Chef
Nominee
Birmingham, Alabama

2015

Highlands Bar and Grill
Outstanding Restaurant
Nominee
Birmingham, Alabama

Rob McDaniel | SpringHouse
Best Chef: South
Semi-finalist
Alexander City, Alabama

Dolester Miles | Highlands Bar and Grill
Outstanding Pastry Chef
Semi-finalist
Birmingham, Alabama

Chris and Anna Newsome | Ollie Irene
Best Chef: South
Semi-finalist
Birmingham, Alabama

Nick Pihakis | Jim 'N Nick's Bar-B-Q
Outstanding Restaurateur
Semi-finalist
Birmingham, Alabama

2014

Highlands Bar and Grill
Outstanding Restaurant
Nominee
Birmingham, Alabama

Rob McDaniel | SpringHouse
Best Chef: South
Semi-finalist
Alexander City, Alabama

Dolester Miles | Highlands Bar and Grill
Outstanding Pastry Chef
Semi-finalist
Birmingham, Alabama

Nick Pihakis | Jim 'N Nick's Bar-B-Q
Outstanding Restaurateur
Semi-finalist
Birmingham, Alabama

2013

Highlands Bar and Grill
Outstanding Restaurant
Nominee
Birmingham, Alabama

James Lewis | Bettola
Best Chef: South
Semi-finalist
Birmingham, Alabama

Rob McDaniel | SpringHouse
Best Chef: South
Semi-finalist
Alexander City, Alabama

Nick Pihakis | Jim 'N Nick's Bar-B-Q
Outstanding Restaurateur
Semi-finalist
Birmingham, Alabama

2012

Christopher Hastings | Hot and Hot Fish Club
Best Chef: South
Winner
Birmingham, Alabama

Highlands Bar and Grill
Outstanding Restaurant
Nominee
Birmingham, Alabama

James Lewis | Bettola
Best Chef: South
Semi-finalist
Birmingham, Alabama

Ollie Irene
Best New Restaurant
Semi-finalist
Mountain Brook, Alabama

Nick Pihakis | Jim 'N Nick's Bar-B-Q
Outstanding Restaurateur
Semi-finalist
Birmingham, Alabama

Wesley True | True
Best Chef: South
Semi-finalist
Mobile, Alabama

2011

Chris Dupont | Café Dupont
Best Chef: South
Semi-finalist
Birmingham, Alabama

Christopher Hastings | Hot and Hot Fish Club
Best Chef: South
Nominee
Birmingham, Alabama

Highlands Bar and Grill
Outstanding Restaurant
Nominee
Birmingham, Alabama

Nick Pihakis | Jim 'N Nick's Bar-B-Q
Outstanding Restaurateur
Semi-finalist
Birmingham, Alabama

Frank Stitt | Highlands Bar and Grill
Outstanding Chef
Semi-finalist
Birmingham, Alabama

Frank Stitt
Who's Who of Food and Beverage in America
Winner
Birmingham, Alabama

Wesley True | True
Best Chef: South
Semi-finalist
Mobile, Alabama

2010

Stacey Craig, Jimmy Koikos, Nicky Koikos | The Bright Star
America's Classics
Winner
Bessemer, Alabama

Christopher Hastings | Hot and Hot Fish Club
Best Chef: South
Nominee
Birmingham, Alabama

Highlands Bar and Grill
Outstanding Restaurant
Nominee
Birmingham, Alabama

Nick Pihakis | Jim 'N Nick's Bar-B-Q
Outstanding Restaurateur
Semi-finalist
Birmingham, Alabama

Frank Stitt | Highlands Bar and Grill
Outstanding Chef
Semi-finalist
Birmingham, Alabama

2009

Christopher Hastings | Hot and Hot Fish Club
Best Chef: South
Semi-finalist
Birmingham, Alabama

Highlands Bar and Grill
Outstanding Restaurant
Nominee
Birmingham, Alabama

Frank Stitt | Highlands Bar and Grill
Outstanding Chef
Semi-finalist
Birmingham, Alabama

2008

Christopher Hastings | Hot and Hot Fish Club
Best Chef: South
Nominee
Birmingham, Alabama

Frank Stitt | Highlands Bar and Grill
Outstanding Chef
Nominee
Birmingham, Alabama

2007

Christopher Hastings | Hot and Hot Fish Club
Best Chef: South
Nominee
Birmingham, Alabama

2006

Frank Stitt | Highlands Bar and Grill
Best Chef: Southeast
Winner
Birmingham, Alabama

2001

Frank Stitt | Highlands Bar and Grill
Best Chef: Southeast
Winner
Birmingham, Alabama

2000

Frank Stitt | Highlands Bar and Grill
Best Chef: Southeast
Nominee
Birmingham, Alabama

DOWNTOWN MENTONE

Martie's Alabama
RESTAURANT ROAD TRIP

★ **ABBEVILLE**
Huggin' Molly's, 162

★ **ALABASTER**
Full Moon Bar-B-Que, 196
Jim 'N Nick's BBQ, 84

★ **ALEXANDER CITY**
SpringHouse, 64, 66

★ **ANNISTON**
Classic on Noble, 153
Top O' The River, 90

★ **AUBURN**
Acre, 32, 52
Ariccia Trattoria, 146
Baumhower's Victory Grille, 54
Jim 'N Nick's BBQ, 84
Steel City Pops, 218
The Depot, 176
The Hound, 70

★ **BESSEMER**
The Bright Star, 174

★ **BIRMINGHAM**
Baumhower's Victory Grille, 54
Big Spoon Creamery, 188
Bistro V, 148
Bottega & Bottega Café, 190
Brick and Tin, 108
Chez Fonfon, 48
Dyron's Lowcountry, 154
Full Moon Bar-B-Que, 196
Highlands Bar & Grill, 100
Homewood Gourmet, 116
Hot and Hot Fish Club, 118
Jim 'N Nick's BBQ, 84
John's City Diner, 86
Little Savannah Restaurant and Bar, 200
Melt, 128
Niki's West, 206
Ocean, 164
Post Office Pies, 130
Saw's Soul Kitchen, 168
Steel City Pops, 218
The Atomic Bar and Lounge, 42

★ **CAMDEN**
Gaines Ridge Dinner Club, 198

★ **CULLMAN**
Jim 'N Nick's BBQ, 84

★ **DAPHNE**
Baumhower's Victory Grille, 54
Guido's, 60
Southwood Kitchen, 134

★ **DECATUR**
Big Bob Gibson's Bar-B-Q, 76
Curry's on Johnston Street, 112

★ **DOTHAN**
Full Moon Bar-B-Que, 196
Hunt's Seafood Restaurant and Oyster Bar, 62
Zack's Family Restaurant, 216

★ **ELKMONT**
Belle Chevré Cheese Shop and Tasting Room, 56

★ **FAIRHOPE/ POINT CLEAR**
Grand Hotel Golf Resort & Spa, 38
Panini Pete's, 210
Sunset Pointe, 40, 136
Wash House Restaurant, 220

★ **FLORENCE**
Odette, 88
Ray's at the Bank, 132, 212
Ricatoni's, 166
The Factory Café at Alabama Chanin, 105

★ **FOLEY**
Wolf Bay Lodge, 184

★ **FULTONDALE**
Full Moon Bar-B-Que, 196

★ **GADSDEN**
Top O' The River, 90

★ **GARDENDALE**
Jim 'N Nick's BBQ, 84

★ **GREENSBORO**
Pie Lab, 208

★ **GULF SHORES**
King Neptune's Seafood Restaurant, 158
Lulu's Gulf Shores, 124, 126
The Hangout, 44

★ **GUNTERSVILLE**
Top O' The River, 90

★ **HARTSELLE**
Freight House, 194

★ **HUNTSVILLE**
Baumhower's Victory Grille, 54
Below the Radar Brewing Company, 180
Commerce Kitchen, 192
Cotton Row Restaurant, 142
Hildegard's German Cuisine, 160
Jim 'N Nick's BBQ, 84
Steel City Pops, 218

★ **IRONDALE**
Irondale Café, 82

★ **JASPER**
Full Moon Bar-B-Que, 196
Jim 'N Nick's BBQ, 84

★ **LAKE MARTIN**
SpringHouse, 64, 66

★ **LAVACA**
Ezell's Fish Camp, 80

★ **MENTONE**
Wildflower Café, 214

★ **MOBILE**
Baumhower's Victory Grille, 54
Dauphin's, 114
Dauphin's Bar 424, 35
Panini Pete's, 210
Southern National, 172
The Noble South, 72
The Trellis Room at the Battle House Hotel, 145

★ **MONTGOMERY**
Baumhower's Victory Grille, 54
Central, 150
Full Moon Bar-B-Que, 196
Jim 'N Nick's BBQ, 84
Martin's Restaurant, 202
Vintage Year, 92

★ **MUSCLE SHOALS – SHEFFIELD**
Champy's Famous Fried Chicken, 110

★ **NEW MARKET**
New Market BBQ, 204

★ **OPELIKA**
Full Moon Bar-B-Que, 196

★ **ORANGE BEACH**
Buzzcatz Coffee & Sweets, 78
Fisher's at Orange Beach Marina, 157
Flora-Bama Lounge, Package & Oyster Bar, 36
Playa, 68
The Gulf, 46
Voyagers at Perdido Beach Resort, 182
Wolf Bay Lodge, 184

★ **PRATTVILLE**
Jim 'N Nick's BBQ, 84

★ **SPANISH FORT**
Ed's Seafood Shed, 122

★ **THEODORE**
Bayley's Seafood Restaurant, 107

★ **TRUSSVILLE**
Crazy Horse, 58
Full Moon Bar-B-Que, 196
Jim 'N Nick's BBQ, 84

★ **TUSCALOOSA**
Baumhower's Victory Grille, 54
Full Moon Bar-B-Que, 196
Jim 'N Nick's BBQ, 84
Steel City Pops, 218
The Waysider, 94

Caroline Ward Sayre, artist | Hometown: Montgomery

Life is made better by food.

I've said it before and I'll say it again: We put up with a lot to live where we do. The summers are oppressively hot and those of us on the coast have been raised to keep a watchful eye on the Gulf of Mexico at all times. Depending on where you live, winters can be equally as bad, especially if you have ever attempted to drive up Monte Sano Mountain in the snow. And who can forget the constant threat of being toted off by a horde of rampaging mosquitoes, deer flies and no-see-'ums.

Why, then, do we live here? That's easy—for the food. A mess of fresh Gulf shrimp or a bushel of fresh-picked Silver King corn can go a long way toward making our home feel a little more like home. Or a pile of succulent Chilton County peaches and a tote sack of Bon Secour oysters will make even the warmest day seem cooler.

I'm speaking, of course, for myself. But I'm certain that a goodly number of you agree that life in the Yellowhammer State is made better by food. We are more than happy to put up with a bit of inconvenience for the sake of a good meal. I have written often of the restorative power of food—how it acts as a balm for our blistered souls and binds communities together in a way that politicians can only dream of. We continue to have our differences (Roll Tide/War Eagle), but we are joined by our collective desire for a good meal. It's one thing to argue over the Iron Bowl, but it's something else altogether to argue over who gets the last piece of fried chicken. (I never win that argument, by the way.)

So, as we pause to celebrate the majesty of Alabama's culinary past and present, I am especially thankful that we live in a state where food can bring us together in ways that some folks may not understand. Yes, we put up with a lot to live here, but we are also fortunate to live in a state where the only real debate worth having is whether to serve biscuits or cornbread for supper.

You know my answer on that one—cornbread.

Since 1998, David Holloway has explored Alabama's culinary backroads and byways with a knife, fork, and a notepad. He writes a weekly food-related column for AL.com, *Mobile Press-Register*, *Birmingham News*, and *Huntsville Times*.

Alabama Cravings

FAMOUS FOLKS CRAVE...

I have discovered if you ever want to break the ice or get somebody talking, bring up food. More specifically, bring up the food they were raised on. Asking somebody what food their mama made or what Alabama food they crave most will even get super-famous folks to answer your e-mail and talk to you on the phone.

Thank you to some of our most celebrated native sons and daughters for taking the time to share your favorite Alabama cravings with me. It makes me smile to know a little more about you—and it makes me feel like what those Yankees say about us might be true. We really are all kin to each other—through our food.

xo
Martie

"You won't find in these pages a recipe for my **grandmother's biscuit**. Notice I use the singular form of the word. Outside the cities of Alabama, biscuits have always been referred to as 'biscuit,' as in: Lord, don't that girl know how to make good biscuit, or "We'll be eatin' just soon as the biscuit's done." I believe this linguistic curiosity arises from the fact that, in the country places, biscuit has always constituted its own separate food group. We ate biscuit with breakfast, dinner, and supper. Alone or with butter or fig preserves or scuppernong jelly. Stuffed with salty-sweet country ham or peppery patty sausage from Conecuh County. When a finger-hole was poked in the side and filled with sorghum syrup, a biscuit became a "boley holey," a kind of portable dessert, the Alabama equivalent of a Twinkie. Sometimes biscuit was crumbled in milk, and eaten with a spoon. Sometimes on a Sunday the biscuit dough was rolled out flat, cut into little crinkle-edged strips, and lodged deep inside a chicken pie, where it magically transformed itself into a dumpling. The reason you won't find my grandmother's recipe for biscuit is that she never worked from a recipe. She just knew how to do it."

MARK CHILDRESS, author
Hometown: Monroeville

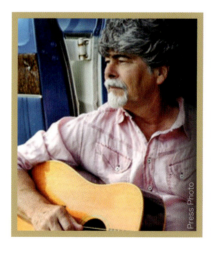

"My sister's and granny's (my Moma's) **biscuits**; Moma's are cathead; sister's are equally incredible: and amazingly edible!!! Now, if you add some homemade butter and sorghum to those hot biscuits, they are even better!"

RANDY OWEN, lead singer, Alabama (Country Music Hall of Fame, Alabama Music Hall of Fame)
Hometown: Fort Payne

"Love, love **Taco Casa**. It was a frequent Chi O (sorority) meal spot when I was at 'Bama. It takes me right back to college days, and to this day, whenever I drive through Tuscaloosa, Taco Casa is a must stop."

SELA WARD, Emmy award-winning actress
Hometown: Tuscaloosa (by way of Meridian, MS)

"From Pogo, Alabama, *'Mama' Ferrell's homemade Butter Roll dessert* is one of my favorites, only because she's gone and it primarily exists in my loving memory. As for what we can still enjoy every day but Sunday….I am gonna stand and brag on the hot dogs from Bunyan's BBQ in Florence. There's no explanation for how red they are but they are simply perfect and at the same time not like any other hot dog on earth. I constantly hear from fellow musicians when telling them where I'm from… "Y'all got that Hot Dog." I've bought as many as 200 at a time. My boss Jimmy Buffett has landed his plane just for this hot dog. Shoot—now I've given myself a craving and I'm 2,000 miles away."

MAC McANALLY, musician, singer, songwriter (Alabama Music Hall of Fame)
Hometown: Red Bay

"If I could get anything I wanted, it would be a *tomato sandwich* with Duke's mayonnaise and salt and pepper. And some Golden Flake barbecue potato chips and a big glass of milk. Man, that's good."

RICK BRAGG, author
Hometown: Piedmont

"Crab. There isn't anything better than soft shell crab. But if you can't get a soft shell, here's the next best thing. First, you split the crab and clean out the cavity. You fold it open, completely flat. Just use the body. Heat up a cast iron skillet and sauté that crab—just pan fry it in just a little butter and a little olive oil. Gertie Pearl used to cook crab like this on the beach at Battles Wharf when I was a kid. I never forgot it. And that's all I got to say about that." Find Jimbo and get him to take you on a Mobile Tensaw Delta tour: JimbosDeltaExcursions.com

JIMBO MEADOR, outdoorsman, Delta guide, photographer, the real Forrest Gump?
Hometown: Point Clear

"Of course, my Alabama craving is *Alabama Gulf shrimp*! You can barbecue it, boil it, broil it, bake it, sauté it. Dey's uh, shrimp-kabobs, shrimp creole, shrimp gumbo. Pan-fried, deep-fried, stir-fried. There's pineapple shrimp, lemon shrimp, coconut shrimp, pepper shrimp, shrimp soup, shrimp stew, shrimp salad, shrimp and potatoes, shrimp burger, shrimp sandwich. And always with an ice-cold beer."

WINSTON GROOM, author
Hometown: Point Clear

Famous Folks Crave | 15

Alabama Cravings

FAMOUS FOLKS CRAVE...

FAME Recording Studio founder Rick Hall, center, with grandson Jackson (L), and son Rodney (R).

"My favorite Alabama craving has got to be my parents' **homemade peach ice cream**. My mom and dad perfected the ice cream recipe over the years. The peaches need to come from Chilton County. He would drive the 3 hours to get down to Durbin's farm just to get peaches when they were in season. Nothing like it on a hot Alabama summer day."

RODNEY HALL, music producer
Hometown: Muscle Shoals

Homemade Peach Ice Cream

Hall Family recipe courtesy Rodney Hall

4 large eggs
1 cup sugar
1 teaspoon almond extract
1/2 pint whipping cream
2 cans Eagle Brand sweetened condensed milk
10-12 Chilton county peaches, peeled and diced small
Milk

Makes 1 gallon

Mix together the eggs, sugar, almond extract, whipping cream, and sweetened condensed milk in a bowl. Chill for 1 hour in the refrigerator.

When you are ready to freeze, pour the chilled mixture into an ice cream maker. Add the peaches. Add milk until the freezer is filled 3/4 full; leave room because the liquid will expand in volume as it freezes. Freeze according to manufacturer's instructions.

"Every time I'm in the kitchen, I'm really just trying to re-create my childhood. I want my kids to have the same memories I have. My mom was always cooking. She still is. She grew up cooking enough for my grampa's farm crew in South Dakota. She can whip up a casserole like nobody's business. When it came to birthdays, though, she 'contracted out.' In every birthday picture from my early years, I'm smearing cake on my face from either Savage's Bakery or Waite's (had to be coconut). We are STILL talking about those **coconut cakes**! My parents made me try all of their favorites in Birmingham: Coleslaw at John's, egg rolls at Joy Young, those little steak biscuits at Ireland's, beer cheese soup at Baby Doe's, and milk shakes at the Spinning Wheel. The orange rolls at All-Steak in Cullman or The Club in Birmingham make my list of favorites, too. Isn't it incredible how just one taste can trigger so many incredible memories?"

ANDREA LINDENBERG, journalist, talk show host
Hometown: Birmingham

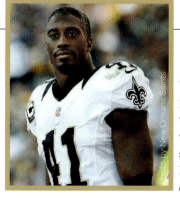

"I crave my **mama's fried pork chops**. I'd know she was going to make them when I saw her cast iron skillet out on the stove, so I wouldn't eat all day, so I could save up to eat 8 of those things. Man, now I'm hungry!"

ROMAN HARPER, Former University of Alabama & NFL football player
Hometown: Prattville

"We lived on a residential street in eastern Birmingham where summers were spent looking for adventure in the neighborhood. One summer, I spotted millions of plump, blackish-red berries. They were beautiful and miraculous, and I ran inside to show my mother. She said they were **blackberries**, handed me a small bucket, and said if I could fill it, she'd make a pie. She emphasized the 'if.' I'm sure her bet was placed on the thorns wearing me down. I went back out and in the thorny, prickly shadows, fell in love. That pie hooked me—I'm helpless against anything blackberry. I can't make biscuits without making a pot of blackberry preserves with nothing but sugar and a squeeze of lemon. I remember the glistening crystals of sugar my mother had sprinkled over the crust of that first pie, and I thought it was the prettiest pie I'd ever seen. I was transfixed by blackberries off the branch, but it was the sugar and heat and berry juices bubbling and thickening and conspiring, that completely did me in."

BIANCA "BIBI" BORGES HENRY, chef
NBC Today, *PBS Milk Street* Season 2
Hometown: Birmingham

Bibi was my classmate at Birmingham's Banks High School. Martie

"As a Gulf Coast gal living at the Southern-most edge of Sweet Home Alabama, I am mightily blessed. Just a few miles inland from the Gulf of Mexico, Baldwin County sports some of the most prodigious farmland in the entire country. The black dirt fields lining miles of two-lane country roads yield luscious summer harvests including Silver Queen corn, soybeans, and acres of red-skinned new potatoes grown by farming families for generations. Sprinkled among these large tracts are private homes on a few acres, many of them sporting wonderful kitchen gardens full of okra, home-grown tomatoes, all kinds of peas and pole beans and almost always, there is a gorgeous **watermelon** patch, slap on the edge of the property, next to the road.

As a mischievous teen, it was common practice for my "pack" of pals to dare each other to poach one of the huge succulent melons peeking through shiny green ribbons of vines, when passing a patch. Chain smoking Tareytons and slurping Icees, we'd inevitably spot a row of ripe melons and one of us would holler, 'Stop the car!' The bravest of the bunch or in hindsight, maybe the baddest, would sprint into the field and snatch the best looking, most humongous melon she could find. Then, we would high tail it down the road, our adrenaline pumping in fear, relief, and heavenly anticipation.

Straight to a friend's home on Mobile Bay we would speed, sneaking around the outside of the house to the end of their pier. There were no knives, plates, napkins or finery. Just a gray weathered walkway and a ripe melon. With childlike delight, we simply dropped that melon onto the pier, 'bustin it wide open' and scooped the brilliant red fruit out with our bare hands, plucking the sweet fruit promptly in to our salivating mouths. Oh my! The taste was sublime. Super sweet yet sill warmish from the constant midday sun in the field, it quenched our parched throats. The juice, sliding down our arms to our elbows and covering our chins, was the badge of courage we wore for our stolen treasure. Afterwards, full of watermelon and even more full of our young selves, we would jump into the Bay, washing away the sticky and frolic in the warm brackish water for hours, telling secrets and sharing the dreams that teenage girls dream. To this day, a bite of watermelon immediately takes me back to the wild and crazy girl I once was and just for a brief moment, I stop and bask in the glow of this honeysweet memory without a care in the world."

LUCY BUFFETT, author, restaurateur & entrepreneur
Hometown: Mobile

Alabama Cravings

FAMOUS FOLKS CRAVE...

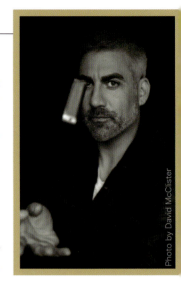

"**Hot and Sour Soup at Shangri-La Chinese** is the best I've ever had in my life. I bet you're thinking, "Why in the world would he start with Chinese food in Alabama?" My answer: Why not? It's that good, folks. This dish has saved marriages, formed unions, cured hangovers. It's nothing short of the state's Culinary Fountain of Youth, Bama's version of House of Nanking in San Francisco. (Google it.) The most difficult culinary accomplishment in this country is properly cross-pollinating the South with the Far East. Shangri-La has done just that. Insider tip: Get extra shrimp in the soup. (Did I mention it cures hangovers?)"

TAYLOR HICKS, musician, *American Idol* winner
Hometown: Birmingham

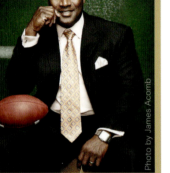

"I had nine brothers and sisters and about seven of us were at the house at any given time. **Cornbread** was a staple because there were days when we didn't have anything to eat but cornbread. I watched my mother make cornbread in an 11-pound cast iron skillet every day. The first time I made cornbread I was five and a half years old and my sister gave me a quarter, a whole quarter in 1968, to make that cornbread, and when I got that quarter, in my mind, I had more money than Jeff Bezos."

BO JACKSON, Former Auburn University and NFL football & MLB player, and entrepreneur
Hometown: Bessemer

"My favorite Alabama food memories center around growing up on a farm in McCalla. My Mama and Daddy were both amazing cooks with amazing hearts. Every week the family gathered at our house for Sunday dinner. I can still smell the **fried chicken** coming from the kitchen in that perfect cast iron skillet. To this day I compare everyone's chicken to Mamas. It's funny how food can take you right back there—right with the ones you love."

JANICE ROGERS, news anchor and producer
Hometown: McCalla

"For me in Alabama it's always been about peach **cobbler**. The cobbler from Niki's West in Birmingham has always been top notch! The only place that seems to nail the proper peaches/crust ratio. The peaches in Clanton, Alabama are world class. And anything you find at a Clanton gas station with peaches Is DELICIOUS. Chick-Fil-A used to have a GREAT peach milkshake. But now it's gone. I cry myself to sleep about it every night."

ROY WOOD, Jr., comedian and correspondent for *The Daily Show* on Comedy Central. Find him at RoyWoodJr.com
Hometown: Birmingham

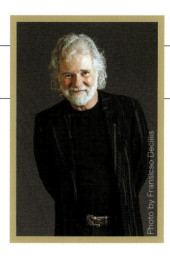

"When I think of craving food from my home state of Alabama, I think of black-eyed peas, butter beans, collard greens, cornbread, mac and cheese, country-fried steak (or maybe fried chicken), rice and gravy, and sweet tea. Maybe peach cobbler for dessert. Then a nice nap. Ahhhh."

CHUCK LEAVELL, musician (Alabama Music Hall of Fame)
Hometown: Birmingham

"I'm a transplant from south Louisiana and we've got many a food cravings from that side of the family. When I moved to Alabama, I was introduced to white sauce and pulled pork, which has become a weekly staple in the appetite. There are various versions around the state, but it never seems to disappoint."

BILLY REID, fashion designer
Hometown: Florence

I knew anyone who would design a baseball cap with a gravy boat on it certainly had an Alabama craving I needed to know about for this book. Martie

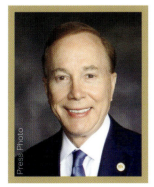

"When my twin sister and I were about 10, our family would occasionally ride with Daddy to go to Birmingham where my grandfather was in the independent gasoline business. We liked to eat at Britling's Cafeteria since the manager was from Clay County. I ate hamburger steak, shrimp cocktail and chocolate milk. (I hope Frank Stitt doesn't see this.) My first memory of a white-tablecloth restaurant where a waiter actually wrote down our orders was upstairs at Joy Young. I always used a fork there and didn't master chopsticks until college."

LEE SENTELL, director, Alabama Department of Tourism
Hometown: Ashland

Alabama Cravings

FAMOUS FOLKS CRAVE...

"My favorite Alabama food memory is from growing up in Camden, eating my mother's congealed tuna fish salad for lunch on a hot summer day."

KAY IVEY, Alabama Governor
Hometown: Camden

"I love the Christmas season at the Governor's mansion; it is the time of year when we open the doors and invite everyone in. Taking in all the decorations, listening to Alabama musicians, and seeing the dining room table loaded with Alabama foods is the highlight of the year for me; I serve a lot of **Alabama Gulf seafood** including whole roasted fish, pickled shrimp, and a variety of Alabama's farmed oysters. Since it is the Governor's Alabama craving, there may even be a congealed tuna salad on the table this holiday season."

JIM SMITH, Alabama Executive Chef, Bravo's *Top Chef* Season 14
Hometown: Troy

Lane Cake

ALABAMA GOVERNOR'S MANSION

Recipe courtesy Alabama Executive Chef Jim Smith

Cake:

3 1/2 cups cake flour

2 teaspoons cream of tartar

2 teaspoons baking soda

1/4 teaspoon kosher salt

1 cup buttermilk, room temperature

1 teaspoon vanilla extract

2 sticks unsalted butter, room temperature

2 cups granulated sugar

8 egg whites, room temperature

Icing:

12 egg yolks, room temperature

1 1/2 cups granulated sugar

1 1/2 sticks unsalted butter, room temperature

1 1/2 cups chopped and toasted pecans

1 1/2 cups chopped golden raisins

1 1/2 cups fresh coconut, sliced very thin on a mandolin

1/2 cup good-quality Alabama whiskey

1 teaspoon vanilla extract

1/4 teaspoon salt

Makes 1 (9-inch) three layer cake This cake is best if you make it the day before you want to serve it so that the icing has time to permeate the cake.

Preheat the oven to 350° Fahrenheit. Coat 3 (9-inch) cake pans with cooking spray and set aside.

For the cake: Using a whisk and a large mixing bowl, mix the flour, cream of tartar, baking soda, and salt. In a separate bowl, combine the milk and vanilla. Set both the flour and milk mixtures aside.

Using a stand mixer fitted with the paddle attachment, beat the butter and sugar on medium speed until light and fluffy, scraping down the sides of the bowl with a rubber spatula as needed. Reduce the mixer speed to low and add the flour mixture to the butter mixture, alternating with the milk mixture, beginning and ending with the flour mixture. Beat until smooth and set aside.

Using the stand mixer fitted with the whisk attachment, whip the egg whites on medium-high speed until they form soft peaks. Using a rubber spatula, fold the egg whites into the flour mixture in three batches. Gently mix until completely combined.

Pour the batter into the prepared pans and bake at 350° 30 minutes or until the tops spring back when touched and a pick inserted in the center of the cakes comes out clean, rotating halfway through the bake. Remove from the oven and let cool on a wire rack.

For the icing: In a medium saucepan, combine the egg yolks and sugar and whisk until smooth. Add the butter and cook over medium heat, stirring constantly until the mixture coats the back of a spoon, about 5 minutes. Make sure not to overcook or boil. Add the pecans, raisins, and coconut and cook another minute. Remove from the heat, add the whiskey vanilla, and salt; let cool to room temperature.

Decorate the cake with the icing, spreading it between the stacked cake layers or on top of the mini cakes. Let stand 4 hours or overnight after decorating.

Note: The Lane Cake is the state cake of Alabama. Its roots go back to Clayton, Alabama where it is reported to have been created by Emma Rylander Lane. It found fame within the pages of Harper Lee's novel, *To Kill a Mockingbird* when, in Chapter 13, Scout relates that "Miss Maudie Atkinson baked a Lane cake so loaded with shinny it made me tight." Anyone from Alabama knows that shinny is a reference to moonshine. I doubt I need to tell anyone what Scout meant by the term "tight."

Alabama Cravings

FAMOUS FOLKS CRAVE...

"**Quail with pepper gravy and rice and collard greens**, that was one of my favorite dinners. Beddie Harris, who was our family cook, was like our Calpurnia, and she cooked it in an iron skillet, like you do fried chicken. You present the quail on a bed of rice and you pour gravy over it and put the collard greens on the side, and it's just heaven on a plate as far as I'm concerned."

MARY BADHAM, Academy Award-nominated actress, activist
Hometown: Birmingham

Spooner's favorite craving is his "mama's **biscuits and chocolate gravy** with a lot of butter on the biscuit." His wife Karen responded: "When Spooner took me to meet his mama for the first time, she made biscuits and chocolate gravy. I knew at that moment I had found my people!" Spooner: "Don't forget the butter!"

SPOONER OLDHAM, musician (Muscle Shoals Swamper, Rock and Roll Hall of Fame, Alabama Music Hall of Fame)
Hometown: Center Star

"**Banana Pudding** is my favorite Alabama dish. Growing up, I never had a birthday cake. Everyone knew to put my candles on a big dish of homemade banana pudding!"

GENE HALLMAN, CEO, Bruno Event Team
Hometown: Birmingham

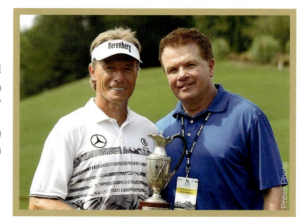

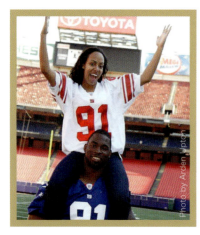

"I grew up running from the school bus to my grandmother's kitchen to watch her cook every day. She never used measuring cups. She would always say, "You only need to add love." She taught me all of her tricks; her **Red Velvet Cake** caused many fights between my cousins and me."

JUSTIN TUCK, Former University of Notre Dame and NFL professional football player with 2 Super Bowl wins (shown with his wife, Lauran)
Hometown: Kellyton

"You could smell the chicken grease for blocks away. On a back street alley just off Main Street in Roanoke, Alabama, once stood a simple white cinderblock walk-up chicken joint called Big Chick. Rain or shine there was always a line. It was **grease-soaked-through-the-paper-bag good fried chicken**. People would not even wait to drive it home. They would just sit on the curb and eat it on the spot. And though there are fine examples of that Southern staple throughout Alabama, there are none that smell like my childhood more than the Big Chick."

LELAND WHALEY, journalist, talk show host
Hometown: Roanoke

"Living in the Shoals area, we are blessed to have so many great places to eat for such a small town. My favorites are Georges Steak Pit, Bunyan's Barbeque, and Odette. If I could just find some grilled calves liver and onions my life would be complete!"

DAVID HOOD, Swamper, musician
(Alabama Music Hall of Fame)
Hometown: Sheffield

AND ONE OF MY OWN ALABAMA FOOD CRAVINGS:

"One of my favorite Alabama food cravings is from childhood—**boiled peanuts**. Every summer, we'd pack up the car and head to Panama City Beach (which I know is technically Florida) for one blissful week on the Gulf of Mexico in a cinder block house with 1 bathroom for six people and no air-conditioning. My dad would never want to stop on the drive down until we got near Dothan and there would be boiled peanut stands lining the side of the road. Dad would let us get a small bag of hot boiled peanuts and a cold drink, I'd climb back in the station wagon with my boiled peanuts and Grapico and savor those boiled peanuts for the rest of the drive. I was always told it was good luck when you got a boiled peanut with 4 good (not squishy) peanuts in the shell."

Martie

Famous Folks Crave

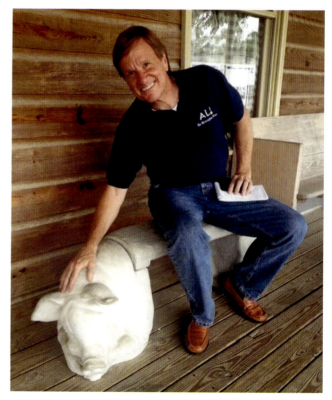

24 | Alabama Cravings

Food...the main character

I grew up in a Linden, a tiny town in Alabama's Black Belt. It had about 2,500 people back then, and it was, and still is, a long way from anywhere. It wasn't until several years later—decades, even—that I came to understand how much the food of our great state was always the main character in most of my childhood memories.

In those days, going out to eat meant a cheeseburger and a chocolate shake at the Dairy Queen down the hill from our house, or, on a special occasion, a road trip to Ezell's Fish Camp in Lavaca for fried catfish and hushpuppies. A trip to far-away Birmingham, where that big iron man kept watch over the city from the top of that steep mountain, was like going to New York City for us.

It wasn't until I went away to college in Tuscaloosa that I began to think of certain foods (i.e., vegetables) as not something that you had to eat, but something you could actually enjoy. At the City Café in Northport, where a student could get five vegetables for under two bucks after the lunch rush had died down, I cultivated a liking for turnip greens and fried okra, two vegetables that you couldn't pay me to eat as a teenager but are two of my favorites now.

When I moved to Birmingham right out of college to go to work for *The Birmingham News*, we would get our lunchtime meat-and-three fixes at the Social Grill, Andy's on the Green and La Paree, all of which were within walking distance of our downtown office but all of which, like our office building, are long since gone now.

One of our favorites, though, was the original John's Restaurant, a downtown fixture for 60 years. What I loved most about John's—and still miss the most about it—were those hot, fluffy cornbread sticks, which reminded me of when I was a little boy and would sit on the kitchen counter and help our family cook, Earlene, make the batter for "cornsticks," as I called them. Earlene would heat up a little bacon grease in the molds of a cast iron cornstick pan before she poured the batter in them, and the cornbread would practically jump out of the pan after it came out of the oven. Daddy, who I do believe ate cornbread every day of his life, would take that cornbread, crumble it up into little pieces, and soak it in the "potlikker" from Earlene's turnip greens. It was another Southern delicacy that I did not come to appreciate until I was grown.

See, I've done it again. I started reminiscing about John's cornbread, and somehow, it took me all the way back home to Linden again. My favorite memories always do.

Bob Carlton is an Alabama journalist who has written about food and culture for AL.com, *Mobile Press Register*, *Birmingham News*, and *Huntsville Times* since 1980.

Martie's ALABAMA Playlist

▶ **Sweet Home Alabama / Lynyrd Skynyrd**
The best-known song about Alabama wasn't even recorded here. Lynyrd Skynyrd pays tribute to the "Swampers" in the 4th verse of the song. Their early tracks were produced by Swamper and Sheffield native Jimmy Johnson.

▶ **I'll Take You There**/Staple Singers**
FYI: Mavis Staples is not singing "baby, little baby" as she encourages David Hood, the bass player on the track. Mavis is actually singing "David, little David," as Hood lays down one of the most memorable bass riffs ever.

▶ **Sweet Soul Music*/Arthur Conley**
I dare you not to dance.

▶ **Never Loved a Man*/Aretha Franklin**
That's Spooner Oldham on the famous electric piano intro. (Read his Alabama craving on page 22)

▶ **Keep on Truckin'/Eddie Kendricks**
Eddie's first solo #1 hit without the Temps.

▶ **When a Man Loves a Woman*/Percy Sledge (from Leighton, AL)**
Percy's anthem to loving the one your friends can't stand still rings true!

▶ **Steal Away*/Jimmy Hughes (from Leighton, AL)**
One of my all-time favs. Jimmy is Percy Sledge's cousin.

▶ **Slip Away*/Clarence Carter (from Montgomery, AL)**
This was tough. "Patches" is another great one.

▶ **Tell Mama*/Etta James**
Etta's rendition of the Clarence Carter song, "Tell Papa".

▶ **One Bad Apple*/The Osmond Brothers**
Don't judge me. I loved Donny Osmond in 1971.

▶ **Fancy*/Bobbie Gentry**
This was the first album I bought with my own money.

▶ **Hey Jude*/Duane Allman & Wilson Picket**
There's a very funny story about this song in the documentary *Muscle Shoals*.

▶ **Mustang Sally*/Wilson Pickett**
Everybody sing along: "All you wanna do is ride around, Sally. Ride, Sally, ride..."

▶ **Loan Me a Dime**/Boz Scaggs**
Duane Allman, Eddie Hinton, and Jimmy Johnson play guitar on this blues classic along with David Hood on bass and Barry Beckett on keyboards.

▶ **Brown Sugar**/Rolling Stones**
Recorded during a 3-day session in Muscle Shoals along with *Wild Horses*, which Keith wrote in the studio's bathroom. True.

▶ **Kodachrome**/Paul Simon**
Check out another funny Jimmy Johnson story about the Paul Simon Muscle Shoals sessions in the film *Muscle Shoals*.

▶ **Mainstreet**/Bob Seger**
The Swampers play on most of the B-side tracks on Seger's *Night Moves* LP.

▶ **True Love**/Glenn Frey**
Vince Gill covers this one on Muscle Shoals tribute album, *Small Town, Big Sound*.

▶ **Come and Go Blues/The Allman Brothers Band**
Produced by Decatur native Johnny Sandlin, features Birmingham native Chuck Leavell on keyboards. See Chuck's Alabama craving on page 19.

*Songs recorded at FAME **Songs recorded at Muscle Shoals Sound St

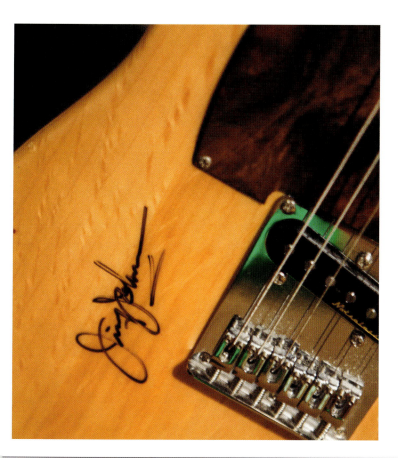

I drove a lot of miles as I ate my way around Alabama for this book. Photographer Mo Davis was with me for many of those miles. Luckily, we had the common bond of music to help pass the time. This is a playlist of some of my favorite songs with Alabama roots—songs that were either recorded in Alabama or recorded by or with artists from Alabama. Many were recorded by the 'father of the Muscle Shoals sound' Rick Hall and/or feature the Muscle Shoals Rhythm Section, session players better known as the Swampers: David Hood, Jimmy Johnson, Barry Beckett, and Roger Hawkins along with Spooner Oldham and Pete Carr.

▶ **Shake a Leg/Sea Level**
Chuck Leavell is a Birmingham native. He has been the keyboardist and music director for the Rolling Stones since 1982. Read his Alabama craving on page 19.

▶ **Easy/Commodores (from Tuskegee, AL)**
And *Brick House* because there is no other song that fills a dance floor faster.

▶ **All Night Long/Lionel Richie (from Tuskegee, AL)**
Yes, I really did sing this on stage with Lionel at my friend Stevie's birthday party.

▶ **After All These Years/Mac McAnally (from Red Bay, AL)**
Also a huge hit for Sawyer Brown. Find Mac's Alabama food craving on page 15.

▶ **Bama Breeze/Jimmy Buffett (from Mobile, AL)**
Said to have been written from some of Jimmy's experiences at the Flora-Bama. Get their Bushwacker recipe on page 37.

▶ **Old Flame/Alabama (Fort Payne, AL)**
Written by Mac McAnally & Donny Lowrey, this was Alabama's third #1 hit.

▶ **Keep on Smilin'/Wet Willie (from Mobile, AL)**
Lead singer Jimmy Hall was born in Birmingham and raised in Mobile, AL

▶ **Boulder to Birmingham/Emmylou Harris (from Birmingham, AL)**
Emmylou is the coolest girl ever—because she is from Birmingham and friends with Linda Ronstadt and Dolly.

▶ **Alabama Pines/Jason Isbell (from Green Hill, AL)**
Jason's song *Maybe It's Time* is covered by Bradley Cooper in the remake of *A Star is Born* with Lady Gaga.

▶ **Hold On/Alabama Shakes (from Athens, AL)**
Brittany Howard and the boys formed the band in Athens, Alabama, where she is from.

▶ **Done/The Band Perry (from Mobile, AL)**
Written by my friends, Birmingham songwriters John Davidson and Jacob Bryant of The Brummies—it was a #1 hit for The Band Perry.

▶ **Just My Imagination/The Temptations**
Temps Eddie Kendricks and Paul Williams are from Birmingham. Melvin Franklin is from Montgomery. When David Ruffin left the group, he was replaced by Dennis Edwards from Fairfield. Birmingham has an Eddie Kendricks Memorial Park with a sculpture tribute to The Temptations.

▶ **Renegade/Styx**
Guitar player and vocalist Tommy Shaw is from Montgomery. He wrote and sings lead on this song—the band's biggest hit.

▶ **Take Me There/Rascal Flatts**
Written by songwriter Neil Thrasher from Birmingham. Neil has also written #1 songs for Jason Aldeen, Kenny Chesney, and others.

Wanna Go?

FAME Recording Studio | Muscle Shoals
Fame2.com

Muscle Shoals South Studio | Muscle Shoals
MuscleShoalsSoundStudio.org

Alabama Music Hall of Fame | Tuscumbia
Alamhof.org

SUNSET POINTE AT FLY CREEK MARINA | Fairhope

The Atomic's mural is a riff on the iconic Sgt. Pepper's Lonely Hearts Club Band album cover. It highlights several dozen famous, infamous and coming up people in Alabama. Highlands Bar and Grill's Chef Frank Stitt is in the center.

THE ATOMIC BAR AND LOUNGE | Birmingham

Cocktails

Call Me Old-Fashioned, 33
ACRE

Thyme Out Martini, 35
DAUPHIN'S BAR 424

Alabama Bushwacker, 37
FLORA-BAMA LOUNGE, PACKAGE & OYSTER BAR

1847 Cocktail, 38
GRAND HOTEL GOLF RESORT & SPA

Lavida Royale, 41
SUNSET POINTE

Skylar Brown, 43
THE ATOMIC BAR AND LOUNGE

Shark Attack, 45
THE HANGOUT

Fresh Fruit Mojito, 47
THE GULF

French Blonde, 49
CHEZ FONFON

ACRE
Auburn

Chef & Owner David Bancroft

David Bancroft, a James Beard Award semi-finalist in the Best Chef: South category, has received a variety of accolades since opening Acre in 2013. The beautifully styled restaurant is set on an acre of land where Bancroft and his team plant and harvest many items found on their menu. Acre's robust bar program has received high praise of its own. You'll find a wide selection of craft beer on tap and a collection of signature and classic cocktails created with house-made syrups, infusions, shrubs, bitters, and garnishes from the garden. The spirited "brown water" menu includes hard-to-find bottles from Pappy Van Winkle, Four Roses, and E.H. Taylor.

DON'T MISS: The lunch specials Thursday through Saturday and Sunday Brunch. You'll find items such as Rice and Gravy, Fried Chicken Friyay, and Chicken and Waffles. Order from the snack menu: Acre Pimento Cheese, Chicken Fried Bacon (see the recipe on page 53), and Cornmeal Fried Okra with Remoulade Sauce will make you think your mom is cooking in the kitchen. The Half-Pound Hereford Beef Tenderloin alone is worth a drive to the Plains.

ACRE
210 East Glenn Avenue | Auburn, Alabama 36830
334-246-3763 | AcreAuburn.com

Call Me Old-Fashioned

ACRE

Ham-Fat Whiskey:

4 ounces aged country ham skin

1 quart Woodford Reserve bourbon

Bourbon-Cherry Simple Syrup:

1 cup bourbon-cherry juice (from 1 jar Jack Rudy Bourbon Cocktail Cherries)

1 cup distilled water

1/2 cup sugar

Ice

2 ounces Ham-Fat Whiskey (See recipe above.)

2 teaspoons Bourbon-Cherry Simple Syrup (See recipe above.)

1 dash Stirrings Blood Orange Bitters

1 Jack Rudy Bourbon Cocktail Cherry for garnish

Orange peel for garnish

Makes 1 This recipe requires 3-5 days for the bourbon to infuse properly. You may choose to make less of the bourbon or simple syrup—if you choose to make less, simply reduce the proportions.

For the Ham-Fat Whiskey: Put the ham skin in a jar with a tight-fitting lid, such as a Mason jar. Pour the Woodford over the top. Seal and age 3-5 days before use. Makes a quart of ham-fat-infused bourbon.

For the Bourbon-Cherry Simple Syrup: Bring the bourbon-cherry juice and distilled water to a simmer in a pot; remove from the heat. Stir in the sugar until dissolved. Allow to cool. This will keep in the refrigerator in a jar with a tight-fitting lid for up to 2 weeks. Makes 2 cups of simple syrup.

To serve: Add ice to a rocks glass to chill. In a shaker with a strainer, add ice, 2 ounces Ham-Fat Whiskey, 2 tablespoons Bourbon-Cherry Simple Syrup, and a dash bitters. Shake until chilled. Strain into the prepared glass. Garnish with the cherry and orange peel.

Tip

Making simple syrup is simple. The standard ratio is 1 part sugar to 1 part water. You may also substitute another sweetener for part of the sugar, as Chef Bancroft did for this recipe by adding the juice from the cherries.

DAUPHIN'S BAR 424
Mobile

Perched atop the 34th floor of Mobile's RSA Tower, Bar 424 at Dauphin's has one of the very best views you will experience anywhere in the state of Alabama. You will experience spectacular views of Mobile Bay from every angle, watch the ships on the water, and behold wonderous sunsets that streak the sky in glorious shades of magenta, gold, and scarlet. There's a grand piano so you'll often find live music; plan to meet early or stay for a nightcap after dinner. The bar program includes classic cocktails and seasonal creations with fresh ingredients. There is room for any group or occasion—perfect for a happy hour meeting or holiday party. Dauphin's cuisine is by Executive Chef Steve Zucker who has partnered with Alabama restaurant icon and Alabama football legend Bob Baumhower to bring new glory to the old Bienville Club.

DON'T MISS: Dauphin's offers weeknight happy hour drink and food specials like $2 sliders and $6 specialty cocktails in the bar.

You can sit at the bar, at one of the high-top bar tables, or secure one of the comfy lounge seating groups—it's quite the place to be after work in Mobile. Local celebrities, sports heroes, politicians, and movie folks can be found here. Try the 'Bama Buzz mixed with bourbon, ginger beer, and muddled blackberries or the Vieux Carre with rye whiskey and cognac. The Smoked Gulf Fish Dip and the Hawaiian Style Poke with Yellowfin tuna are two of the bar appetizers you'll want to try.

DAUPHIN'S BAR 424
107 St. Francis Street, Suite 9400 | Mobile, Alabama 36602
251-444-0200 | GoDauphins.com

Thyme Out Martini

DAUPHIN'S BAR 424

Thyme-Infused Simple Syrup:

1 cup water

1 cup sugar

1 large bunch fresh thyme

Juice from 3-4 lemons

Ice

3 ounces thyme lemonade (See instructions at right.)

2 ounces Ketel One Vodka

1/2 ounce Pama brand liqueur

1 ounce St-Germain elderflower liqueur

Fresh thyme sprig for garnish

Lemon slice for garnish

Makes 1

For the Thyme-Infused Simple Syrup: Add the water and sugar to a pot and bring to a boil. Remove from the heat and stir to dissolve the sugar; add the thyme and allow to cool completely. Strain to remove the thyme. Store the syrup in a glass jar; refrigerate and use as needed.

Thyme lemonade: In a small pitcher, mix the lemon juice with Thyme-Infused Simple Syrup to taste to make lemonade.

To serve: In a cocktail shaker filled with ice, add 3 ounces lemonade, the vodka, and the liqueurs; shake until well chilled and strain into a chilled martini or coupe glass. Garnish with a fresh thyme sprig and lemon slice.

Owner Bob Baumhower

Cocktails | 35

FLORA-BAMA LOUNGE, PACKAGE & OYSTER BAR

Alabama-Florida State Line near Orange Beach

Consistently voted the best beach bar in America, the sprawling Flora-Bama entertainment complex located on the state line between Florida and Alabama has inspired movies, songs, television shows, and legend since it opened in 1964. Technically, the Flora-Bama is in Perdido Key, Florida, but it is an Alabama institution. Some of the country's biggest musical acts got their start on the stages of the Flora-Bama—Jimmy Buffett among them. The Flora-Bama has become synonymous with fun in Lower Alabama. Events such as Flora-Bama's annual Interstate Mullet Toss bring 30,000+ people from around the world to watch competitors toss a mullet (the fish, not the haircut) across the state line of Florida and Alabama to see who can toss it the furthest. Each November, singer-songwriters descend on the Flora-Bama for the Frank Brown Songwriter Festival.

DON'T MISS: The Flora-Bama's Bushwhacker is Alabama's unofficial state cocktail. The restaurant sells over a million of the creamy concoctions each year, and a few of those are made for me. At the Ole River Grill, the Flora-Bama's sister restaurant across the street, you will find a wide variety of other frozen drinks. Order the popular Key Lime Colada, made with Blue Chair Bay Key Lime Rum Cream—it tastes just like key lime pie. As far as the food goes, the Flora-Bama is known for oysters, both raw and grilled and the Flora-Bama Yacht Club has quite a following for their shrimp nachos. There's something for everyone at the Flora-Bama, including a really good time.

FLORA-BAMA LOUNGE, PACKAGE & OYSTER BAR
17401 Perdido Key Drive | Pensacola, Florida 35207
251-980-5118 | FloraBama.com

Alabama Bushwacker

FLORA-BAMA LOUNGE, PACKAGE & OYSTER BAR

Chocolate syrup

2 ounces white rum, chilled

1 ounce dark rum, chilled

1 ounce spiced rum, chilled

1 ounce Amaretto, chilled

1 ounce crème de cacao, chilled

1 pint vanilla ice cream

1/2 cup milk

Whipped cream and maraschino cherries for garnish

Makes 2 The Flora-Bama makes their famous frozen drinks in massive quantities in commercial freezing units, so your results at home may taste slightly different than the original. The result is best if all the ingredients are chilled before blending. The traditional method of serving includes chocolate syrup drizzled on the inside walls of the glass.

Drizzle the interior walls of two chilled glasses with the chocolate syrup; set aside.

Using a blender: Add the rums, Amaretto, crème de cacao, ice cream, and milk to the blender. Blend on high for 10-20 seconds or until slushy.

Using an immersion blender: Add the rums, Amaretto, crème de cacao, ice cream, and milk to a tall pitcher and blend until slushy.

Using an ice cream maker: Add a pint of milk (instead of 1/2 cup) and the ice cream and spin until the milk is slushy; add the rums, Amaretto, crème de cacao, and spin until well incorporated.

Pour into the prepared glasses. Garnish with the whipped cream and cherries.

Greek Shrimp Nachos

Bacon and BBQ Fire-Roasted Oysters

1847 Cocktail

GRAND HOTEL GOLF RESORT & SPA

Honey-Mint Syrup:

1 cup water

1 cup honey

2 large bunches fresh mint leaves—a lot of mint!!

Ice

1.5 ounces Alabama Dettling cask-strength bourbon

1 ounce homemade Honey-Mint Syrup (See recipe above.)

1 ounce fresh-squeezed lemon juice

Fresh mint and lemon for garnish

Makes 1 This is the new signature cocktail for the 1847 Bar at the Grand Hotel. It is made with mint grown in the chef's garden and with Alabama's Dettling cask-strength bourbon made with Alabama corn.

For the Honey-Mint Syrup: Bring the water and honey to a boil and stir to dissolve. Remove from the heat and add the mint. (Make sure to use only leaves, not stems.) Let the mint seep until the color turns dark green, about 20 minutes. Strain into a glass container with a lid; cover and chill. The syrup will keep for 1-2 weeks in the refrigerator and is also lovely as a sweetener for iced tea.

To serve: Add ice to a rocks glass. Add the bourbon, Honey-Mint Syrup, lemon juice, and ice to a cocktail shaker fitted with a strainer. Shake until well chilled. Pour over the ice in the glass. Garnish with the lemon and mint.

Located on 550 of the most beautiful acres in the state, the Grand Hotel stands over the shores of Mobile Bay as the grande dame of Alabama hospitality, welcoming guests from around the world since 1847. Many have made a stay at the Grand a family tradition, returning each year for summer vacations, holiday celebrations, and special occasions. Boasting unparalleled resort amenities like pools, a spa, golf, tennis, fishing, and boating, the Grand has a notable military past and pays tribute to its history daily with the firing of a cannon and a drum corps parade around the grounds. The resort has recently undergone a $32 million renovation which includes an impressive culinary operation with stunning new restaurants and the new 1847 bar. The newly refurbished Bucky's is named for the resort's revered bartender, Bucky Miller. Bucky's statue overlooks the lawn; order one of his signature Mint Juleps with mint picked from the chef's garden on the grounds. Bucky's often features live music; guests take a spin around the dance floor or gather around the piano to sing along. Many prefer to relax outside by one of the firepits overlooking the bay.

DON'T MISS: Locals and guests alike have made the Grand's Sunday brunch—which is particularly lavish during holiday celebrations—a tradition for decades. The new high tea service each afternoon boasts house-made sweets and savories, an extensive selection of Champagne and sparkling wines, and a carefully curated selection of tea; it makes afternoon tea at the Grand a most regal experience. The new Local café in the lobby has a variety of house-baked sweets—try a French canelé with a cup of cappuccino to start the morning or as an afternoon pick-me-up.

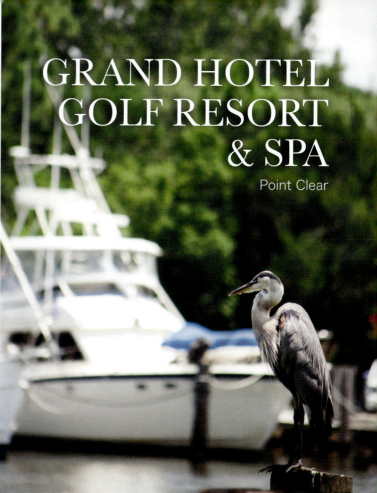

GRAND HOTEL GOLF RESORT & SPA
Point Clear

GRAND HOTEL GOLF RESORT & SPA
One Grand Boulevard | Point Clear, Alabama 36564
251-928-9201 | Grand1847.com

SUNSET POINTE
Fairhope

Chef & Owner 'Panini' Pete Blohme

SUNSET POINTE
831 North Section Street at Fly Creek Marina | Fairhope, Alabama 36532
251-990-7766 | SunsetPointeFairhope.com

Lavida Royale

SUNSET POINTE

Pom Syrup:

2 parts pomegranate juice

1 part sugar

Large ice sphere

Ice

1 1/2 ounces Cuestión or tequila of choice

3/4 ounce Pom Syrup (See recipe above.)

3/4 ounce lime juice

Champagne

Fresh mint sprig for garnish

Makes 1

For the Pom Syrup: Combine the pomegranate juice and sugar in a saucepan. Heat and stir to dissolve the sugar. Remove from the heat and cool completely. (Use as needed and store in a tight-fitting jar in the refrigerator up to 2 weeks.)

To serve: Add the ice sphere to a wine glass. Fill a cocktail shaker with ice. Add the tequila, Pom Syrup, and lime juice to the shaker. Shake and strain into the glass over the ice sphere. Top the drink with the Champagne. Slap the mint sprig to release its oils and add as garnish.

Note: You may use any ice in place of the ice sphear.

I used to go to Fly Creek Marina back in the day for a cold beer and the sunsets, and I hated when it closed. That is, until Panini Pete bought it, renovated it, and opened it under the name Sunset Pointe, where the sunsets are free with the food and drinks. Some locals come to Sunset Pointe via boat and dock at Fly Creek Marina. After visits by Guy Fieri on his shows *Diners, Drive-Ins and Dives* and *Guy's Family Road Trip*, it is not surprising to find as many tourists as locals at Sunset Pointe. Pete is also the owner of one of Guy's other favorite restaurants Panini Pete's in Fairhope's French Quarter. Pete has also appeared (and won) Fieri's show *Guy's Grocery Games*! Whether you go for a light bite or dinner, the menu has a lot of variety for whatever mood you're in. The Crab Mac 'n Cheese with blue crab in a cream sauce, pecorino, and crunchy panko topping; the Seared Tuna Nachos; and the Southern Mediterranean Crudo with tuna, cucumber, feta, and fried capers are all highlights on the small-plates list.

DON'T MISS: The cocktail list has something for everyone. Favorites include the Cool as a Cucumber with Tanqueray, cucumber, basil, rosemary, and lemon; the Point Clear Tea with vodka, lemon, mint, and sweet tea; and the Jodi's Mojito (named for Pete's wife) with rum, pineapple, mint, and lime. Be sure to make it to "the Pointe" in time for sunset when Pete rings the bell to toast the end of the day.

THE ATOMIC BAR AND LOUNGE
Birmingham

Owners Feizal Valli & Rachael Roberts

What will it be? A bumble bee? Elvis? A shark? I'm not talking about the cocktail list—I'm talking about the crazy costumes you'll find (and can wear) while cocktailing at The Atomic Bar and Lounge in Birmingham. Feizal Valli and Rachael Roberts met in 2013 and married three years later. They also decided to marry their love of craft cocktails and dive bars to create The Atomic. Rachael and Feizal have history with some of Birmingham's top restaurants, so they know their way around a cocktail shaker. The Atomic has a list of cutting-edge drinks and a fittingly quirky-chic mid-century-modern interior design. Not long after The Atomic opened, the James Beard Foundation gave Feizal and Rachael the shock of their lives when it named their bar a semi-finalist for Outstanding Bar Program, one of the most prestigious honors in the industry.

DON'T MISS: The bar is known for The Legendary Sex Panther cocktail composed of bourbon, blackstrap rum, Cynar, demerara, and bitters and is accompanied by a temporary panther tattoo. The Atomic's Instagram feed is full of photos of guests showing off their panther ink. My favorite cocktail is the Brad Green, made with Cathead Honeysuckle Vodka, St-Germain elderflower liquor, and Aperol. It's the perfect blend of bitter and sweet. Make sure to get a good look at the mural behind the bar of the adapted Beatles' Sgt. Pepper's album cover in which Frank Stitt and other famous Birmingham faces appear in place of the originals. How many of these Birmingham folks you can identify?

THE ATOMIC BAR AND LOUNGE
2113 1st Avenue North | Birmingham, Alabama 35203
205-983-7887 | TheAtomicLounge.com

Skylar Brown

THE ATOMIC BAR AND LOUNGE

Ginger Syrup:

1 cup sugar

1 cup boiling water

1/2 cup fresh ginger

Ice

1 1/4 ounces Cathead vodka

3/4 ounce lemon juice

1/2 ounce Combier Crème de Framboise (raspberry liqueur)

1/2 ounce Ginger Syrup (See recipe above.)

Prosecco

Makes 1

For the Ginger Syrup: Combine the sugar and boiling water and stir until the sugar is dissolved. Let cool. Slice the ginger and place in a blender along with the syrup. Process until the ginger is finely chopped. Strain through a fine strainer, reserving the syrup and discarding the solids. The leftover syrup will keep refrigerated for a few weeks.

To serve: Fill a cocktail shaker with ice. Add the vodka, lemon juice, raspberry liqueur, and Ginger Syrup to the shaker. Shake and strain into a Collins glass. Top with the Prosecco.

THE HANGOUT
GULF SHORES

I have been a big fan of The Hangout since my first Alabama food tour with the Alabama Tourism Department in 2012, when I was lucky enough to encounter Shaul Zislin, the man and magic behind The Hangout. Zislin is the visionary who created this world-renowned music and entertainment destination located at the "T" where I-59 intersects with Beach Boulevard. The Hangout may be best known for its Hangout Music Festival each May, with superstar acts headlining the 3-day festival right on the beach. It also hosts thousands of oyster-lovers and chefs who descend on The Hangout for the Hangout Oyster Cook-Off each November. The complex boasts three permanent stages, a DJ booth, and giant televisions broadcasting sports. The food is comfort food, with great burgers, salads, sandwiches, and signature dishes, including anything with The Hangout's Shaka Sauce, named for their symbolic shaka logo (aka the "hang loose" sign).

DON'T MISS: The Hangout is a great place for spicy peel-and-eat Gulf shrimp by the pound and the Seafood Boil is a favorite with locals and tourists alike. Everyone raves about the Smoked-Fish Dip, Bacon-Crab Dip, Gulf Shores Gumbo, and Chicken Nachos on the appetizer menu. Order apps at the bar and pair with a cold brew from their large selection of craft beers. The cocktail menu is extensive, making The Hangout one of the best places to have a cocktail overlooking the water. And watch out for the sharks—The Hangout's Shark Attack is quite possibly the most-popular cocktail on the beach.

THE HANGOUT
101 East Beach Boulevard | Gulf Shores, Alabama 36542
251-948-3030 | TheHangout.com

Shark Attack

THE HANGOUT

Ice

3/4 ounce Malibu rum

1/2 ounce peach schnapps

3/4 ounce blue curaçao

1 1/2 ounces sour mix

1/2 ounce pineapple juice

1/4 ounce grenadine for garnish

Maraschino cherry for garnish

Serves 1 The Shark Attack is colored like a Gulf Shores sunset and is perfect for a summer party. It's easy to make in large quantities, and you can also freeze it and serve as a slush.

Fill a glass with ice and set aside. Fill a cocktail shaker with ice and add the rum, schnapps, blue curaçao, sour mix, and pineapple juice to the shaker. Shake and strain into the glass. If you happen to have a plastic shark, fill it with the grenadine and put a cherry in its mouth for garnish. Squeeze the grenadine into the cocktail for the "shark attack" effect and stir.

THE GULF
Orange Beach

The shipping containers that house The Gulf restaurant on Perdido Pass might look cool from the front, but when guests walk "in" for the first time, their reaction is always WOW! There is no "in" at The Gulf since the space is all outside. The Gulf was the first restaurant built from shipping containers in the area and is another of entrepreneur Shaul Zislin's jewels on the beach. (He also owns The Hangout.) Truckloads of pristine white sand were brought in and grass was planted to create the beach and lounge areas overlooking the Pass; there are also private cabanas and lounge areas on the beach. The Gulf prides itself on its chef-driven menu created with fresh, local ingredients and seafood right out of the water. The bars are a gathering place for local folks and visitors alike to watch boats sail by or the sun go down with a cold beverage and vintage vinyl tunes on the turntable.

DON'T MISS: The Grouper Sandwich. Long thought to be the best grouper sandwich on the beach, it has been a menu staple since The Gulf opened in 2012. Ask my favorite bartender, Victor, for his signature fresh fruit mojito. It might be blackberry, blueberry, strawberry, or raspberry, or a combination of these, muddled with fresh mint. They infuse the vodka for the Bloody Mary; pair one up with the Red Snapper Ceviche or the Grilled Shrimp Tacos. Don't leave without a t-shirt or some supercool swag from the carefully curated gift shop.

THE GULF
27500 Perdido Beach Boulevard | Orange Beach, Alabama 36561
251-424-1800 | TheGulf.com

The Gulf's Signature Fresh Fruit Mojito

THE GULF

2 mint leaves, torn

2 fresh local blackberries (or use blueberries, raspberries)

1 tablespoon fresh lime juice

1 1/2 ounces Bacardi Superior Rum (or your favorite brand)

1/2 ounce sugar cane simple syrup (Torani brand or make your own)

3 ounces club soda

Ice

1 1/2 ounces citrus soda (like Sprite)

Fresh mint sprig for garnish

Fruit for garnish as desired

Lime wedge for garnish

Makes 1

Add the mint, berries, and lime juice to a cocktail shaker. Muddle well to crush the berries and bruise the mint. Add rum, simple syrup, club soda and ice. Shake until well chilled. Pour into a tall glass filled with ice. Top with the citrus soda. Garnish with the mint sprig, additional fresh fruit, and a lime wedge.

CHEZ FONFON
Birmingham

Chez Fonfon, part of Chef Frank Stitt's restaurant group, evokes memories of a week in Paris and a quaint café on a remote side street. Though it is situated in the middle of Birmingham's Southside entertainment district, you feel transported. Trees line the street, and church bells ring on the hour. There's also a boule court on the back patio, if you'd fancy a game. The food is flawless, and the service is, too. Casual French fare like Moules et Frites, Escargots, and homemade charcuterie, share the menu with Birmingham's best burger, seasonal soups, hearty braises, and side dishes featuring ingredients from area farmers. *Southern Living* magazine claims the bar at Chez Fonfon is the best restaurant bar in Alabama, and I agree. My friends and I like to gather there over cocktails and charcuterie. My favorite is the French Blonde. Served in a classic Champagne coupe, it feels quite elegant to sip on while sitting at the bar.

DON'T MISS: They really know how to make a fantastic soup at Chez Fonfon, and I always order it, even in the summer. The Shrimp and Avocado Salad is my mainstay except on Thursdays when I opt for the crab cake special. Desserts are made by Dolester Miles, the James Beard Foundation award winning pastry chef who creates the desserts for Stitt's Highlands Bar and Grill and Bottega restaurants. Your experience would not be complete without Mrs. Dol's Lemon Meringue Tart, her celebrated Coconut Pecan Cake (recipe found on page 191), or any of the other seasonal desserts on the menu.

CHEZ FONFON
2007 11th Ave South | Birmingham, Alabama 35205
205-939-3221 | FonfonBham.com

French Blonde

CHEZ FONFON

Ice

1/2 ounce St-Germain elderflower liqueur

1 ounce Bombay Sapphire (or other dry gin)

2 ounces Lillet Blanc

2 ounces fresh grapefruit juice

A few dashes lemon bitters

Thin, spiral lemon twist for garnish

Makes 1

Add ice to a Champagne coupe to chill.

Add the St-Germain, gin, Lillet Blanc, grapefruit juice, and bitters to a cocktail shaker. Shake until well chilled. Discard the ice from the glass. Strain the cocktail into the glass. Garnish with a lemon twist.

Note: This cocktail is served 'up'—meaning the drink is served chilled but without ice, as are most martinis. Bartenders will usually chill the service glass by filling it full of ice while mixing the drink. They discard the ice before pouring the cocktail into the glass. This step insures the cocktail is served well chilled.

Appetizers & Snacks

Chicken Fried Bacon with Sawmill Gravy, 53
ACRE

Bam Bam Gulf Shrimp, 55
BAUMHOWER'S VICTORY GRILLE

Belle Chévre Goat Cheese Fondue, 57
BELLE CHEVRE CHEESE SHOP AND TASTING ROOM

Shrimp Isabel, 59
CRAZY HORSE

Crab-Stuffed Bacon-Wrapped Shrimp, 61
GUIDO'S

Hunt's Oysters Supreme, 63
HUNT'S SEAFOOD RESTAURANT AND OYSTER BAR

SpringHouse Pimento Cheese, 65
SPRINGHOUSE

SpringHouse Famous Boiled Peanuts, 67
SPRINGHOUSE

Playa Gulf Ceviche, 69
PLAYA

Heirloom Tomato Pie, 71
THE HOUND

The Noble South Pickled Shrimp, 73
THE NOBLE SOUTH

ACRE
Auburn

Chef & Owner David Bancroft

Acre offers a modern spin on timeless Southern recipes. Chef David Bancroft has his roots deep in the rich soil of Hartford, Alabama, where his grandparents farmed. He had a unique vision for the acre of land in the heart of Auburn's historic district, just a few blocks from the city's renowned Toomer's Corner. Bancroft built his restaurant in the middle of the property and surrounded it with an edible landscape, planting an orchard of fruit trees around the parking lot. What they don't grow at Acre they source from local farms. The restaurant walls are wrapped in solid oak sourced from Ten Mile Creek Farms, owned by Bancroft's grandfather. The exposed beams are salvaged from the 100-year-old Crawford General Store, and there is an authentic Toomer's oak tree outside, propagated from one of Auburn's famous trees. Chef Bancroft's new restaurant, Bow & Arrow, is scheduled to open in the fall of 2018.

DON'T MISS: A drink at the bar. In August 2018, Acre was named one of the outstanding restaurant-bars in the South by *Southern Living* magazine. See Acre's Call Me Old-Fashioned recipe on page 33; crafted with ham-infused bourbon, this cocktail is uniquely satisfying. If it's chilly, ask for a seat by the fireplace and order the Solid Oak Sampler so you may sample Acre's many meats, cheeses, and fixin's. I now crave the Chicken Fried Bacon with Sawmill Gravy—it is like none other. Homemade desserts are made with the same "fresh-local" ingredients for a sweet ending to a wonderful experience.

ACRE
210 East Glenn Avenue | Auburn, Alabama 36830
334-246-3763 | AcreAuburn.com

Chicken Fried Bacon with Sawmill Gravy

ACRE

Chicken Fry Mix:

1 cup all-purpose flour

1/2 teaspoon baking powder

3 teaspoons kosher salt

3 teaspoons garlic powder

2 teaspoons black pepper

2 teaspoons paprika

1/8 teaspoon dried thyme

4 strips smoked bacon

1 cup whole buttermilk

Sawmill Gravy:

1/3 cup all-purpose flour

1/4 cup unsalted butter

1 cup half-and-half

2 cups whole milk (Add more for a thinner consistency, if desired.)

1/2 teaspoon kosher salt

1/4 teaspoon black pepper

1/4 teaspoon onion powder

1 quart peanut oil

1 cup Chicken Fry Mix (See recipe at right.)

4 ounces Sawmill Gravy (See recipe above.)

4 ounces maple syrup

Toasted pecans, crushed, for garnish

Serves 2 You'll need a fryer or a large Dutch oven and a thermometer for this recipe. Preheat the oven to 400° Fahrenheit to render (pre-cook) the bacon.

For the Chicken Fry Mix: Combine all the ingredients in a bowl. Set aside.

Place the bacon on a baking sheet and render the bacon slightly in the oven to cook out some of its moisture. Place on a paper towel to drain. Cool the bacon completely and soak in the buttermilk. While the bacon is cooling, make the Sawmill Gravy.

For the Sawmill Gravy: Heat the flour and butter in a saucepan. Whisk and cook to a blonde roux. Add the half-and-half while whisking. Add the whole milk and bring to a simmer. Cook for 3 minutes. Season with the salt, pepper, and onion powder to taste. Remove from the heat. Taste and season as desired. Keep warm.

Heat the peanut oil in a fryer (or a large Dutch oven) to 350°. Dredge the bacon in the Chicken Fry Mix and drop into the hot oil. (Try to keep the bacon flat in the fryer.) Remove to a serving plate when golden brown.

Top with the gravy, as desired; add the syrup around the outside edges of the bacon. Garnish with the crushed pecans.

Appetizers & Snacks

BAUMHOWER'S VICTORY GRILLE

Mobile and nine other locations

Spencer Baumhower

University of Alabama All-American and six-time NFL Miami Dolphin Pro Bowler Bob Baumhower was one of the first to bring Buffalo-style hot wings to Alabama when he opened the first Baumhower's Wings in Tuscaloosa in 1981. Since then, the famed chain known for the best wings in the state has expanded and the menu has grown to include made-from-scratch sports bar favorites and Southern specialties. These days, Bob's oldest son, Spencer, has joined the business, truly making Baumhower's a family restaurant. Baumhower's signature burgers are made with a combination of fresh USDA choice chuck and beef brisket and served on a custom brioche bun, branded on top with the Baumhower's logo. Their Hot Bama Brown is featured on the list of 100 Things to Eat in Alabama Before You Die. A spin on the iconic Kentucky Hot Brown, Baumhower's version includes oven-roasted turkey, bacon, and tomato smothered in mushroom gravy and served open-faced on Texas Toast.

DON'T MISS: Wings. Wings. Wings. The restaurant uses fresh, never frozen hormone-free chicken wings and fries in 100% vegetable oil. The sauce options range from mild to 911 to Bring Da-Pain, their hottest option. Order an array of appetizers to share and save room for the scratch-made desserts. Their Banana Pudding Ala'Bama is wrapped in pastry and deep fried, while the Strawberry Shortcake is made with macerated strawberries piled high on a biscuit topped with ice cream.

BAUMHOWER'S VICTORY GRILLE
Auburn, Daphne, Huntsville, Lee Branch-Birmingham, Mobile, Montgomery, Montgomery Downtown, Patton Creek-Birmingham, Tuscaloosa North, Tuscaloosa South
Baumhowers.com

Bam Bam Gulf Shrimp

BAUMHOWER'S VICTORY GRILLE

Oil for frying (canola recommended)

6 ounces all-purpose flour

1 teaspoon kosher salt

1 teaspoon ground black pepper

1 teaspoon garlic powder

4 ounces buttermilk

16 large (21/25 count) Alabama Gulf shrimp

8 ounces Baumhower's Thai Sweet Chili Sauce for dipping*

3 ounces ranch dressing for dipping, optional

1 tablespoon chopped Italian flat-leaf parsley for garnish, optional

Lemon wedges for garnish

Serves 2

Heat the oil in deep skillet or fryer to 350° Fahrenheit.

In a shallow bowl or container, mix the flour with the salt, pepper, and garlic powder.

Add the buttermilk to a separate container and soak the shrimp for a few moments; tap to remove the excess buttermilk and toss in the seasoned flour.

Fry the shrimp for 2 minutes; then place the shrimp on paper towels to remove the excess grease.

To serve: Coat the shrimp with the chili sauce and place on a plate. Garnish with the parsley, if desired and serve with ranch dressing and a lemon wedge.

*You can find a sweet Thai chili sauce at your local market on the international foods aisle.

Appetizers & Snacks

BELLE CHÈVRE CHEESE SHOP AND TASTING ROOM

Elkmont

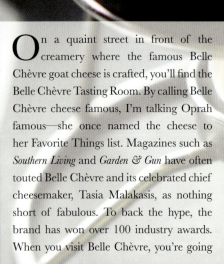

On a quaint street in front of the creamery where the famous Belle Chèvre goat cheese is crafted, you'll find the Belle Chèvre Tasting Room. By calling Belle Chèvre cheese famous, I'm talking Oprah famous—she once named the cheese to her Favorite Things list. Magazines such as *Southern Living* and *Garden & Gun* have often touted Belle Chèvre and its celebrated chief cheesemaker, Tasia Malakasis, as nothing short of fabulous. To back the hype, the brand has won over 100 industry awards. When you visit Belle Chèvre, you're going to want to arrive hungry and try everything on the menu. French press coffee with toast and one of their breakfast cheeses are a great way to start the day. If you are there on Friday or Saturday, be sure to take the creamery tour and meet the goats. Tell the head goat Jenny, (pictured at right) that I said hello.

DON'T MISS: The Five-Cheese Grilled Cheese with fig chèvre, Cheddar, aged Gouda, smoked Gouda, and Gruyère with caramelized onions and prosciutto. It is, without a doubt, one of the best sandwiches I had while traveling the state to compile this book. The cheesecake is as creamy and luscious as any you've ever tasted. Make sure to pick up a copy of Tasia's cookbooks, *Tasia's Table* and *Southern Made Fresh*. Both are full of goat cheese recipes, Southern classics, and Greek-inspired dishes.

Tip Take a few cheesecakes home because you will not stop craving them once you've tried them.

BELLE CHÈVRE CHEESE SHOP AND TASTING ROOM
18849 Upper Fort Hampton Road | Elkmont, Alabama 35620
256-732-3577 | BelleChevre.com

Belle Chèvre Goat Cheese Fondue

BELLE CHÈVRE CHEESE SHOP AND TASTING ROOM

11 ounces Belle Chèvre goat cheese (Find it at most grocery stores or online.)

1/4 cup heavy cream

1/4 cup dry white wine

Freshly cracked black pepper

1 tablespoon finely chopped fresh chives

For dipping:

1 apple, cut into wedges

Summer sausage, cut into chunks

1/2 loaf sourdough bread, cut into 1-inch cubes and toasted

Serves 4-6

Place the goat cheese in a small saucepan over low heat. Add the heavy cream, white wine, and black pepper to taste. Cook, stirring occasionally, until the cheese is melted and the wine has cooked off, 8-10 minutes. The fondue will be thick and creamy.

Remove from the heat and stir in the chives.

Serve warm in a fondue pot with skewers for the sliced apple, summer sausage, and bread.

Owner Tasia Malakasis

CRAZY HORSE
Trussville

East of Birmingham, you'll find a Greek chef with a lifetime of experience in the restaurant industry and a local guy who grew up in a family known for supplying the state's best restaurants with the best seafood and meat available. That is the crack team behind Crazy Horse, a Trussville restaurant that is part high-end steakhouse, part neighborhood eatery. Hunter Evans (of the Evans Meats family) along with Executive Chef Brian Karadimos are delivering big city cuisine to the small town of Trussville complete with the Greek specialties for which the chef has become known. Steaks are the big draw. (Evans Meats supplies the meat, so Crazy Horse has the best cuts available.) The 18-ounce Porterhouse is enough for two to share—one gets the filet, and the other gets the strip. Shrimp Isabel is the recipe Crazy Horse diners asked me to score; I am certain it has something to do with the seared cheese!

DON'T MISS: The gumbo. Chef Karadimos's Seafood Gumbo is new to the Crazy Horse menu and has won awards in Baldwin County, where they know a thing or two about gumbo. The Beer Cheese Soup is a local favorite; people remember it from Birmingham's Baby Doe's Matchless Mine restaurant, which closed in 1993. Saturday breakfasts at Crazy Horse are quite the thing to do. Folks stand in line for the Orange Rolls, an iconic recipe that Crazy Horse has made their own. Don't sleep in next Saturday. Get there early and arrive hungry!

CRAZY HORSE
8885 Gadsden Highway | Trussville, Alabama 35173
205-655-2040 | CrazyHorseArgo.com

Shrimp Isabel

CRAZY HORSE

Tzatziki:

1/4 cup Greek yogurt

1/4 cup diced cucumber

1 teaspoon chopped fresh oregano

1 teaspoon chopped fresh dill

1 teaspoon chopped fresh mint

2 garlic cloves

1 tablespoon extra-virgin olive oil

1 tablespoon lemon juice

1 tablespoon red wine vinegar

Salt and pepper to taste

Olive's Salad:

1/2 cups pitted Greek olives

Zest of 1 orange

2 garlic cloves

1 tablespoon extra-virgin olive oil

1 teaspoon chopped fresh dill

1 teaspoon chopped fresh mint

Shrimp:

1/2 pound (16/20 count) Gulf shrimp, peeled and deveined

4 cherry tomatoes, halved

1 teaspoon chopped fresh oregano

1 teaspoon chopped fresh dill

1 teaspoon chopped fresh mint

1 teaspoon roasted garlic (roast the garlic in the oven until soft or use store-bought

1/8 cup lemon juice

1/8 cup ouzo

2 tablespoons extra-virgin olive oil

2 ounces Manchego cheese, cut 1/2-inch thick

2 tablespoons Tzatziki (See recipe above.)

2 tablespoon Olive's Salad (See recipe above.)

Makes 1 appetizer to serve 2

For the Tzatziki: Purée all the ingredients in a food processor until smooth. Set aside. (You may keep the leftover Tzatziki in the refrigerator for up to a week.)

For the Olive's Salad: Purée all the ingredients in a food processor until smooth. Set aside.

Sauté the shrimp, tomatoes, oregano, dill, mint, and roasted garlic in a hot pan for 2 minutes. Deglaze the pan with the lemon juice and ouzo. Set aside.

In a separate pan, heat the olive oil. Sear the cheese until golden brown. Flip and repeat. Remove from the pan and set aside to rest.

To serve: Place the Tzatziki on a plate and top with the seared cheese. Then top with the shrimp, tomato, and pan sauce. Top it all off with Olive's Salad. (Reserve the remaining Tzatziki and Olive's Salad for another use.)

Owner Hunter Evans & Chef Brian Karadimos

GUIDO'S & COUSIN VINNY'S PIZZERIA

Daphne

If you wonder why people drive for hours to eat at this small restaurant on Daphne's Main Street, simply stop by. The vibe is friendly and the food tastes like an Italian grandmother is cooking in the kitchen. The Italian grandmother in this case is Chef Kris Conlon, the outgoing chef/owner who uses fresh ingredients in old-world Italian recipes. Dishes such as Linguini and Clams, Veal Parmigiana, Chicken Cannelloni, and coastal creations such as Soft Shell Crab Picatta and Bacon-Wrapped Shrimp with Crab Stuffing are just a few of the many favorites. You will find an oddity at Guido's that you won't find in any other Alabama restaurant I have visited: There is an upside-down Christmas tree hanging from the ceiling in the corner, a tradition started by Chef Kris's mother. It is always decorated for the upcoming holiday or season.

DON'T MISS: Fans rave about the Eggplant Parmigiana. The antipasto bowl, full of Italian ham, olives, roasted red peppers, artichoke hearts, pepperoni, cheeses, and sun-dried tomatoes, is a great starter and is enough food for the table to share. We tried a lot of dishes, but the Veal Picatta with lemony caper sauce was my favorite. Don't leave without trying the fried bread pudding—it has a legion of fans. The day we were there, a couple drove 2 hours to order it and ate it before their entrées to make sure they had room—I'm a big fan of eating dessert first!

GUIDO'S & COUSIN VINNY'S PIZZERIA
1709 Main Street | Daphne, Alabama 36526
251-626-6082 | Facebook.com/GuidosDaphne

Crab-Stuffed Bacon-Wrapped Shrimp

GUIDO'S

Olive oil

1 large yellow onion, finely diced

3 ribs celery, finely diced

3 tablespoons garlic, minced

2 large eggs, beaten

1/2 cup Zatarain's Creole Mustard

1 large roasted red bell pepper, finely chopped

1 bunch green onions, finely chopped

1 pound fresh blue crab claw meat, carefully picked to remove the shell

1 tablespoon coarse ground black pepper

6 cups fresh breadcrumbs (not dried breadcrumbs; make from day-old bread)

2 pounds large (21/25 count) Gulf shrimp

48 slices good-quality smoked bacon

Cooking spray

Serves 6-8 as an entrée or can be served as an appetizer

Heat the olive oil over high heat in a skillet. Sauté the onion and celery until translucent. Add the garlic and reduce the heat to medium. Cook until the onions are lightly caramelized. Cool.

In a bowl, whisk the eggs and mustard together. Stir in the red bell pepper, green onions, crab, black pepper, and cooled onion mixture. Lightly fold in the breadcrumbs, a few handfuls at a time. The mixture should be moist but not wet, so add more breadcrumbs as needed. Set the crab mixture aside in the refrigerator.

Preheat the oven to 425° Fahrenheit.

Butterfly the shrimp. Remove the crab mixture from the refrigerator and spoon some of the mixture into each shrimp. Wrap each shrimp from head to tail with a bacon slice, covering as much of the shrimp as possible. (At this point, you can refrigerate the shrimp until ready to cook.)

Line a large baking sheet with parchment paper and spray with cooking spray. Place the bacon-wrapped shrimp flat on the prepared baking sheet; don't overcrowd. Bake at 425° until the bacon is cooked to the desired degree of doneness. Serve drizzled with the warm pan drippings.

Tip Be certain to visit Guido's Cousin Vinny's Pizzeria next door for some of the best pizza in Baldwin County.

Chef & Owner Kris Conlon

Appetizers & Snacks | 61

HUNT'S SEAFOOD RESTAURANT AND OYSTER BAR

Dothan

Hunt's Seafood Restaurant & Oyster Bar started as a three-stool oyster bar inside a gas station in the early 1960s. The building and the menu have changed a lot over the years, but one thing remains constant: The oysters are still hand selected and shucked, and all the food is made from scratch and cooked to order. You'll find fresh Gulf seafood, shrimp, and crab along with the best steaks in the area. The dressings are all made from scratch as are the yeast rolls, which are huge and fluffy—just like the ones the lunchroom ladies used to make at school! On the oyster bar side, you'll find some of the fastest oyster shuckers you've ever seen. They shuck and serve hundreds of oysters on the half shell and dozens of their popular Oysters Supreme a day. Original sports murals and memorabilia cover the walls, a very fitting setting for the many Auburn and Alabama players and coaches who have dined at this Dothan landmark over the years.

DON'T MISS: The hot dogs. Yes, that is right. The hot dogs aren't even on the menu but Hunt's sell hundreds of them each week. Served with Hunt's secret hot dog sauce, they are a decades-old local custom. The oysters are another "don't miss"—get them baked, steamed, Cajun baked, or raw on the half shell. Get the owner, Tim Reeves, to tell you about his family's history—his parents started the restaurant, and many of the recipes are his mother's.

HUNT'S SEAFOOD RESTAURANT AND OYSTER BAR
177 Campbellton Highway | Dothan, Alabama 36301
334-794-5193 | HuntsRestaurant.com

Hunt's Oysters Supreme

HUNT'S SEAFOOD RESTAURANT AND OYSTER BAR

18 fresh oysters on the half shell (Retain as much oyster liquor as possible in each shell.)

1/4 cup fresh-squeezed lemon juice

1/4 teaspoon finely ground black pepper

1 stick butter cut into 18 pieces

1/2 cup Parmesan cheese, grated

Makes 18 oysters

Working in batches, place the oysters in a microwave-safe dish lined with paper towels to stabilize the oysters. Mix the lemon juice and pepper together in a bowl; divide the mixture evenly among the oysters, adding it to the reserved oyster liquor in the shells. Place a piece of the butter on top of each oyster. Top each oyster with the Parmesan cheese. Microwave on HIGH for 3 minutes or until bubbly and the cheese is melted.

 Tip Hunt's cooks these oysters in the microwave, but you can also grill them. Take care when cooking oysters in the shell; not only are they extremely hot, but the shell may burst, or a shell fragment may break off during cooking. It is always a good idea to scrub oyster shells well before you cook or eat them.

Owner Tim Reeves

SPRINGHOUSE
Alexander City

SPRINGHOUSE
12 Benson Mill Road | Alexander City, Alabama 35010
256-215-7080 | SpringHouseAtCrossroads.com

SpringHouse Pimento Cheese

SPRINGHOUSE

2 red bell peppers (You can substitute store-bought roasted red peppers or jarred pimentos, if desired.)

1 large egg yolk

1 teaspoon water

1 cup oil (Use olive, grapeseed, or vegetable.)

1 pound freshly grated white cheese (Use Thomasville Tomme or good-quality white cheddar.)

Pinch of salt

1/4 teaspoon cayenne pepper

2 tablespoons Sriracha

Makes about 4 cups

Roast the bell peppers over a wood fire or flame 5 minutes per side. Remove the peppers to a bowl and cover with plastic wrap. Set aside and allow to cool completely. Once cooled, use a paring knife to remove the pepper skins; discard. Slice the peppers and remove the seeds. Dice the peppers very small. Set aside.

Add the egg yolk and water to a large glass bowl. Whisk until the mixture is pale yellow. Pour the oil in a glass measuring cup with a spout so you can pour it easily. Vigorously whisk the yolk mixture as you drizzle in the oil in a very slow and steady stream, about 1 teaspoon at a time, until the yolk mixture is thickened and emulsified. Set aside.

In a medium mixing bowl, combine the diced bell peppers and grated cheese. Fold in 1/2 cup of the egg mixture until well incorporated. Repeat with the remaining 1/2 cup egg mixture. Add the salt, cayenne, and Siracha. Mix well.

Chill the pimento cheese in the refrigerator at least 30 minutes to allow the seasonings to come together.

Before serving, temper the pimento cheese by allowing it to sit out 15-20 minutes. This makes it more cracker friendly.

Executive Chef Rob McDaniel

One of the state's prettiest restaurant settings combined with stunning interior design, a relaxed ambiance, and James Beard recognition for its excellent cuisine from the time it opened, SpringHouse at Lake Martin is under the direction of Executive Chef Rob McDaniel, a five-time semi-finalist for the James Beard Foundation's Best Chef: South award. SpringHouse is a fine dining destination for food aficionados who come to Alexander City in droves for Chef McDaniel's interpretation of classic Southern dishes prepared with local and seasonal ingredients. Chef McDaniel worked as sous chef to Birmingham's Chef Chris Hastings at Hot and Hot Fish Club and teamed with him on national television to win Food Network's *Iron Chef America*. Chef McDaniel's passion for foraging and sustainability has influenced the culinary style for which he is known today. SpringHouse has a garden on the property where the resident farmer grows ingredients the restaurant uses. He even grows the peppers used for their most-beloved pimento cheese.

DON'T MISS: In the summer, order Mr. Jim's Vegetable Plate. It was one of the prettiest and most delicious vegetable plates I ate throughout my restaurant tour across the state. For an unforgettable experience on special occasions, book the Well House, a private 12-seat, circular dining room within the subterranean wine cellar and 'secret" entrance for an unforgettable experience. Chef's version of the childhood favorite, S'mores, has made it onto the 100 Dishes to Eat in Alabama Before You Die list; order it without hesitation!

Appetizers & Snacks

SPRINGHOUSE
Alexander City

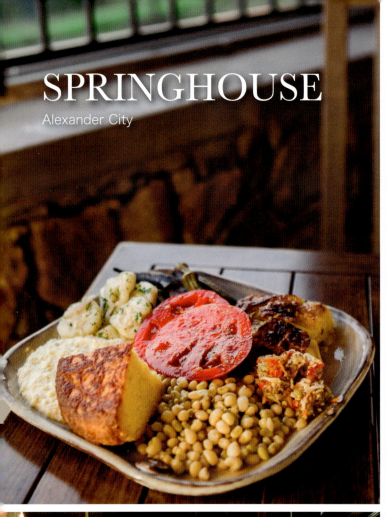

SPRINGHOUSE
12 Benson Mill Road | Alexander City, Alabama 35010
256-215-7080 | SpringHouseAtCrossroads.com

SpringHouse Famous Boiled Peanuts

SPRINGHOUSE

25 pounds green peanuts in the shell

3 pounds Morton's kosher salt

5 heads garlic, cut in half horizontally

20 bay leaves

10 dried whole hot chiles

Note: If you use dried peanuts instead of green peanuts, the cooking time will be much longer.

Serves about 50 This recipe is party sized and the equipment necessary for 25 pounds of peanuts would not be found in most homes. Feel free to reduce the recipe to an amount that best suits your needs and kitchen equipment. Simply reduce the ratio of peanuts to salt. You'll need 1 pound (about 2 cups) of salt for every 8 1/2 pounds of green peanuts.

Place all the ingredients in a very large pot and cover with cold water. Bring to a rolling boil and reduce the heat to a simmer.

Simmer the peanuts, uncovered, 2-3 hours, making certain to stir the pot every 10-15 minutes. After 2 hours, taste the peanuts and continue to cook until the desired doneness is reached. Remove the peanuts from the heat. Strain the peanuts, retaining a quart of the cooking liquid for later. Discard the remaining cooking liquid, garlic heads, bay leaves, and chiles, and chill 24 hours before serving. Serve the boiled peanuts cold or heat them back up to serve hot. You may add want to use a bit of the reserved cooking liquid to heat up the peanuts.

Tip Green peanuts are raw, uncooked peanuts. Most peanuts you find in grocery stores are dry roasted. If you can't find green peanuts at your local grocer, order online from an Alabama grower. Peanut season in Alabama runs from late August through early November.

PLAYA
Orange Beach

Executive Chef Bill Briand

Playa is the latest super hip, super fun, and super beautiful Orange Beach waterfront restaurant by Lower Alabama restaurateur Johnny Fisher and Executive Chef Bill Briand of Fisher's restaurant fame. The location that formerly housed Shipp's Harbor restaurant has been totally transformed into an elegant Cuban-Caribbean hot spot. The top deck offers incredible sunset views, and the interiors are bathed in the subdued coastal colors of sunset pink, sea-glass green, and marine blue. The main dining room showcases a gorgeous beach mural in soft pink tones by Alexander City, Alabama, artist Lila Graves. Chef Briand's menu is Caribbean-meets-Southern, and his dishes, such as Grilled Royal Reds with Chimichurri and Gulf Ceviche with charred corn, jalapeño, and cilantro, have plenty of fans. You'll also find Lower Alabama standards, such as grilled fish of the day and traditional fried seafood platters, on their inspired seafood menu. If you're looking for excellent local fish in Orange Beach, you'll find it here.

DON'T MISS: Grouper in Banana Leaf and Coconut Grouper with sweet-corn grits are both excellent. The Street Tacos are extremely popular. I had the pork with cabbage-and-apple slaw and the grilled shrimp tacos—both were delicious and served on Gaby's house-made tortillas. Add on the Street Corn, which is another "don't-miss" dish. The cocktails are fun and inventive. Sit on the porch upstairs with a Pink Pineapple or Frosé cocktail and an order of Guacamole Your Way. It is the perfect way to enjoy one of Playa's signature sunsets.

PLAYA
27842 Canal Road | Orange Beach, Alabama 36561
251-981-9891 | PlayaOBA.com

Playa Gulf Ceviche

PLAYA

1 pound diced snapper

1/2 cup lemon juice

1/2 cup red wine vinegar

1 cup grilled corn kernels

1/2 cup small-diced red onion

1/4 cup small-diced sweet peppers

2 tablespoons chopped cilantro

1 teaspoon smoked paprika

1 teaspoon paprika

1 teaspoon cumin

1 tablespoon chile powder

1/4 cup orange juice

1 tablespoon extra-virgin olive oil

Salt

1 tablespoon honey

Fresh bread or crackers for serving

Serves 4-6 depending on portion size

Marinate the snapper in the lemon juice and red wine vinegar 2 hours or until the fish turns white and is "cooked" by the acid.

Drain all the liquid from the fish. Discard the liquid and set aside the fish.

In a bowl, mix together the corn, red onion, sweet peppers, cilantro, smoked paprika, paprika, cumin, chile powder, orange juice, olive oil, salt to taste, and honey. Gently stir in the fish and keep cold until ready to serve.

Serve with the fresh bread or crackers to mop up the delicious ceviche juices.

Owner Johnny Fisher

THE HOUND
Auburn

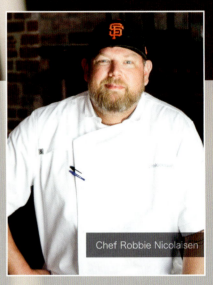
Chef Robbie Nicolaisen

Any restaurant that focuses on bacon, bourbon, and community is okay by me. Jana and Matthew Poirier own the place—Jana is an Auburn grad. Between the elevated Southern comfort-food menu by Chef Robbie Nicolaisen and the rustic, hunting-lodge-chic décor, The Hound is a very good find in a town with a lot of good food. Chef Nicolaisen's menu is elevated, casual cuisine—and you must say "cuisine" because a lot of care goes into delivering The Hound's American comfort-food classics. The Berkshire Pork Chop is juicy and tender, and the Chicken Fried Steak is served with mashed potatoes and a pan gravy that is just sooo good. Try the Bacon and Bourbon Caramel Popcorn—my new addiction—or the Pail-o-Pork Rinds to pair with one of the 28 craft beers on tap. The Meatloaf Burger is a big, juicy 6-napkin burger and tastes like your mama made the meatloaf. The sautéed mushrooms and onion jam take it over the top.

DON'T MISS: The Hound's brunch on Saturdays and Sundays that offers favorites such as homemade Biscuits and Gravy and Lowcountry Shrimp and Grits. Many people told me about The Hound's Heirloom Tomato Pie. Its fantastically flaky crust, as well as the dessert crusts, are all made in house. (If you use the crust recipe for a dessert, add 2 tablespoons sugar.) The Hound's Chocolate Chess Pie with Bourbon Caramel was one of my top five desserts on my road trip for this book that included sampling over 100 desserts!

THE HOUND
124 Tichenor Avenue | Auburn, Alabama 36830
334-246-3300 | TheHound-Auburn.com

Heirloom Tomato Pie

THE HOUND

Crust:

1 1/2 cups White Lily all-purpose flour, plus more for dusting

3/4 teaspoon sea salt

1/4 cup shortening

1/4 cup unsalted butter, plus more for pie plate

4-5 tablespoons ice-cold water

Filling:

2 3/4 pounds assorted large tomatoes, divided

2 teaspoons kosher salt, divided

1 1/2 cups (6 ounces) freshly shredded extra-sharp Cheddar cheese

1/2 cup (2 ounces) freshly shredded Parmigiano-Reggiano cheese

1/2 cup mayonnaise

1 large egg, lightly beaten

1 tablespoon fresh dill, chopped

1 tablespoon chopped fresh thyme, leaves picked and chopped

1 tablespoon chopped fresh tarragon, leaves picked and chopped

1 tablespoon apple cider vinegar

1 green onion, thinly sliced

2 teaspoons sugar

1/4 teaspoon freshly ground black pepper

1 1/2 teaspoons yellow cornmeal

Makes 1 (9-inch) pie

For the crust: Butter a 9-inch pie plate or skillet and set aside.

In a large bowl, combine the flour and salt. Cut in the shortening and butter with a pastry blender or two forks until the mixture resembles a coarse meal. While mixing with a wooden spoon, gradually add enough of the cold water to the mixture until a ball of dough is formed.

Turn out the dough onto a lightly floured piece of plastic wrap and form into a disc. Lightly flour the top of the dough and place another sheet of plastic wrap on top. Starting from the center, roll until the dough is about a 1/8-inch thick.

Remove the top piece of plastic wrap, invert the dough into the pie plate, and remove the remaining piece of plastic wrap. Lightly press the pie dough into the bottom and sides of the pie plate. Cover the pie plate with plastic wrap and freeze at least 30 minutes to overnight.

For the filling: Cut 2 pounds of the tomatoes into 1/4-inch-thick slices and remove their seeds. Place the tomato slices in a single layer on paper towels and sprinkle evenly with 1 teaspoon of the salt. Let stand 30 minutes.

Preheat the oven to 425° Fahrenheit.

Stir together the cheeses, mayonnaise, egg, dill, thyme, tarragon, apple cider vinegar, green onion, sugar, pepper, and remaining 1 teaspoon salt in a large bowl until combined. Set aside. Pat the tomato slices dry with a paper towel.

To assemble: Sprinkle the cornmeal evenly over the pie crust. Lightly spread 1/2 cup of the cheese mixture onto crust and layer with half of the tomato slices in slightly overlapping rows. Spread 1/2 cup of the cheese mixture over the tomatoes. Repeat the layers using the remaining tomato slices and cheese mixture.

Cut the remaining 3/4 pound tomatoes into 1/4-inch-thick slices and arrange on top of the pie. Bake at 425° 40 to 45 minutes, cover the edges with foil during the last 20 minutes to prevent excessive browning. Let stand 1-2 hours before serving.

THE NOBLE SOUTH
Mobile

Chef and owner Chris Rainosek of The Noble South creates exceptional Southern food with flair and style in his downtown Mobile farm-to-table restaurant. The rustic yet chic interior with exposed brick walls and warm wood floors makes for a friendly setting. Sit at the huge, welcoming bar or snag one of the window seats overlooking bustling Dauphin street. If you like to sample a variety of different dishes, this is the perfect place to do it. The Noble South has an exciting and diverse snack and small plates menu. Try the 48-Hour Beef Short Rib, Pickled Shrimp, and the Crab Salad with smoked oysters, Royal Red shrimp, hominy, and poblano, or, for brunch, try Noble's Deviled Eggs. The Vegetable Plate is a bargain and one of the best you'll find anywhere. It tastes like your grandma's home cooking with 4 sides of your choice, such as fried whole okra, field peas, heirloom tomatoes, succotash, fried green tomatoes, squash, and mac and cheese, and pairs perfectly with a glass of iced tea.

DON'T MISS: Of course, you must try Chef Rainosek's Pickled Shrimp. Also order the Pepper Jelly with blue cheese mousse, served on toast. The Noble brunch offers classic mid-morning fare, but you'll also discover original dishes like Chicken Bog, a Gullah-style chicken stew often found in South Carolina, or Baked Egg with creole tomato sauce. You cannot get more local than a plate of Noble's Shrimp and Grits with Gulf shrimp, Claude's Grits, and bill e's bacon. Definitely order that one!

THE NOBLE SOUTH
203 Dauphin Street | Mobile, Alabama 36602
251-690-6824 | TheNobleSouthRestaurant.com

The Noble South Pickled Shrimp

THE NOBLE SOUTH

1 cup lemon juice

1 cup apple cider vinegar

2 cups canola oil

6 garlic cloves, smashed

8 bay leaves

1 lemon, cut into thin half moons

1 medium yellow onion, cut into thin strips

1 tablespoon salt

2 teaspoons cracked black pepper

1 tablespoon mustard seeds

1 tablespoon celery seeds

1/4 cup fresh parsley, chopped

1 tablespoon fresh tarragon, chopped

1 tablespoon Tabasco

2 quarts water

2 tablespoons Creole seasoning

1 pound large (21/25 count) Gulf shrimp, peeled and deveined

Saltine crackers for serving

Makes 1 pound, about 6 appetizer servings

Combine the lemon juice, apple cider vinegar, oil, garlic, bay leaves, lemon, onion, salt, pepper, mustard seeds, celery seeds, parsley, tarragon, and Tabasco in a large glass or plastic bowl to make a marinade. Mix thoroughly and set aside.

Bring the water to a boil in a saucepan and add the Creole seasoning. Add the shrimp to the boiling, seasoned water and immediately turn off the heat. Let the shrimp sit until just cooked through, about 2 minutes.

Drain the shrimp and add to the warm marinade. Refrigerate, stirring occasionally, at least 4 hours and preferably overnight. Serve chilled with the saltine crackers.

Chef & Owner Chris Rainosek

BIG BOB GIBSON BAR-B-Q | Decatur

Sauces, Sides & Breads

Big Bob Gibson's Original Alabama White Sauce, 77
BIG BOB GIBSON BAR-B-Q

Pimento Cheese Biscuits, 79
BUZZCATZ COFFEE & SWEETS

Ezell's Fish Camp's Famous Hush Puppies, 81
EZELL'S FISH CAMP

Fried Green Tomatoes, 83
IRONDALE CAFÉ

Jim 'N Nick's Coleslaw, 85
JIM 'N NICK'S BAR-B-Q

Championship Bar-B-Q Rib Rub, 85
JIM 'N NICK'S BAR-B-Q

Not Your Mama's Macaroni & Cheese (The Original), 87
JOHN'S CITY DINER

Odette Red Curry Deviled Eggs, 89
ODETTE

Top O' The River's Famous Pickled Onions, 91
TOP O' THE RIVER

Vintage Mac and Cheese, 93
VINTAGE YEAR

Waysider Biscuit Gravy, 95
THE WAYSIDER

Sauces, Sides & Breads | 75

Big Bob Gibson's Original Alabama White Sauce

BIG BOB GIBSON BAR-B-Q

- 1 1/4 cups mayonnaise
- 3/4 cup distilled white vinegar
- 1 teaspoon fresh lemon juice
- 1 tablespoon coarsely ground black pepper
- 1 teaspoon granulated sugar
- 1 teaspoon kosher salt

Makes 2 cups

In a medium bowl, combine the mayonnaise, vinegar, lemon juice, pepper, sugar, and salt. Use immediately or store in an airtight container in the refrigerator for up to 2 weeks.

Tip — Alabama White Sauce is great on fried chicken or as a dipping sauce for wings. Add a few dashes of your favorite hot sauce for an extra kick.

Big Bob Gibson's lobby is full of waist-high trophies, including five Grand Champion trophies from the famed Memphis in May World Championship Barbecue Cooking Contest.

I've been a fan of Big Bob Gibson Bar-B-Q since my first visit in 1977. As far as recipes go, nothing much has changed, but in the past 20 years, BBQ guru Chris Lilly and the Big Bob Gibson competition BBQ team have risen to international prominence as one of the best barbecue teams in the world. Customers trek to this barbecue mecca from across the globe for world-championship pulled pork shoulder, ribs, and their award-winning red and white barbecue sauces. Big Bob Gibson is credited with creating the state's iconic Alabama White Sauce. This barbecue sauce is so legendary that most barbecue restaurants around the state (and even beyond) offer a version on their menus. At BBG, the chicken comes off the grill and is immediately dunked in the white sauce. Certainly, this recipe will help you up your own barbecued chicken game!

DON'T MISS: The pie. As tempting as it may be to fill up on the barbecue and sides, save room for pie. Which one? I always go for the Peanut Butter. It's a top-secret recipe made of creamy peanut butter swirled into a rich custard and topped with meringue that's sprinkled with toasted peanuts. I've never had another peanut butter pie like it. If you don't have a sweet tooth, be sure to have the chicken sandwich with Big Bob's famed Alabama White Sauce. It alone is worth the trip.

Chef Chris Lilly

BUZZCATZ COFFEE & SWEETS
Orange Beach

2017 was a big year for biscuit maker and pastry chef Kim Asbury. She partnered with Brian and Jodi Harsany to open their Orange Beach bakery, and soon thereafter, she was named the winner of the 2017 International Biscuit Festival Baking Championship in Knoxville, Tennessee. In other words, you need to put Buzzcatz on your list of breakfast spots to visit next time you're at the beach. Buzzcatz offers homemade pastries, baked goods, ice cream, desserts, and a great cup of coffee—one of the best on the beach. There is always a case of freshly baked cupcakes, croissants, turnovers, and, yes, biscuits and other treats you can eat in or take home. If you have a special occasion, they will bake to your needs; cakes and cupcakes are their forte.

DON'T MISS: Biscuits and gravy, French toast, or omelets for breakfast or brunch on the front porch. There are also weekday breakfast specials including Flap Jack Monday, Tortilla Tuesday, Waffle Wednesday, French Toast Friday, and Cinnamon Roll Sunday, which are local favorites. While Chef Asbury is extremely generous to share her famous biscuit recipe, you'd be well advised to stop by Buzzcatz and have a piping hot biscuit from her oven. Take some home, they are scrumptious toasted. They freeze well, too!

BUZZCATZ COFFEE & SWEETS
25689 Canal Road | Orange Beach, Alabama 36561
251-980-2899 | BuzzcatzOrangeBeach.com

Pimento Cheese Biscuits

BUZZCATZ COFFEE & SWEETS

1 1/2 pounds all-purpose flour

1 1/2 ounces granulated sugar

1 1/2 ounces baking powder

1/2 ounce iodized salt

8 ounces unsalted butter (very cold, cubed) plus more (melted) for brushing

3 large eggs

14 ounces whole buttermilk

12 ounces pimento cheese (Use your favorite brand.)

Makes 24 small to medium biscuits or 12 large biscuits

Preheat the oven to 425° Fahrenheit. Line a baking sheet with parchment paper.

Sift the dry ingredients together in a large mixing bowl. Cut in the cubed butter by hand until it is the size of small peas. Mix the eggs and buttermilk together. Make a well in the flour and pour in the egg mixture.

Using your clean hands, gently mix the dough for 10 seconds, taking care not to overmix. The dough will be shaggy and wet when ready. Flatten the dough on a generously floured table and add a generous dollop of pimento cheese on top.

Fold the dough over on top of itself three times until it has come together. Adding a little more flour to the top of the dough, pat out the dough to 3/4-inch thickness. Cut out the biscuits with a floured cutter and place on the prepared baking sheet.

Bake at 425° in a conventional oven (or preheat to and bake at 400° if using a convection oven) for 12 minutes. Brush with the melted butter immediately after removing from the oven.

Chef Kim Asbury

EZELL'S FISH CAMP
Lavaca

Owners Agnew & Mary Ann Ezell

What started out as a two-room dog-trot cabin and trading post on the Tombigbee River has grown into a restaurant chain that is synonymous with catfish, coleslaw, and one-of-a-kind hush puppies. Ezell's Fish Camp is not the easiest place to find, so it is smart to take your first trip in the daylight. Original owner Charles Agnew Ezell's small cabin has expanded over the years, and today the building holds over 300 guests but retains the same charm and warm hospitality of the original. It includes a porch overlooking the Tombigbee and is outfitted with mounted fish, deer, and fowl. The wood-paneled walls create a warm and rustic hunt-camp ambiance. Owner and General Manager Mary Ann Ezell Hall's family has owned Ezell's through the generations. Her son, Agnew, is the 4th generation to carry on the Ezell family's culinary tradition. While catfish is the menu mainstay at Ezell's, there are often specials. Friday night date-night features ribeye steaks for two.

DON'T MISS: The catfish is what brings in the crowds. You'll find guests from Mobile and Birmingham and as far as Jackson, Mississippi, among the locals on any given night. Ezell's serves more than 300 pounds of catfish per week. The catfish are popular, but the whole catfish is preferred by traditionalists who have been eating at Ezell's for decades. Homemade pies include Lemon Icebox, Buttermilk, and Chocolate Chess. Go for the Buttermilk, my favorite. Until now, Ezell's has never disclosed their Famous Hush Puppies recipe. Thank you, Mary Ann and Agnew, for sharing it with me.

EZELL'S FISH CAMP
776 Ezell Road | Lavaca, Alabama 36904
205-654-2205 | EzellsFishCamp.com

Ezell's Fish Camp's Famous Hush Puppies

EZELL'S FISH CAMP

2 1/2 pounds onions

1 pound tomatoes

1/2 gallon canned corn, drained

1/2 pint whole buttermilk

6 large eggs

1 pound granulated sugar

1 tablespoon baking soda

2 tablespoons seasoning salt

1 tablespoon garlic powder

5 tablespoons black pepper

3 tablespoons baking powder

2 1/2 pounds self-rising flour

2 1/2 pounds self-rising cornmeal

1 (12-ounce) can beer (Add the beer a little at a time until it is mixed thoroughly but is not soupy. Use what you need and drink the rest!)

Oil for cooking (Canola or vegetable oils work best.)

Makes 80 or more hush puppies, depending on the size of the scoop. This recipe can be reduced for a smaller yield.

Finely mince the onions, tomatoes, and corn. Set aside.

Mix together the buttermilk and eggs in a very large bowl.

In a separate bowl, mix together the sugar, baking soda, seasoning salt, garlic powder, pepper, and baking powder, making certain they are mixed together well.

Add the sugar mixture to the buttermilk mixture, making certain they are equally distributed throughout. Add the minced onions, tomatoes, and corn and stir. Add the flour and cornmeal and stir. (The mixture should be very thick and hard to stir.) Drizzle in the beer, a little at a time, using only what you need until the batter is loosened but not soupy.

Let the batter rise, uncovered, 45 minutes. (It will double in size.) After it has risen, cover the bowl with plastic wrap and transfer the batter to the refrigerator to chill 4-5 hours.

When ready to cook, heat the oil in a fryer or Dutch oven to 325° Fahrenheit.

Working in batches, use a small ice cream scoop or a teaspoon to scoop the batter into small balls. Drop directly into the hot oil and fry until golden brown. Do not overcrowd the pan or you will reduce the oil temperature and the hush puppies will become soggy.

Drain the hush puppies on a baking sheet lined with paper towels. Serve hot.

Note: For extra-spicy hush puppies, add a cup of chopped jalapeños and reduce the sugar by half.

IRONDALE CAFÉ
Irondale/Birmingham

When your restaurant's signature dish has a movie and book written about it, your signature dish better be incredible. Fans have been lining up for Irondale Café's Fried Green Tomatoes for decades, made even more famous by Fannie Flagg's book and the movie of the same name. Owner Jim Dolan and his crew serve 600-800 slices of the iconic dish each day to locals and movie fans from all over the globe looking for the original Whistle Stop Café's fried green tomatoes. Grab a tray and walk down the lengthy steam table for Birmingham's traditional "meat and three" lunch. There are daily specials along with homemade breads and desserts. Irondale Café frequently serves cornbread dressing and gravy, so you no longer have to wait for Thanksgiving when that craving hits!

DON'T MISS: The mac 'n' cheese, the cornbread, and the homemade pies all have their fair share of fans. Perhaps nothing on the menu at Irondale Café—aside from the Fried Green Tomatoes, of course—is as popular as the fried chicken. People have been standing in line for the Buttermilk Fried Chicken since the restaurant opened in 1928. Other favorites are Chicken and Dumplings. If you love that classic carrot and raisin salad, this is one of the few places you can still order it. For dessert, the Buttermilk Pie and the Chocolate Chess Pie are equally fantastic.

IRONDALE CAFÉ
1906 1st Avenue North | Irondale, Alabama 35210
205-956-5258 | IrondaleCafe.com

Fried Green Tomatoes

IRONDALE CAFÉ

1 1/4 cups cream meal*

3/4 cup corn flour*

1 cup self-rising flour

1 1/2 cups whole buttermilk

1/2-3/4 cup water, added a little at a time until the desired consistency is reached

Canola oil for frying

4 medium-size green tomatoes, cut into 1/3-inch slices

Salt and pepper

Makes 12-15 tomato slices

Combine the cream meal, corn flour, self-rising flour, buttermilk, and water in a bowl and stir until smooth and lump free. Set the batter aside.

Pour the frying oil into a large skillet to a depth of about 1/2 inch and heat to 320° Fahrenheit.

Dip the tomato slices in the batter and tap to remove the excess batter. Fry the slices on both sides until golden brown. (Do not overcrowd the pan or the oil temperature will drop, resulting in a soggy exterior. You will need to fry the tomatoes in batches.) Drain the slices on a paper towel for 10 seconds. Season with salt and pepper to taste.

*You can find cream meal and corn flour online and in most organic grocery stores in the flour aisle. Bob's Red Mill brand was used for this recipe.

Sauces, Sides & Breads | 83

JIM 'N NICK'S BAR-B-Q
Located in 14 Alabama Cities

Birmingham's Nick Pihakis and his dad, Jim, opened the first Jim 'N Nick's Bar-B-Q in Birmingham in 1985. Today, Jim 'N Nick's boasts 36 locations in 7 states. Although they have grown outside the state, the corporate culture, the recipes, and the time-honored barbecue techniques retain the Pihakis family standards. While known for their barbecue pork, ribs, and sides, the restaurant's most popular item may just be their fluffy Cheese Biscuits. I didn't score the recipe, but the mix is sold online, in their restaurants, and in grocery stores. The championship rub is used by the Jim 'N Nick's team for food events and barbecue competitions across the country. The tangy-sweet coleslaw has many loyal fans who begged me to get the recipe, saying it is the only coleslaw they will eat.

DON'T MISS: Okay, don't judge me, but Jim 'N Nick's is my favorite place to order chicken fingers! They have a crunchy exterior, are so juicy inside, and are served with the best honey mustard dipping sauce. My other favorites are the Baby Back Ribs and the Loaded Bar-B-Q Baker, which is a giant baked potato stuffed with pulled pork and classic toppings. The Bar-B-Q Nachos are also worth the splurge. Get an order of the Cheese Biscuits to go; toast them with some jam or jelly for breakfast.

JIM 'N NICK'S BAR-B-Q
Alabama locations include Alabaster, Auburn, Birmingham, Cullman, Gardendale, Greystone, Homewood, Huntsville, Jasper, Montgomery, Prattville, Riverchase, Trussville, Tuscaloosa.
JimnNicks.com

Jim 'N Nick's Coleslaw

JIM 'N NICK'S BAR-B-Q

1 (2-pound) head green cabbage, quartered, cored, and cut crosswise into 1/8-inch-thick slices (about 14 cups)

1 1/4 cups apple cider vinegar

1 cup sugar

1 cup peeled, grated carrot

4 green onions, thinly sliced

1/4 cup mayonnaise

Salt and pepper to taste

Serves 8 to 10   This slaw is perfect as a side dish or added on top of a pulled-pork sandwich.

Place the cabbage in a large bowl. Combine the vinegar and sugar in a small bowl, stirring until the sugar is dissolved. Add the vinegar mixture to the cabbage; toss to coat. Cover and let stand 30 minutes. Toss the cabbage mixture well; cover and let stand 30 minutes longer. Drain the cabbage. Cover and chill. This can be made and chilled for up to 8 hours.

Transfer the drained cabbage to another large bowl. Add the carrots, green onions, and mayonnaise; toss to coat. Season to taste with the salt and pepper.

Championship Bar-B-Q Rib Rub

1 cup kosher salt

1/2 cup granulated sugar

1/2 cup brown sugar

1/2 cup paprika

2 tablespoons ground black pepper

1 teaspoon cayenne pepper

Makes 2 cups   Combine all the ingredients in a mixing bowl and whisk together to evenly blend all the ingredients. The rub will store well for several months, covered and away from heat. This is a great stand-alone seasoning to use on any meat, but it also a good base recipe. Add your own spices to create a unique rub starring your favorite flavors.

JOHN'S CITY DINER
Birmingham

The story of the original John's Restaurant is what legends are made of. It was opened in 1944 by restaurateur John Proferis, the father of Zoë Cassimus of the famed Zoë's Kitchen chain. Proferis created dishes that became so iconic on the Birmingham restaurant scene that they are considered standards almost 70 years later. Shannon and Shana Gober bought John's in 2004 and are the caretakers of the Birmingham icon and they honor the restaurant's iconic recipes with their own spin. The original John's was known for trout almondine, and people still talk about it. The new version of that classic is their Parmesan Crusted Trout served over Roasted Corn Grits. The meatloaf is another revised classic with a red wine mushroom gravy and topped with fried onions. John's uses only locally grown or organic produce and every meat is hormone, GMO, and antibiotic free. All recipes served are comfort-food favorites with John's unique spin.

DON'T MISS: The macaroni and cheese, of course. Whether you sample each of their three macaroni-and-cheese recipes or go for the award-winning Three Little Pigs rendition, you'll discover John's is the bomb when it comes to mac and cheese. John's is also one of the few Birmingham restaurants serving duck; their Crispy Duck has a perfectly crisp outside and is succulent inside. Try the beer-crusted Fish and Chips made with Good People Brewing Company draft or the Hong Kong-style Chicken and Waffles with honey-soy sauce syrup. All have legions of return fans for a very good reason.

JOHN'S CITY DINER
112 Richard Arrington Jr. Boulevard North | Birmingham, Alabama 35203
205-322-6014 | JohnsCityDiner.com

Not Your Mama's Macaroni & Cheese (The Original)

JOHN'S CITY DINER

Serves 4-6 depending on portion size

1 cup panko (Japanese breadcrumbs)

1 (4-ounce) package thinly sliced prosciutto

1 (16-ounce) package penne pasta

1/2 cup unsalted butter

1 shallot, minced

1/4 cup dry white wine

1/4 cup all-purpose flour

2 cups whole milk (You can substitute 2% or non-fat but the taste will be different.)

2 cups heavy cream or whipping cream

1 bay leaf

1/2 teaspoon salt

1/4 teaspoon ground red pepper

2 (10-ounce) blocks sharp white Cheddar cheese, shredded

1 cup shredded smoked Gouda cheese (You may substitute regular Gouda.)

1/2 cup shredded Parmesan cheese

Preheat the oven to 400° Fahrenheit.

Toast the panko in a single layer on a baking sheet 5-7 minutes or until golden, stirring once after 2 1/2 minutes. Set aside.

Cook the prosciutto in batches in a lightly greased large skillet over medium heat 3-4 minutes on each side or until crisp. Drain on paper towels. Crumble. Set aside.

Prepare the pasta according to the package directions. Drain. Set aside.

Melt the butter in a Dutch oven over medium heat; add the shallot, and sauté 3 minutes or until tender. Add the wine, stirring to loosen the particles from the bottom of the Dutch oven, and cook 1 minute more.

Gradually whisk in the flour until smooth; cook, whisking constantly for 2 minutes. Gradually whisk in the milk, heavy cream, bay leaf, salt, and red pepper. Cook, whisking constantly, 12-14 minutes or until the mixture thickens and begins to bubble. Remove and discard the bay leaf.

Place 4 cups of the Cheddar cheese in a large, heatproof bowl. Reserve the remaining Cheddar for another use. Add the Gouda and Parmesan cheeses to the bowl.

Gradually pour the sauce over the cheeses, whisking until the cheeses are melted and the sauce is smooth.

Stir in the pasta and prosciutto until blended. Pour into a lightly greased 13- x 9-inch baking dish; sprinkle with the toasted panko.

Bake at 400° for 15 minutes or until golden brown and bubbly. Serve immediately.

Note: Don't use pre-shredded cheese; it doesn't melt as smoothly.

ODETTE
Florence

Chef Josh Quick

The historic main street in the small college town of Florence offers several unexpected experiences. One is the flagship retail store of New York fashion designer and hometown hero Billy Reid. The other is Odette, a New York–style neighborhood restaurant with a globally inspired menu created by Chef Josh Quick. The menu changes frequently but you will always find locally sourced ingredients and Southern classics infused with unique flavors from around the world. (These Red Curry Deviled Eggs are a great example of Chef Quick's culinary style.) There's a nice bar where you might rub elbows with music-industry professionals having cocktails after a day in the studio. There is a snack hour each weekday with small-bite specials like BBQ Pork Rinds and Crispy Chicken Bao Buns. Chef Quick was invited to cook at the James Beard House in New York City and won the 2016 Alabama Seafood Cook-Off in Orange Beach.

DON'T MISS: The Bluewater Creek Farm cheeseburger. Odette keeps late-night-burger hours on Friday and Saturday. Get the French Onion Dip and Ranch Chips to go with your burger. Brunch happens on Saturdays from 11am-3pm, and many turn out for it. Try the Peruvian Chorizo and Eggs. Odette's Wedding Soup with Cottonwood Farm Italian sausage, kale, Parmesan, and pastina is also one of the local favorites. I had an incredible ice cream sandwich when I was last there. The ice cream is made in house, and the cookie is a perfect combo of crunchy and soft. Order two—one to eat there and one for the ride home.

ODETTE
120 North Court Street | Florence, Alabama 35630
256-349-5219 | OdetteAlabama.com

Odette Red Curry Deviled Eggs

ODETTE

12 cage-free eggs

2 tablespoons red curry paste

3 tablespoons rice vinegar

1/4 cup mayonnaise

1/4 cup sour cream

1/4 teaspoon sesame oil

Salt and pepper

1 tablespoon toasted sesame seeds for garnish

24 pieces cut fresh chive for garnish

Makes 24 deviled egg halves

Bring a medium pot of water to a boil, leaving enough room for 12 eggs. Once the water is at a low boil, add the eggs. Cook at a low boil for 11 minutes.

While the eggs are cooking, make an ice bath to cool the eggs. Once the eggs have boiled 11 minutes, remove them with a slotted spoon and place them in the ice bath. When cool, peel the eggs and cut them in half through the thickest part of the egg instead of from end to end. Remove and reserve the yolks.

Place the yolks, red curry paste, rice vinegar, mayonnaise, sour cream, sesame oil, and salt and pepper in a food processor and blend until combined and smooth; take care not to over-process the mixture so it doesn't get too thin. Place the egg yolk–mixture into a piping bag.

Season the egg whites with a pinch of the salt and pipe the egg yolk–mixture into the cavity of each egg white. Garnish each filled egg with the sesame seeds and a piece of chive.

TOP O' THE RIVER
Anniston, Gadsden, & Guntersville

Specializing in U.S. farm-raised catfish, this family-owned and operated Alabama chain has been bringing in crowds for fried catfish since 1982 when they opened their first location in Anniston. Top O' The River is an Alabama landmark and people drive from everywhere for their hearty portions of fried catfish, skillet cornbread, side dishes, and their famous pickled onions. I had so many requests for this prized recipe and I'm very happy we were able to talk owner Johnny Phillips into sharing it with us. They make their pickled onions in huge batches at Top 'O The River; we reduced the amounts, so you can easily make it at home. The Pot O' Greens are just a bit spicy and are made using another one of the family's top-secret recipes. If you're a fan of crawfish, Top O' The River is where to order it. The Broiled Crawfish platter comes to the table without the shell, so you get all crawfish meat without having to work so hard to peel them.

DON'T MISS: The coleslaw is another favorite; pair it with the pickled onions, cornbread, and the greens. Add a platter of the Creole Boiled Shrimp and you've got a Southern-style feast right there. The famous Fried Dill Pickles are made with a secret family recipe and are on almost every order. They use very thin dill pickle slices for their fried pickles and that gives the pickles such a nice crunch.

TOP O' THE RIVER
3330 McClellan Boulevard | Anniston, Alabama 36201
256-238-0097 | TopoTheRiverRestaurant.com/Anniston

1606 Rainbow Drive | Gadsden, Alabama 35901
256-547-9817 | TopoTheRiverRestaurant.com/Gadsden

7004 Val Monte Drive | Guntersville, Alabama 35976
256-582-4567 | TopoTheRiverRestaurant.com/Guntersville

Top O' The River's Famous Pickled Onions

TOP O' THE RIVER

4 large sweet onions (such as Vidalia)

2 cups distilled white vinegar

1 1/2 tablespoons granulated sugar

1 tablespoons celery salt, plus more for garnish

1/4 cup olive oil

This makes a lot. You'll eat more of these tart and tangy onions than you'd imagine—ask any fan of Top O' The River!

Peel and cut the onions into wedges or quarters. Place the onions in a deep glass bowl or a large canning jar with a tight-fitting lid. Set aside.

To make the pickling liquid, add the vinegar to a saucepan and bring to a boil. Add the sugar and the celery salt and stir to dissolve. Let cool completely. Once cool, whisk in the olive oil.

Pour the pickling liquid over the onions; cover, and place in the refrigerator to marinate overnight.

The onions should be tangy and slightly firm; they should still have some "bite" left in the texture after marinating.

Tip

Serve pickled onions with a light sprinkle of celery salt to pair with vegetables like collard greens, turnip greens, fried or stewed okra, or with cornbread as they do at Top O' The River.

Sauces, Sides & Breads | 91

VINTAGE YEAR
Montgomery

The Old Cloverdale area of Montgomery is trendy in the best sense of the word, with new restaurants and swanky shops generating a lot of buzz. But there is one spot that isn't new. It is old, in fact, but it still has that swagger of a new kid on the block, sort of like a Sinatra song. A popular Montgomery special-occasion destination for decades, Vintage Year has been the hub of Old Cloverdale since the 80s. Their interiors have recently undergone an extensive renovation, but the vibe is still totally Rat Pack; sleek and sophisticated but warmly welcoming. The menu is classic; worldly flavors share the stage with Southern favorites. The seared scallops are an excellent choice, as is the risotto; both dishes are found on the menu but may change with the seasons and availability of ingredients. Beef is done well here, as are oysters. You'll usually find oysters served on the half shell with a seasonal mignonette or a cocktail sauce with some sass to it such as the Meyer Lemon Mignonette and Jerk Cocktail Sauce.

DON'T MISS: Try the Tenderloin Carpaccio; it is a very good way to start your meal, or just order it at the bar with a glass of wine. The short rib and the CAB Filet are also excellent choices in the beef department. Order a side of the Brussels and Bacon and the Vintage Mac and Cheese to go with it. Stop by for Tuesday Burger Night, a Montgomery after-work tradition.

VINTAGE YEAR
405 Cloverdale Road | Montgomery, Alabama 36106
334-819-7215 | VYmgm.com

Vintage Mac and Cheese

VINTAGE YEAR

8 ounces dry elbow macaroni

3 tablespoons butter

2 tablespoons all-purpose flour

1/2 cup whole milk

2 cups heavy cream

1 1/2 cups aged white Cheddar

1 cup smoked Gouda

1/2 cup Parmesan, plus more for garnish

1/2 teaspoon white pepper

Chopped fresh chives for garnish

Serves 4-6 depending on portion size

Cook the macaroni to the package directions, just to al dente. Set aside.

Heat the butter in small pot. Add the flour and cook over medium heat 1 minute. Add the milk and heavy cream while stirring constantly.

Once the milk mixture begins to simmer, mix in the cheeses, gradually adding in small handfuls, until the sauce is smooth and free of chunks.

Add the white pepper and reduce 3 minutes, continuing to stir so the cheese sauce does not scorch on the bottom.

Fold the cooked macaroni into the cheese sauce, taking care not to break up the noodles.

Pour into individual ramekins. Serve with a bit of extra grated Parmesan and garnish with a sprinkle of the fresh chives.

THE WAYSIDER
Tuscaloosa

When you are touted as "the best breakfast in Tuscaloosa" by the mother of all Southern media, *Southern Living* magazine, your breakfast better be good. And when you routinely serve breakfast to University of Alabama luminaries and its many sports heroes, you can bet the food lives up to the hype. Alabama's beloved coach, Paul "Bear" Bryant, used to frequent The Waysider for breakfast; he had a regular table by the door, and his favorite menu item is said to have been country ham. The Waysider is universally known for their biscuits and gravy, tall, fluffy stacks of pancakes, and Southern-style cooking. They offer a traditional "meat and three" lunch during the week, but on the weekends, it's breakfast only. If it's gameday in Tuscaloosa, you better get there early. UA alums from around the globe will be standing in line for a Waysider "Breakfast of Champions" biscuit and gravy fix.

DON'T MISS: The chicken and dressing, if they have it when you visit. It is so good, you are going to want to get some to take home. Breaded pork chops are not something you see much these days, and I love 'em. If they are on the menu, I'll order those for sure with some mashed potatoes and gravy and turnip greens. (Yep, I'm that country.) They make great beignets, too. Order those with a cup of coffee, and that, in my opinion, is the real breakfast of champions.

THE WAYSIDER
1512 Greensboro Avenue | Tuscaloosa, Alabama 35401
205-345-8239 | Facebook.com/TheWaysider

Waysider Biscuit Gravy

THE WAYSIDER

6-8 pork sausage patties or pork sausage cut into 1 1/4-inch patties

4 tablespoons sausage drippings

2 cups whole milk

1/2 cup all purpose flour

Salt and pepper

12 buttermilk biscuits (make your favorite recipe or use store bought)

Serves 6 or more depending on portion size

Add the sausage to a skillet and cook until it is done. Remove to a plate lined with paper towels to drain. Set aside. Retain the sausage drippings in the skillet. You need about 4 tablespoons. Add a bit of butter if you don't have enough drippings.

Heat the milk in a saucepan over medium low heat.

Over medium-high heat, whisk the flour into the hot drippings. Whisk and cook the flour for 2-3 minutes to cook out the flour taste. (Don't brown the flour too much as milk gravy is meant to be a light color.) Reduce the heat to medium-low. Whisk in the milk, 1/2 cup at first and then a little at a time until it is all incorporated, scraping up any browned bits from the bottom of the pan as you go. Cook the gravy about 3 minutes, whisking constantly to achieve a smooth consistency with no lumps. Reduce the heat to low. Crumble the sausage and stir it into the gravy, stirring to heat it through. Taste the gravy and season with salt and pepper, if desired.

Serve warm over hot buttermilk biscuits sliced in half.

Note: As the mixture cooks, it will thicken. If the gravy is too thick for your taste, you can thin it with a bit of chicken broth or milk.

Tip: The Waysider makes their biscuits from scratch, and you'll have to visit them to get one as the biscuit recipe is a closely guarded family secret. I was able to get Julie to part with the gravy recipe and as everybody knows, you can even make a canned biscuit taste like homemade with the right gravy!

VIEW FROM ED'S SEAFOOD SHED | Spanish Fort

VIEW FROM SUNSET POINTE AT FLY CREEK MARINA | Fairhope

Soups, Salads, Sandwiches & Stews

Tomato Salad
with Cucumbers, Basil, and Lady Pea Vinaigrette, 102
HIGHLANDS BAR AND GRILL

Gram Perkins' Egg Salad, 104
THE FACTORY CAFÉ AT ALABAMA CHANIN

Bayley's Famous West Indies Salad, 106
BAYLEY'S SEAFOOD RESTAURANT

Butternut Squash Soup, 109
BRICK & TIN

Champy's Shoals Homemade Chicken Stew, 111
CHAMPY'S

Curry's Southern BLT, 113
CURRY'S ON JOHNSTON STREET

Mobile Bay Stew, 115
DAUPHIN'S

Baby Blue Salad, 117
HOMEWOOD GOURMET

Hot and Hot Tomato Salad, 119
HOT AND HOT FISH CLUB

Ed's Famous Crab Bisque, 123
ED'S SEAFOOD SHED

Lucy Buffet's Famous Seafood Gumbo, 125
LULU'S GULF SHORES

LuLu's L.A. (Lower Alabama) Caviar, 127
LULU'S GULF SHORES

Melt Mac-n-Cheese Sandwich, 129
MELT

Brussels and Kale Salad, 131
POST OFFICE PIES

Ray's Firehouse Chili, 133
RAY'S AT THE BANK

Pork Belly and Watermelon Salad, 135
SOUTHWOOD KITCHEN

Sunset Pointe Bouillabaisse, 137
SUNSET POINTE

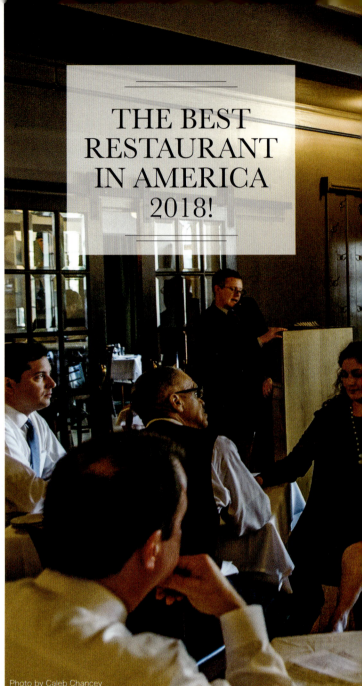

THE BEST RESTAURANT IN AMERICA 2018!

Photo by Caleb Chancey

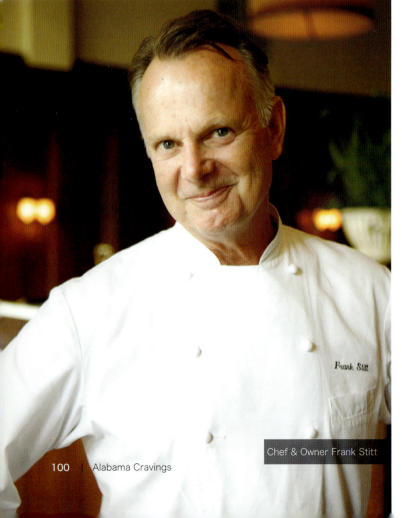

Chef & Owner Frank Stitt

Pastry Chef Dolester Miles

Alabama Cravings

HIGHLANDS BAR AND GRILL
Birmingham

In May 2018, Chef Frank Stitt and his wife and business partner, Pardis, along with the Highlands Bar and Grill team won the highest culinary honor in the land when the James Beard Foundation named Highlands Bar and Grill the best restaurant in the country. During the same ceremony, the Foundation also recognized Highlands' Dolester Miles as the country's best pastry chef. Highlands has earned many other accolades over the years, including Chef Stitt's James Beard Foundation win in 2001 for Best Chef: Southeast and his induction into the Foundation's Who's Who of Food and Beverage in America. As one of the fathers of the country's farm-to-table movement, Chef Stitt's is constantly changing his menu, filling it with seasonal vegetables and herbs, many from his own Paradise Farm. You'll always find a selection of oysters on the half shell; going to Highlands for a cocktail and oysters after work has long been a Birmingham tradition.

DON'T MISS: The experience. Highlands is cozy, elegant, and timeless. On any given day, farmers arrive at the restaurant to unload their harvest for the evening's menu. Start with the Stone Ground Baked Grits, a dish that has been on the menu from the beginning. Finish with a slice of Mrs. Dol's legendary Coconut Pecan Cake served with vanilla anglaise. The cake can be ordered whole. (Find the recipe on page 191.) Be sure to place your order early for Thanksgiving and Christmas. You will also find it on the menu at Stitt's other Birmingham restaurants: Bottega, Bottega Café, and Chez Fonfon.

HIGHLANDS BAR AND GRILL
2011 11th Ave South | Birmingham, Alabama 35205 | 205-939-1400 | HighlandsBarAndGrill.com

Tomato Salad with Cucumbers, Basil, and Lady Pea Vinaigrette

HIGHLANDS BAR AND GRILL

Vinaigrette:

1/2 cup sherry vinegar

2 shallots, minced

1 teaspoon fresh thyme, chopped

2 teaspoons Dijon mustard

1/2 cup extra-virgin olive oil

1/2 cup canola oil

Kosher salt and freshly ground black pepper to taste

Salad:

1 pound fresh lady peas, shelled

1 yellow onion, peeled and cut in half

1 carrot, peeled and cut in half

2 celery stalks, cut in half

3 bay leaves

3 fresh thyme sprigs

1 teaspoon salt

1 red onion, cut into 1/2-inch slices

Kosher salt and freshly ground black pepper to taste

Extra-virgin olive oil

2 small cucumbers, peeled with seeds removed, cut lengthwise into 4 strips and then into 1/4-inch dice

2 pounds locally sourced heirloom tomatoes, preferably a variety of colors, cored, and thickly sliced

2 fresh basil sprigs, leaves picked

1 pint locally sourced cherry tomatoes, preferably an assortment, halved

Sherry vinegar for garnish

Serves 4

For the Vinaigrette: Combine the sherry vinegar, shallots, and thyme in a mixing bowl, and let sit for 1 hour. Add the mustard and mix well. Slowly whisk in the oils and season with the salt and pepper to taste. Set aside.

For the Salad: Combine the peas, yellow onion, carrot, celery, bay leaves, thyme sprigs, and salt in a large pot; add water to cover by 3 inches, and bring to a simmer over high heat. Reduce the heat to medium and simmer 20-25 minutes or until tender. Skim the foam from the peas and discard. Allow the peas to cool in the liquid.

Meanwhile, preheat the grill. Season the red onion slices with the salt and pepper to taste and drizzle with the olive oil. Place the onion slices on the hot grill and slightly char, about 5 minutes on each side. Remove from the grill and set aside to cool.

Drain the cooled lady peas and place in a large mixing bowl. Cut the cooled grilled onion slices into 1/2-inch dice and add to the bowl, along with the cucumbers. Mix the Vinaigrette well and add 1/2 cup to the lady pea mixture. Season with the salt and pepper to taste and let stand 10 minutes.

Place the heirloom tomato slices on a baking sheet and season with the salt, pepper, and remaining vinaigrette.

To assemble: On a large plate, attractively stack the sliced heirloom tomatoes, beginning with the larger slices on the bottom and alternating the lady pea vinaigrette and basil leaves between the slices. Scatter the cherry tomatoes over and around the stack, and garnish with a drizzle of sherry vinegar and freshly ground black pepper.

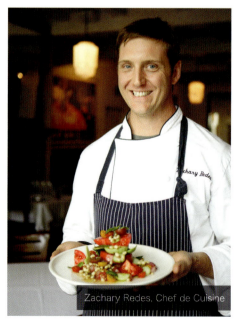

Zachary Redes, Chef de Cuisine

HIGHLANDS BAR AND GRILL
Birmingham

HIGHLANDS BAR AND GRILL
2011 11th Ave South | Birmingham, Alabama 35205
205-939-1400 | HighlandsBarAndGrill.com

Gram Perkins' Egg Salad

THE FACTORY CAFÉ AT ALABAMA CHANIN

5 eggs

2 tablespoons bread-and-butter pickles, coarsely chopped

2 tablespoons Duke's mayonnaise

1/2 teaspoon dry mustard

1/8 teaspoon ground cayenne

1/4 teaspoon kosher salt

Chives, for garnish (optional)

Makes 2 cups Hard boil the eggs using your favorite method. Peel and allow to cool. Once cool, coarsely chop the eggs and set them aside.

Combine the chopped pickles, mayonnaise, mustard, cayenne, and salt in a mixing bowl. Stir together using a whisk. Gently fold in the chopped eggs using a rubber spatula.

Garnish with the chives, if desired.

Store in an airtight container and refrigerate until ready to serve. Serve on top of toasted crostini or as a sandwich.

Natalie Chanin began Alabama Chanin in 2000, using locally sourced and sustainable fabrics and utilizing hand quilting and other "slow" production techniques in her designs. Florence, Alabama, is home to the company's design and production studios as well as the Factory Café. The café holds to the highest standard of quality for their dishes, sourcing local, seasonal ingredients. The menu frequently changes but always includes fresh soup, salads, and sandwiches plus Southern favorites such as Ms. Shirley's Tomato Pie. Gram Perkins' Egg Salad is everyone's favorite for a light bite. They also offer a mouthwatering burger and an assortment of homemade desserts.

DON'T MISS: The Factory tour at 2pm each day. If you are crafty, pick up one of the DIY kits to make your own "Natalie" creation at home. If you go on a Saturday, make sure to hit the brunch, where you'll find breakfast favorites such as Buttermilk French Toast made with house-made ciabatta bread, cinnamon custard, maple syrup, and whipped cream. You will also find Biscuits and Chocolate Gravy, a regional specialty. Bonus: The Factory Café is one of the few places you can get premium Alabama Fatback Pig Project bacon.

THE FACTORY CAFÉ AT ALABAMA CHANIN
Florence

THE FACTORY CAFÉ AT ALABAMA CHANIN
462 Lane Drive | Florence, Alabama 35630
256-760-1090 | AlabamaChanin.com

Bayley's Famous West Indies Salad

BAYLEY'S SEAFOOD RESTAURANT

1 medium onion, finely chopped, divided

1 pound fresh lump crab meat

Salt and pepper to taste

4 ounces Wesson oil

3 ounces apple cider vinegar

4 ounces ice-cold water

Salt and pepper to taste

Saltine crackers

Makes 1 pound

Spread half of the onion over the bottom of a large mixing bowl. Place the crab meat over the onions; add the remaining onions over the crab.

Add the salt and pepper to taste. Pour the oil, vinegar, and cold water, in that order, evenly over the onions. Cover, place in the refrigerator, and allow to marinate for 2-12 hours.

When ready to serve, remove from the refrigerator and toss lightly, but do not stir. Add salt and pepper to your taste.

Serve with saltine crackers.

Owner Bill Bayley, Jr.

Nita's Gumbo

Soft Shell Crab

BAYLEY'S SEAFOOD RESTAURANT
Theodore

If Lower Alabama is known for any one dish, it may well be West Indies Salad. Bill Bayley of the legendary Bayley's Seafood Restaurant is the person credited with creating this Gulf-coast classic decades ago. Now, tourists and locals alike flock to Bayley's for one of Alabama's most crave-worthy recipes, and many restaurants around the South have a version of this iconic dish on their menu. Bill Bayley, Jr., runs Bayley's just like his father did, using only the freshest local seafood in his 60-year-old family recipes. You'll find Bayley's on the way to Dauphin Island; stop in if you're driving from Mobile. In addition to their signature West Indies Salad, folks line up for the fried flounder when it is available.

DON'T MISS: Try any of their fried foods but especially the flounder, old-school-style hushpuppies, hand-dipped onion rings, and soft-shell crab when it's in season. Make sure to order the gumbo, which is made daily from Bill's late wife Nita's recipe and is chock-full of shrimp. The coleslaw is also a local favorite and a perfect accompaniment to the fried seafood platter. Say hello to Mr. Bill when you go—he's as much of an institution as the West Indies recipe.

BAYLEY'S SEAFOOD RESTAURANT
10805 Dauphin Island Pkwy | Theodore, AL 36582
251-973-1572 | Facebook.com/bayleysseafood

BRICK & TIN
Birmingham

Chef Mauricio Papapietro refined his culinary chops in the kitchens of chefs Frank Stitt and Chris Hastings before opening Brick & Tin, his artisanal restaurant where the bread is the star of the show. While the vibe at Brick & Tin is fashionably casual, the menu is elegantly upscale, created with locally sourced produce and ingredients. The menu offers silky smooth seasonal soups, crisp and clever salads, and the once lowly sandwich is elevated to mouthwatering new heights—constructed on their house-baked flatbread, potato rosemary, and focaccia breads. The Mountain Brook location offers a full bar with craft cocktails, local brews, and a well-curated wine list that complements the ever-evolving menu which frequently includes seared salmon, steaks, and house-made pasta with hearty sauces.

DON'T MISS: The bakery. Take home loaves of one of their freshly baked breads, and don't forget the cookies! The Mac 'n Cheese is a perpetual favorite as are the deviled eggs with house-made pickles. In the summer, you'll find a stellar veggie plate on the menu, filled with local peas, tomatoes, corn, okra, and other Southern favorites, and the soups are popular year 'round. Order the bread pudding from the catering menu for your next dinner party or holiday soirée. It is out of this world!

BRICK & TIN
Mountain Brook Village: 2901 Cahaba Road
Mountain Brook, Alabama 35223 | 205-502-7971

Downtown: 214 20th Street North
Birmingham, Alabama 35203 | 205-297-8636

BrickAndTin.com

Butternut Squash Soup

BRICK & TIN

Homemade Crème Fraîche:

1 1/2 tablespoons whole buttermilk

1 cup whole milk

1/4 pound unsalted butter

1 large yellow onion, peeled and thinly sliced

2 tablespoons kosher salt, plus more to taste, divided

2 medium (or 1 large) butternut squash, peeled, seeded, and cut into 2-inch cubes

2 cups heavy whipping cream

Extra-virgin olive oil for garnish

Homemade Crème Fraîche for garnish (See recipe above.)

Serves 6

Note: Make the crème fraîche ahead of time. It requires 48 hours of resting at room temperature before it is used. (Use store-bought if you are short on time.)

For the Homemade Crème Fraiche: Whisk together the buttermilk and milk and place in a glass jar with a tight-fitting lid. Let rest at room temperature 48 hours. After resting, whisk and refrigerate until ready to use. This keeps 5-7 days covered in the refrigerator.

In a heavy pot, melt the butter over medium heat. Add the sliced onion and season with 1 tablespoon of the salt. Slowly sweat the onions over medium heat, stirring occasionally until they're completely soft, translucent, and very fragrant. (There should be no browning or caramelization on the onions.)

Stir the butternut squash pieces into the onion mixture. Gently sauté 5 minutes to release the fragrance of the squash. Cover the vegetables with 1-2 inches of water. Add the remaining 1 tablespoon salt. Turn the heat to high and bring to a simmer. Turn the heat down and gently simmer until all the squash pieces can be easily mashed with a fork, about 15-20 minutes.

Carefully transfer the soup in small batches to a blender and purée until completely smooth or use an immersion blender instead. Be sure to start the blender slowly to avoid the hot liquid coming out the top. You may need to add a little more water if the mixture is too thick, so all of the squash gets puréed. When the mixture is completely combined and smooth, add the heavy cream, whisking to fully combine. Season to taste with more salt as needed.

To serve: Ladle the soup into bowls. Garnish with a drizzle of olive oil and a dollop of Homemade Crème Fraiche, if desired.

CHAMPY'S FAMOUS FRIED CHICKEN
Muscle Shoals

When I visited Muscle Shoals on my first road trip around the state for the Alabama Department of Tourism, I visited Champy's Famous Fried Chicken. I'd heard a lot about Champy's famous fried chicken, their cute interior décor, and their live music. The fried chicken was among the best I found during that 80+ stop tour, and it remains so today. In addition to Champy's Southern staples of fried okra, green beans, potato salad, and hush puppies, you'll find signature additions to the menu that are only served at the Muscle Shoals location. Champy's Shoals Famous Homemade Chicken Stew has many fans who requested I obtain the recipe for this book. Chicken Stew is a very big "thing" in the Shoals; almost every church or organization in the area will host a chicken stew fundraising dinner. Live music on Champy's screened porch might just include one of the famous "Swampers" or any other celebrated local musicians who call Muscle Shoals home. Champy's should absolutely be a stop on your list when visiting Muscle Shoals for both food and fun. Tell the owner, Wade Baker, I sent you!

DON'T MISS: The tamales! Besides the fried chicken, and the chicken stew, the Mississippi Delta Homemade Hot Tamales and the Homemade Key Lime Pie are what I always order at Champy's. It's just tart enough and is so creamy-good. Try the fried green tomatoes, which are perfectly fried. The cocktails are fun at Champy's. Get a mason jar-sized margarita or one of their cocktail specials to sip while you watch one of the incredible musicians perform live on the porch.

CHAMPY'S FAMOUS FRIED CHICKEN
120 Second Street | Muscle Shoals, Alabama 35661
251-389-9985 | ChampysChicken.com

Champy's Shoals Homemade Chicken Stew

CHAMPY'S FAMOUS FRIED CHICKEN

1 large roasting hen or 4 bone-in, skin-on chicken breasts

2 tablespoon salt, plus more to tastes

2 1/2 (28-ounce) cans whole tomatoes, undrained

1/2 teaspoon black pepper, plus more to taste

1 can tomato paste

2 large onions, finely diced

8 large potatoes, peeled

34 ounces corn kernels

2 tablespoons unsalted butter

Makes 10-12 servings depending on portion size

Barely cover the chicken with water. Add a tablespoon salt to the water. Bring to a boil and then reduce to a simmer. Skimming the foam occasionally. When the chicken is done, bone the chicken and discard the bones and skin. Pull the chicken into small pieces and return to the stock.

Mix the tomatoes, 1 tablespoon salt, pepper, and tomato paste into the stock. Break up the tomatoes with a wooden spoon. Add the onions and whole potatoes. When the potatoes are done, remove them from the stock, mash, and return to the stock.

Cook the stew on medium-low heat about 4 1/2 hours. Then add the corn and cook another 30 minutes.

After cooking, stir in the butter. Taste the stew and season with additional salt and pepper as desired.

Owner Wade Baker

CURRY'S ON JOHNSTON STREET

Decatur

CURRY'S ON JOHNSTON STREET
115 1/2 Johnston Street Southeast | Decatur, Alabama 35601
256-350-6715 | CurrysRestaurant.com

Curry's Southern BLT

CURRY'S ON JOHNSTON STREET

---

8 slices thick-cut bacon

Herb Butter:

6 cloves garlic

1/2 cup chopped fresh Italian flat-leaf parsley

Pinch of kosher salt

1 stick salted butter, room temperature

Cajun Aioli:

1/2 cup mayonnaise

1/2 teaspoon blackening seasoning (or Cajun seasoning)

Dredge:

1 cup all-purpose flour

1 tablespoon dried parsley

1/2 teaspoon kosher salt

1/4 teaspoon black pepper

1 teaspoon garlic powder

Dash of cayenne

Tomatoes:

2 eggs, beaten

3 green tomatoes, sliced

Kosher salt and black pepper to taste

2 tablespoons all-purpose flour

4 slices ciabatta bread

Leaf lettuce, shredded

Oil for frying
(Peanut or canola is best.)

Serves 2

Cook the bacon until crispy. Drain on paper towels and set aside until ready to assemble.

For the Herb Butter: Add the garlic, parsley, and pinch of salt to the bowl of a food processor. Pulse to coarsely chop. Add the butter and blend until well combined. Turn out into a small bowl. Use as needed. The leftovers will keep covered in the refrigerator for several weeks.

For the Cajun Aïoli: Combine the mayonnaise and the blackening seasoning. Set aside.

For the Dredge: Combine the flour, parsley, salt, pepper, garlic powder, and cayenne in a shallow dish. Set aside.

Heat the oil in a large cast iron skillet or fryer to 350° Fahrenheit.

For the Tomatoes: Add the beaten egg to another shallow dish. Season the tomato slices with the salt and pepper to taste. Lightly dust the tomato slices with the flour and shake off the excess. Dip the tomato slices in the egg wash and then in the dredge, covering both sides of the slices with the dredge. Place into the hot oil and fry until golden brown and crispy. Drain on paper towels.

Assembly: Brush the bread slices with the Herb Butter and grill to toast. Spread the Cajun Aïoli on one side of the bread slices; top 2 slices evenly with the lettuce, 4 bacon slices, 2-3 slices fried green tomatoes, and the remaining 2 bread slices (aïoli side down). Slice each sandwich in half and serve.

Curry's on Johnston Street is a graceful standard for lunch in Decatur. The gourmet deli is located in a beautiful 1890s building, which used to be the Cotaco Opera House. Owner Meg Curry is known for her scratch-made sandwiches, soups, salads and other Southern favorites; she has been named North Alabama's premier caterer for weddings and social occasions for the past seven years by the Decatur Daily. Homemade desserts, including the popular 'stack' cakes—baked by one of Meg's twin daughters—they are large enough to share. You'll want to make reservations early for holiday celebrations, especially Valentine's Day and New Year's Eve; the tables are draped in white linen and the menu includes specials like Oysters Rockefeller and New Zealand lamb chops.

DON'T MISS: Curry's chicken salad served with their homemade banana bread is by far the most popular menu item—for good reason! The Sweet Broccoli Salad and Strawberry Pretzel Salad are two other local salad favorites. Fried oysters and Po'boys also bring in the crowds, but it is Curry's Southern BLT that was the most-requested sandwich for this book. Finish any meal off with the Peanut Butter and Chocolate Cake, which tastes like a Reese's peanut butter cup—but better!

DAUPHIN'S
Mobile

Alabama restaurateur Bob Baumhower and Executive Chef Steve Zucker have created a sophisticated dining experience on the 34th floor of the Trustmark Building, which once was Mobile's renowned Bienville Club. The restaurant boasts incomparable views of Mobile Bay and the menu marries Baumhower's love of the Caribbean with Chef Zucker's deep Creole roots. Items such as Oysters Bienville, Kingston Rooster, and specials like Creole Beef Daube, and Lechon a la Cubano have won Dauphin's and Chef Zucker several of Mobile's top food awards including a nomination as Chef of the Year for Alabama. His Mobile Bay Stew was nominated for a prestigious Lagniappe "Nappie" award for Best Entrée in Mobile.

DON'T MISS: Chef Zucker's riff on Leah Chase's famous Gumbo Z'Herbes recipe is found on Alabama's 100 Dishes to Eat Before You Die list and is one of my personal Alabama cravings. The Gorgonzola, Pear, and Spinach Salad with Conecuh bacon dressing is wonderful for lunch or dinner, as are the Fried Green Tomatoes and Alabama Shrimp Remoulade. Save room for dessert; order the impressive Leslie's Passion—a tableside flambé of blackberries, blueberries, strawberries, and raspberries in a Chambord-Grand Marnier sauce over vanilla ice cream, which serves 2. Book the Chef's Table for your party of 6 or fewer; it is without question the best table in Mobile. You'll get to watch the chefs in action and enjoy a bird's eye view of Mobile Bay as far as the eye can see.

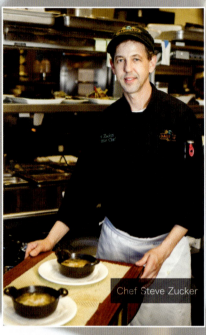
Chef Steve Zucker

DAUPHIN'S
107 St Francis Street | Mobile, Alabama 36602
251-444-0200 | GoDauphins.com

Mobile Bay Stew

DAUPHIN'S

6 ounces Bill E's small-batch bacon, diced small

6 ounces Conecuh sausage, diced small

1-2 large yellow onions, diced small (about 2 cups)

1 cup celery, diced small

1/2 cup green bell pepper, diced small

1/4 cup garlic, minced

4 ounces unsalted butter

4 ounces all-purpose flour

3 tablespoons tomato paste

6 cups shrimp or seafood stock

2 large tomatoes, diced small

1 pound Yukon Gold potatoes, diced small

2 bay leaves

1 tablespoon red pepper flakes or to taste

2 tablespoons fresh thyme, minced

2 ounces Baumhower's hot sauce

1 ounce Lea & Perrins or your favorite Worcestershire sauce

1 tablespoon ground black pepper

1 tablespoon Tony Chachere's or your favorite Creole seasoning

12 large (21/25 count) Gulf shrimp

12 ounces flounder filets

4 eggs

12 fresh Gulf oysters

8 ounces lump crabmeat

1 tablespoon green onions, chopped, for garnish

Serves 4-6 depending on serving size A fan favorite. The key to this recipe is to prep everything in advance and to make sure the ingredients are all diced the same size to ensure even cooking.

Add the diced bacon and sausage to a 3-quart heavy-bottom pot over high heat. Once the bacon is crispy and the sausage is browned, add the onions, celery, bell pepper, and garlic.

Cook while stirring until the onions are translucent. Add the butter. Whisk in the flour and tomato paste, stirring often to make sure the bottom does not burn. Cook for 3 minutes, stirring constantly.

Add the shrimp stock, tomatoes, and diced potatoes. Stir well to make sure nothing is sticking to the bottom of the pot.

Add the bay leaves, red pepper flakes, thyme, hot sauce, Worcestershire, black pepper, and Creole seasoning. Bring to a boil and then reduce to a simmer. Simmer for 15 minutes or until the potatoes are just cooked.

Place the shrimp and fish in the simmering stew.

One by one, gently crack the eggs into the simmering stew. Once the shrimp and fish are cooked and the eggs are poached but have a raw yolk, add the oysters and crabmeat. Boil for 10 seconds and ladle into large bowls, distributing the seafood and eggs evenly. Garnish with the chopped green onions.

HOMEWOOD GOURMET
Birmingham/Homewood

The husband and wife chef team of Laura and Chris Zapalowski made Alabama their home after evacuating to Birmingham during Hurricane Katrina in 2005. They brought their love for creative Louisiana cuisine with them and have developed quite a following for their New Orleans inspired creations. Dine in or pick up one of the popular 'Dinner in a Dash' take-home meals. Chicken and Sausage Jambalaya is one of the most popular dishes and the roll ups are perfect to pick up for get-togethers at home. All components of their recipes are made from scratch, right down to the bread for their many sandwiches. This is where you'll find Birmingham's original Baby Blue Salad; it has been a local standard since it first appeared on the menu.

DON'T MISS: The daily specials. The Chicken Pot Pie on Mondays has a flaky crust and is one of the best comfort food dishes in Birmingham. Guests swear by the Grilled Meatloaf Sandwich. The classic Louisiana recipes have their own fans; the Shrimp Po'boy is one of the best you will find outside of New Orleans. Try the oh-so-decadent Bread Pudding with Whiskey Sauce, made from their fresh-baked bread. Order one for your next special occasion or holiday dinner.

HOMEWOOD GOURMET
1919 28th Avenue South, Suite 113 | Homewood, Alabama 35209
205-871-1620 | HomewoodGourmet.com

Baby Blue Salad

HOMEWOOD GOURMET

Spiced Pecans:

1/4 cup plus 2 tablespoons sugar, divided

1 cup warm water

1 cup pecan halves

1 tablespoon chili powder

1/8 teaspoon ground red pepper

Dressing:

1/2 cup balsamic vinegar

3 tablespoons Dijon mustard

3 tablespoons honey

1 tablespoon chopped fresh garlic

1 tablespoon chopped fresh shallots

1 1/2 cups olive oil

1/2 teaspoon salt

1/4 teaspoon ground black pepper

Salad:

1 (5-ounce) bag mixed spring salad greens

1/4 cup crumbled blue cheese

1 orange, peeled and sectioned

1/2 pint fresh strawberries, hulled and quartered

Serves 2 to 4 depending on portion size

Preheat the oven to 350° Fahrenheit.

For the Spiced Pecans: Stir together 1/4 cup of the sugar and the warm water until the sugar dissolves. Add the pecans; soak 10 minutes. Drain and discard the liquid.

Combine the remaining 2 tablespoons sugar, chili powder, and red pepper. Add the pecans; toss to coat. Place the pecans in a single layer on a lightly greased baking sheet. Bake at 350° for 10 minutes or until golden brown, stirring once. Set aside to cool. (The Spiced Pecans will keep for several weeks in an airtight container. Use leftovers for another use.)

For the Dressing: Whisk together the vinegar, Dijon, honey, garlic, and shallots in a large mixing bowl. Slowly drizzle in the oil while whisking constantly. Season with the salt and pepper. Set aside until ready to use.

For the Salad: Toss together the salad greens, blue cheese, orange segments, and strawberries in a large bowl. Drizzle with 1/3-1/2 cup of the Dressing; gently toss to coat. Reserve the remaining Dressing for another use. Top the salad with 1/2 cup of the Spiced Pecans, and serve immediately.

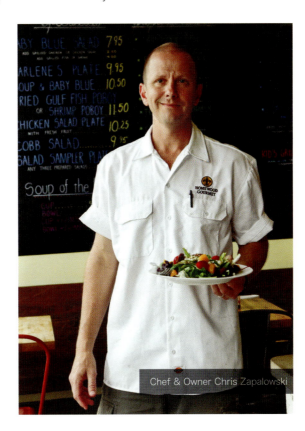

Chef & Owner Chris Zapalowski

HOT AND HOT FISH CLUB
Birmingham

The husband-and-wife team of Chris and Idie Hastings opened their highly acclaimed Hot and Hot Fish Club in Birmingham's historic Upside-Down Plaza in 1995. The restaurant is a tribute to locally grown, sourced, and foraged ingredients. The menu is modern yet steeped in tradition of days gone by, marrying components of French, Californian, and classic Southern cuisines. Hot and Hot has a loyal local following, but the dining room is often filled with tourists and food lovers from all over who know Chef Hastings from his victory over Bobby Flay on *Iron Chef America* or his James Beard Foundation award for Best Chef: South in 2012. The menu at Hot and Hot changes with the seasons, and one dish is always most eagerly anticipated—the Hot and Hot Tomato Salad. Its many fans eagerly await the email announcing its return to the menu each spring, quite an accomplishment in a city that boasts dishes that have inspired books and movies.

DON'T MISS: I ask for a seat at the chef's counter where I can watch the culinary process happen; I always pick up a few tricks watching the chefs at work. You cannot go wrong with any fish dish—there are usually several on the menu as Chef Hastings is as a member of the Alabama Seafood Marketing Commission. The Elton's Chocolate Soufflé is one of the best desserts in town. It takes 30 minutes to bake so make certain to place your dessert order with your entrée. The soufflé is served warm with a decadent Crème Anglaise.

HOT AND HOT FISH CLUB
2180 11th Court South | Birmingham, Alabama 35205
205-933-5474 | HotAndHotFishClub.com

Hot and Hot Tomato Salad

HOT AND HOT FISH CLUB

Balsamic Vinaigrette:

1/2 cup extra-virgin olive oil

1/2 cup olive oil

1 cup fresh chives, finely chopped

1 cup balsamic vinegar

1/2 cup green onions, chopped

1/4 teaspoon kosher salt

1/8 teaspoon freshly ground black pepper

Salad:

6 large beefsteak tomatoes

2 large Golden Delight tomatoes

2 large Big Rainbow tomatoes

3/4 cup plus 3 tablespoons Balsamic Vinaigrette, divided (See recipe above.)

1 1/2 teaspoons kosher salt, plus more to taste

3/4 teaspoon freshly ground black pepper, plus more to taste

1 smoked ham hock

1 large onion, peeled and quartered

1 fresh thyme sprig

1 cup fresh field peas such as black-eye, pink-eye, Crowder, or butter beans

3 ears yellow corn, husked

2 tablespoons peanut oil

Serves 6

For the Balsamic Vinaigrette: Whisk together all the ingredients in a large bowl. The vinaigrette can be used immediately or stored in an airtight container in the refrigerator up to 5 days. Be sure to bring the chilled vinaigrette to room temperature and whisk well before serving. Makes 2 cups.

For the Salad: Core and slice the beefsteak, Golden Delight, and Big Rainbow tomatoes into 1/4-inch-thick slices. Toss the tomatoes with 3/4 cup of the Balsamic Vinaigrette. Season the tomatoes with the salt and pepper and set aside at room temperature to marinate until ready to serve.

Combine the ham hock, onion quarters, thyme sprig, and field peas in a medium stockpot with enough cold water to cover the beans. Bring the peas to a simmer and cook until just tender, 12-15 minutes, stirring occasionally. Remove from the heat, drain, and cool. Remove and discard the ham hock, onion, and thyme. Place the cooled peas in a mixing bowl and set aside.

Shave the kernels off the corn cobs, discarding the silk hairs. Heat the peanut oil in a large skillet over medium-high heat. Add the corn kernels and cook until tender, 8-10 minutes. Season the corn with the salt and pepper to taste, remove from the heat and cool slightly. Toss the corn kernels with the cooked field peas and the remaining 3 tablespoons of the Balsamic Vinaigrette. Set the pea mixture aside to marinate at room temperature until ready to serve.

Recipe continued on next page.

Recipe copyright Chef Chris Hastings.

Recipe continued from previous page.

Hot and Hot Tomato Salad

HOT AND HOT FISH CLUB

Fried Okra:

4 cups vegetable oil

30 pieces whole baby okra

1/4 cup whole-milk buttermilk

1/4 cup corn flour

1/4 cup cornmeal

1/4 cup all-purpose flour

1 teaspoon kosher salt, plus more to taste

1/2 teaspoon freshly ground black pepper, plus more to taste

Chive Dressing:

1 small garlic clove, peeled and finely minced

6 tablespoons fresh chives, finely chopped

1 large egg yolk

2 tablespoons fresh lemon juice

1/2 teaspoon kosher salt

1/4 teaspoon freshly ground black pepper

1 cup olive oil

1/4 cup homemade Crème Fraîche (or store bought)

1/2 pint Sweet 100 tomatoes (Tiny currant tomatoes may be substituted.)

Fried Okra (See recipe above.)

6 slices Applewood smoked bacon, cooked until crisp

3/4 cup Chive Dressing (See recipe above.)

6 tablespoons fresh basil, chiffonade for garnish

Recipe copyright Chef Chris Hastings.

For the Fried Okra: Pour the vegetable oil into a deep-sided skillet to a depth of 3 inches. (Alternately, a deep fryer can be filled with vegetable oil.) Preheat the oil to 350° Fahrenheit.

Trim the okra stems and place the okra pods in a small bowl with the buttermilk. Toss until well coated.

Combine the corn flour, cornmeal, flour, salt, and pepper in medium-size bowl. Drain the okra from the buttermilk and toss in the cornmeal mixture. Shake off any excess cornmeal mixture. Place the okra in the preheated vegetable oil and fry for 2-3 minutes or until golden. Remove the okra from the hot oil with a slotted spoon and drain on a paper towel–lined plate. Season the okra with the additional salt and pepper, if needed. Keep warm until ready to serve.

For the Chive Dressing: Combine the garlic and chives in a small bowl. Add the egg yolk, lemon juice, salt, and pepper and whisk to combine. Add the olive oil in a thin, steady stream while whisking vigorously. This should create an emulsion. Whisk in the Crème Fraîche. You may need to add a drop or two of water if the dressing is too thick. Cover and chill the dressing for at least 20 minutes before serving. The dressing will keep refrigerated in an airtight container for up to two days. Makes about 1 1/4 cups.

To serve: Arrange each of the different types of marinated sliced tomatoes on six plates. Place the whole Sweet 100 tomatoes around the sliced tomatoes. Evenly divide the pea-and-corn mixture among the plates on top of the tomatoes. Arrange 5 pieces of the Fried Okra around each plate and place 1 slice of the crispy bacon on the top of each salad. Drizzle 1-2 tablespoons of the Chive Dressing over the tops of each salad and garnish each with 1 tablespoon of the basil. Serve immediately.

Chef & Owner Chris Hastings

Sedesh Boodran, Chef de Cuisine

Soups, Salads, Sandwiches & Stews

ED'S SEAFOOD SHED
Spanish Fort

A Lower Alabama landmark since the Bridges family opened it on the Causeway (technically Battleship Parkway) in 2000, Ed's Shed, as it is affectionately known, is a great little seafood shack. Except it isn't little. Ed's is a sprawling building with a series of decks overlooking Mobile Bay where the sunsets are without equal. (That's saying a lot for an area that boasts more than its fair share of amazing views.) Chef Pete Blohme of Panini Pete's and Sunset Pointe purchased Ed's in October 2017 and has been steadily adding his own seasoning to the reputation Ed's has enjoyed for almost 20 years. The Yo Mama's Platter, a massive assortment of fried shrimp, oysters, fish, crab, and hush puppies, has a cult following. The gumbo is a new menu addition and quite popular. It shares its top status with the recipe everyone asked me to obtain: Ed's Crab Bisque. Crab bisque has been a Lower Alabama staple for decades. Many families have a version, and many lower Alabama restaurants have it on their menu—but Ed's recipe is said to be the original!

DON'T MISS: Ed's has a nice selection of fun cocktails to sip while watching the sun go down. Made with cream, chocolate syrup, and rum, Ed's Bushwacker is one of their most popular drinks and can double as dessert. The homemade Key Lime Pie is another "don't miss." The crab cakes have the proper crab-to-breadcrumb ratio, and they are served with Panini Pete's famous remoulade sauce and that takes the dish to the next level.

ED'S SEAFOOD SHED
3382 Battleship Parkway | Spanish Fort, Alabama 36527
251-625-1947 | EdsShed.com

Ed's Famous Crab Bisque

ED'S SEAFOOD SHED

1/4 pound sweet cream butter

1 cup diced celery

1 cup diced onion

1 cup diced red onion

1 cup diced green pepper

1 teaspoon Greek seasoning

1 teaspoon Old Bay seasoning

Salt and black pepper

2 ounces white wine

2 quarts heavy cream

6 1/2-7 cups water, plus 2 ounces water for the slurry

20 ounces shrimp or seafood stock

1 pound cream cheese, softened and cubed

2 ounces cornstarch

1 1/2 pounds lump crab, carefully picked over for shell

1 1/2 pounds crab claw meat, carefully picked over for shell

Chopped fresh parsley for garnish

Makes 4 1/2 quarts (18 cups)

Melt the butter in a large stockpot over low heat. Add the celery, onion, red onion, and green pepper to the pot and cook over medium heat 15-20 minutes. (You want to soften the vegetables but not brown them.)

When the vegetables are tender, add the Greek seasoning, Old Bay seasoning, salt and pepper to taste, and white wine; stir. Simmer 5 minutes. Purée the mixture using an immersion blender or regular blender until liquified.

Add the cream and increase the heat to medium-high. Bring to a boil. Reduce the heat.

In a separate pot, heat the water and stock. Whisk into the cream mixture, a few cups at a time. Bring the pot to a simmer. Reduce the heat to low. Add the cream cheese, a few cubes at a time, stirring to facilitate melting.

Once all the cream cheese has melted, whisk approximately 2 ounces cornstarch with 2 ounces of water to form a slurry. Add to the pot. Once combined, bring the pot back to a boil. Reduce the heat to a simmer. Cook 20-30 minutes, stirring frequently to prevent scorching.

Carefully fold in the crab and heat through. Garnish with the parsley.

LULU'S GULF SHORES
Gulf Shores

Photo by Chandler Williams

"Over the years, this is the recipe that I've cooked the most and that has remained a featured specialty at my restaurants. As far as the seafood goes, I use shrimp and crab, but if the season is cool enough for oysters and there are some sweet and pretty ones available, or it's crawfish season, I will toss those in, too. And though I usually use only sausage in my winter gumbo, it's no crime to add a little andouille to the pot, as well."

– Lucy Buffett

LUCY BUFFETT'S LULU'S
200 East 25th Avenue | Gulf Shores, Alabama 36542
251-967-5858 | LuluBuffett.com

Lucy Buffett's Famous Seafood Gumbo

LULU'S GULF SHORES

- 3 pounds medium wild-caught Gulf shrimp, heads on
- 2 pounds cooked blue crab claw meat, picked for shells, handled carefully to keep the meat in big chunks
- 4 large ripe tomatoes, or 1 (28-ounce) can whole tomatoes with their juices reserved
- 3/4 cup vegetable oil or bacon grease
- 1 cup all-purpose flour
- 2 large onions, coarsely chopped
- 1 bunch celery, coarsely chopped, including leaves
- 2 green bell peppers, coarsely chopped
- 8 cups shrimp or seafood stock, heated
- 2 to 3 teaspoons sea salt, or to taste
- 1 tablespoon freshly ground black pepper
- 1/4 teaspoon cayenne pepper
- 2 tablespoons dried thyme
- 4 bay leaves
- 1 teaspoon dried oregano
- 1 teaspoon dried basil
- 2 tablespoons LuLu's Crazy Creola Seasoning or your favorite Creole seasoning
- 1/4 cup hot sauce
- 2 tablespoons Worcestershire sauce
- 4 blue crab bodies, if available (optional)
- 2 1/2 pounds fresh okra, chopped into 1/4-inch pieces, or thawed frozen cut okra
- 2 cups finely chopped green onions
- 1/2 cup finely chopped fresh parsley
- 1/2 cup fresh lemon juice
- Cooked white rice, French bread, and butter, for serving

Serves 14-16 depending on portion size

Peel and devein the shrimp. Refrigerate the shrimp and crabmeat until ready to use.

If using fresh tomatoes, fill a medium saucepan with water. Bring to a boil. Carefully drop the tomatoes into the boiling water and cook for 1 minute, let cool. The skins will slip off easily. Remove the cores and coarsely chop, retaining as much juice as possible. Set aside. (If using canned tomatoes, chop each tomato into eighths and return them to the juice in the can.)

To make the roux, in a large 10-quart stockpot, heat the vegetable oil over medium-high heat. When the oil is hot, gradually add the flour. Whisk continuously, adjusting the heat as necessary to keep it from burning, until the roux is a dark mahogany color, about 25-35 minutes. Be careful: If the roux burns, you will have to start all over again!

Carefully add the onion to the roux and stir with a large wooden spoon 2-3 minutes. (The onion will sizzle and steam when it hits the hot roux, so caution is advised. All seasoned gumbo cooks have roux battle scars on one or both arms.) Add the celery and cook, stirring continuously, 2-3 minutes.

Add the bell pepper and cook, stirring continuously, 2-3 minutes more. The mixture should resemble a pot of black beans in color and texture. Add the heated stock and the tomatoes with their juices. Stir in the salt, black pepper, cayenne, thyme, bay leaves, oregano, basil, Creole seasoning, hot sauce, and Worcestershire sauce. Stir well. Bring the gumbo to a boil and cook 5 minutes, then reduce the heat to maintain a slow simmer. Add the crab bodies (if using) and simmer, uncovered, about 1 hour.

Add the okra and bring the gumbo to a boil. Cook 5 minutes. Reduce the heat to maintain a slow simmer and cook, uncovered, 30 minutes, or until the okra has lost its bright green color and is cooked down like the other vegetables. If the gumbo gets too thick, add a little water. If it is too thin, continue to simmer it, uncovered.

When ready to serve, slowly bring the gumbo to a simmer over medium-low heat. Thirty minutes before serving, add the green onion, parsley, and lemon juice to the gumbo. Cover and cook 15 minutes. Add the shrimp and crabmeat, mix well, and cook 2 minutes. Cover and turn off the heat. Let it sit at least 15 minutes more to cook the seafood. The gumbo will stay hot for a long time. Remove and discard the bay leaves. Taste and adjust the seasonings; serve over cooked white rice with French bread and butter. Gumbo is always better the day after it has been cooked, although I've never had a complaint when I served it the day I made it.

Recipe copyright Lucy Buffett.

LULU'S GULF SHORES
Gulf Shores

Singer, songwriter, and pirate Jimmy Buffett has a crazy younger sister who is a crazy-good cook. Restaurateur and cookbook author Lucy Buffett, a.k.a. the "crazy sista"—is affectionately known as LuLu. Her massive LuLu's restaurant and entertainment complex in Gulf Shores at Homeport Marina offers a laid-back family-friendly atmosphere in a colorful, open-air restaurant. Watch the boats roll in over a cup of LuLu's Famous Seafood Gumbo; Lucy says the roux is hand-stirred "until your arm falls off" to give it that dark color and rich flavor. Other favorites include Lucy's L.A. (Lower Alabama) Caviar and her Fried Green Tomatoes with Wow Sauce. Perhaps you've seen Lucy on *The Today Show*, cooking a recipe from her popular cookbooks, *LuLu's Kitchen* and *Gumbo Love*.

DON'T MISS: Crazy Sista's Crab Toast is a crabmeat and cheese casserole heaped onto French bread and perfectly toasted until the cheese is browned. The Crab Melt Nachos are piled high with crab and traditional nacho toppings. Both dishes are neck and neck for the most-popular item on the menu. I love LuLu's Gouda Grits, especially in her version of the Southern classic Shrimp and Grits. Desserts? Yaaassss. Order the indulgent Hot Fun Krispy Kreme Bread Pudding that's served with Vanilla Custard Sauce or the tart and tangy Key Lime Pie that's one of the best anywhere. All of LuLu's dishes are insanely tasty, especially the seafood, and you'd expect no less from a pirate's crazy sista. P.S. LuLu's now boasts locations in Destin, Florida, and Myrtle Beach, South Carolina!

LUCY BUFFETT'S LULU'S
200 East 25th Avenue | Gulf Shores, Alabama 36542
251-967-5858 | LuLuBuffett.com

LuLu's L.A. (Lower Alabama) Caviar

LULU'S GULF SHORES

Dressing:

3/4 cup balsamic vinegar

1/2 cup extra-virgin olive oil

1/4 cup sugar

2 teaspoons salt

1 teaspoon black pepper

4 (15-ounce) cans black-eyed peas, rinsed and drained

1 cup chopped green bell pepper

1 cup chopped yellow bell pepper

1 cup chopped red bell pepper

1 cup chopped red onion

1 1/2 cups cherry tomatoes, quartered

1 cup chopped fresh parsley

Tortilla chips or saltine crackers for serving

Serves 20-25

For the dressing: Combine the balsamic vinegar, olive oil, sugar, salt, and pepper in a jar; cover tightly and shake vigorously to dissolve the sugar. Set aside.

Rinse and drain peas well. Place in a large glass or aluminum bowl.

Add remaining ingredients and dressing to the bowl. Toss well. Transfer to a plastic container, cover, and refrigerate at least 2 hours before serving.

Serve with tortilla chips or saltine crackers.

During one memorable chapter of my life, I ran with a group of highly disreputable folks who lived in lavish historic homes on Washington Square in Mobile, Alabama. We had weekly soirées complete with costumed cabaret numbers around a white baby grand piano and copious amounts of cocktails and hors d'oeuvres. Right before I opened LuLu's, we had a reunion celebrating my friend Suzanne Cleveland's 60th birthday. One of our "partners in crime," John Coleman arrived with a great black-eyed pea dip. John is a barbecue aficionado, redneck lawyer, and rogue gourmand, so it gave me great pleasure to steal his recipe! I had just returned from living in Los Angeles, so I gave the recipe a little LuLu's twist and the L.A. reference, a perfect fit for my high-class dive. L.A. (Lower Alabama) Caviar has been on the menu at LuLu's since day one and is one of the restaurant's signature dishes. Today, we make it in twenty-gallon batches."

– Lucy Buffett

MELT
Birmingham

Harriet Despinakis and Paget Pizitz claim they were just two cheesy chicks with a food truck. And then came a restaurant. And after that, they captured quite the following of loyal Birmingham foodies, who will readily tell you that the Mac Melt, Melt's signature Mac-n-Cheese stuffed between two pieces of Texas toast and grilled, is Birmingham's best grilled cheese sandwich and has no rival. Melt is on a prominent corner in the Avondale restaurant and entertainment district. You'll often see Matilda, their food truck that started it all, in the parking lot or about town with lines of fans clamoring for their addictive sandwiches. If you like a patty melt, as I do, you'll love the one at Melt that's served on perfectly griddled Texas toast with an Angus beef patty, grilled onions, and, of course, melty Swiss cheese.

DON'T MISS: A drink at the bar. Melt has one of the best bars in Avondale. Their cheekily named cocktails like the Oops, I Did It A Gin with gin, cucumber, and basil and the Get Your Tiki On with Havana Club rum, pineapple, and ginger beer are two of my personal favorites. It is a casual menu, but there's quite a nice wine list and a good variety of packaged craft beers and craft beers on tap. While you're at the bar, order the Mac 'n Cheese Roll: Mac & cheese stuffed egg rolls, served with sweet & spicy chili glaze. Another "don't miss" favorite is the Deep-Fried Double-Stuffed Oreos. Get 5 for $5 and do not share even one of them.

MELT
4105 4th Avenue South | Birmingham, Alabama 35222
205-917-5000 | meltbham.com

Melt Mac-N-Cheese Sandwich

MELT

Mac-N-Cheese:

1/2 cup plus 1 tablespoon unsalted butter, divided

1 pound penne pasta, uncooked

4 cups whole milk

1 sprig of thyme

1 small red onion, finely diced

1/2 cup all-purpose flour

1 cup mozzarella cheese, grated

1 cup sharp Cheddar cheese, grated

1/2 cup Parmesan cheese, grated

Salt

Tabasco sauce

Sandwich:

Unsalted butter

Texas toast slices

American cheese

Mac-n-Cheese (See recipe above.)

Makes 6-8 servings of Mac-N-Cheese This recipe makes enough Mac-N-Cheese for quite a few sandwiches, or you can serve it as a side dish.

For the Mac-N-Cheese: Preheat the oven to 425° Fahrenheit. Butter a 3-quart casserole or baking dish with 1 tablespoon of the butter, and set aside.

Cook the pasta according to the package directions until al dente. Drain well and set aside.

Heat the milk and thyme sprig in a saucepan over low heat; bring to simmer but do not boil.

In a separate large saucepan, melt the remaining 1/2 cup butter with the diced red onion over low heat. Cook until the onions are softened, about 3 minutes. Whisk in the flour, mixing thoroughly, and increase the heat, whisking until the mixture reaches a blondish-brown color, about 3 minutes. Whisk in the hot milk and thyme, adding a little at a time until the mixture is smooth. Cook 2-3 more minutes over low heat until the mixture thickens and reaches a smooth texture. Strain the mixture to remove the onion and thyme; discard the onion and thyme. Return the mixture to the pan and add the cheeses, stirring until melted. Add the salt and Tabasco to taste.

Add the cooked and drained pasta; stir. Transfer the mixture to the prepared dish.

Bake at 425° until golden brown.

For each sandwich: Spread 1 tablespoon of butter over 2 pieces of Texas toast. Top each slice with 1 slice of American cheese and grill. When the toast is golden brown, remove it from the grill, place a scoop of the Mac-N-Cheese between the slices, and serve.

Owners Paget Pizitz & Harriet Despinakis

POST OFFICE PIES
Avondale Neighborhood

Chef & Owner John Hall

Post Office Pies is known for its former post office location in Birmingham's trendy Avondale restaurant and entertainment district and for Chef John Hall's hand-tossed wood-fired pizza, crafted with the freshest local ingredients and cheeses. Partners Brandon Cain and Mike Wilson (of Saw's BBQ fame) teamed up with Chef Hall on Post Office Pies, named one of the 33 Best Pizzerias in America by Thrillist.com. Hand-tossed pies like the Swine with house-made sausage, slab bacon, and Molanari & Sons pepperoni, or the Chicken Pesto with fresh basil and roasted chicken thighs are Birmingham favorites. Post Office Pies has almost as large a following for their salads as for their pizza. After asking for three years for his popular Brussels and Kale Salad recipe, Chef Hall finally gave us the recipe for my book, *Magic City Cravings*. The salad's many fans are happy to be able to make it at home when the salad is not on the menu.

DON'T MISS: There is frequently a pasta special; if it is Mac 'n Cheese, order it. The bar has a good assortment of local brews and cocktails; it is a good spot to wait on your table or a to-go order. You can watch the wood-fire brick pizza oven from that vantage point, too. The House Made Meatballs with marinara, Pecorino Romano, Parmesan, and fresh basil are tender and delicate but hearty, just like your Italian grandmother (if you had one) used to make.

POST OFFICE PIES
209 41st Street South | Birmingham, Alabama 35242
205-599-9900 | PostOfficePies.com

Brussels and Kale Salad

POST OFFICE PIES

1/4 cup Brussels sprout hearts

1 quart Brussels sprout leaves and kale mix

1/2 tablespoon canola oil

Salt and pepper to taste

1/4 cup bacon, cooked and chopped

2 fresh mint leaves, torn

6 fresh cilantro leaves, torn

Red wine vinaigrette (Use homemade or store-bought.)

1 teaspoon crushed red chili flakes for garnish

Serves 2-4 depending on portion size

Preheat the oven to 420° Fahrenheit.

Cut the root ends off the Brussels sprouts. Peel off the outer leaves, discarding any discolored or bruised leaves, and place the fresh leaves in a bowl. Set aside.

Stem the kale and roughly chop or tear it into bite-size pieces. Wash and dry the pieces in a salad spinner. Mix the Brussels sprout leaves with the kale.

Cut the Brussels sprout hearts into quarters, toss in the oil, and season with the salt and pepper to taste. Place on a baking sheet and roast at 420° 12 minutes or until browned and tender. Set aside.

To assemble: In a large bowl, gently toss all ingredients together except the red chili flakes. Sprinkle chili flakes over the top before serving.

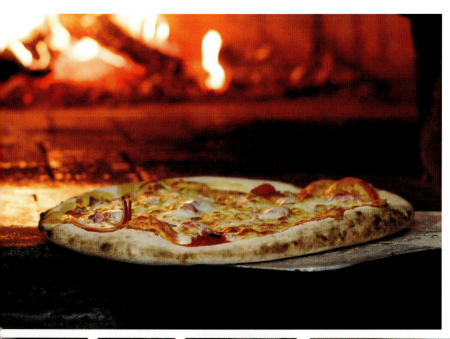

RAY'S AT THE BANK
Florence

Owner Katrina Hudson

The old bank building on Huntsville Road in Florence, Alabama, has new life as Ray's at the Bank, featuring family recipes, brisket, pork, and chicken from the smoker, a very nice wine list, and entertainment from top local musicians. Katrina Hudson has pooled her lifelong restaurant experiences and favorite recipes to create Ray's, the eponymous restaurant named for her father and business partner, Ray. It is Ray's Firehouse Chili recipe that fans asked us to obtain for this book. Lunch at Ray's features soups, salads, and sandwiches. For their popular Salad Trio, pick three "salad" sides from their list—Smoked Gouda Pimento Cheese, Chicken Salad, Potato Salad, Mac Salad, or the locals' favorite, Cornbread Salad. The Dinner menu features surf and turf, prime rib, appetizer specials, and more. West Indies Salad, Sautéed Crab Claws, and fresh oysters from the Gulf are frequently featured.

DON'T MISS: Anything from the smoker. The pulled-pork sandwich topped with coleslaw is made with competition-worthy 'cue. The lunch specials taste like your mama made them. You don't have to wait for Thanksgiving for Ray's Turkey and Dressing, as it is often on the menu in the fall. Dessert? Oh yes, you must! Order the Southern Pecan Bread Pudding—if it is on the menu when you visit—for one of the best bread puddings I've ever had. (Find the recipe on page 213.) The Lava Cake and Crème Brûlée are quite good, so save room!

RAY'S AT THE BANK
1411 Huntsville Road | Florence, Alabama 35630
256-275-7716 | Facebook.com/RaysAtTheBank

Ray's Firehouse Chili

RAY'S AT THE BANK

2 tablespoons oil

1 1/2 pounds ground chuck or lean ground beef (At Ray's, we grind our own.)

1 large onion, chopped, (2 tablespoons reserved for garnish)

4 garlic cloves, crushed

1 1/2 teaspoons salt

1/4 teaspoon cayenne pepper

1/4 teaspoon cumin

1/4 teaspoon dried oregano

2 tablespoons chili powder

1 (28-ounce) can Rotel tomatoes

1 cup tomato sauce

1 cup water

3 (16-ounce) cans dark red kidney beans, undrained

Sour cream for garnish

Cheddar cheese for garnish

Serves 6-8 depending on serving size

Heat the oil in a Dutch oven. Add the meat and cook until browned. Add the onion and garlic and cook until the onion is tender. Drain the grease. Return the drained meat mixture to the Dutch oven. Add the salt, cayenne pepper, cumin, oregano, and chili powder. Add the Rotel, tomato sauce, and water and mix well. Stir in the kidney beans. Bring to a simmer. Cover and simmer 45 minutes-1 hour.

Serve garnished with the sour cream, cheddar, and reserved onions.

SOUTHWOOD KITCHEN
Daphne

If you've ever driven down US 98 from Mobile to Fairhope, you've driven past one of the best restaurants in L.A. (Lower Alabama). Chef Jeremiah Matthews's Southwood Kitchen is just that good. It is fine dining disguised as a casual neighborhood restaurant and bar. After all, you don't often find a 12-hour cured pork belly or Akaushi Wagyu Beef Kalbi with a sunny-side duck egg on the menu at most local joints. Baldwin County, where Southwood Kitchen is located, has some of the richest farmland in the state. Gulf waters are moments away, and Alabama oyster farms are nearby. You'll see all this incredible bounty reflected in Chef Matthews's innovative cuisine. The day I was there, a forager brought in a huge bag of chanterelle mushrooms for his inspection. I saw Chef grin from ear to ear as he went to get his checkbook. The chanterelles were on the menu later that evening—that's the way Chef Matthews rolls.

DON'T MISS: I'm a sucker for BBQ Shrimp, and Chef Matthews's version is stellar. The Pimento Cheese with house-made pork rinds has a cult following. There is always a selection of local oysters, which frequently are Portersville Bay's Murder Point Oysters served with the chef's Alabama mignonette and cocktail sauces. The restaurant boasts an extensive wine selection and seasonal craft cocktail menu. For dinner, the certified Angus beef tenderloin is grilled and served with duck fat–whipped potatoes. (Yes. I said duck fat.) Pair it with an order of the Fried Brussel Sprouts with kimchi, crispy pork belly, and blistered shishito peppers.

SOUTHWOOD KITCHEN
1203 US Hwy 98 Suite 3D | Daphne, Alabama 36526
251-626-6676 | SouthwoodKitchen.com

Pork Belly and Watermelon Salad

SOUTHWOOD KITCHEN

Pork Belly:

1 cup brown sugar

1 cup salt

4 quarts water

1 (10-pound) slab uncured pork belly, skin removed

Vinaigrette:

1/2 cup red wine vinegar

2 tablespoons honey

1 tablespoon finely chopped tarragon

1 tablespoon finely chopped basil

1 teaspoon Dijon mustard

1 cup canola oil, plus more for searing the pork

Salad:

1 large seedless watermelon (seeded, if desired)

3 cups arugula (1/2 cup per serving)

Salt and pepper

12 ounces feta cheese (2 ounces per serving)

3 lunchbox peppers, finely sliced on a bias (substitute pickled peppers, if desired)

Makes 6 servings for the salad. You'll have pork belly leftover for another use.

For the pork belly: Place the brown sugar, salt, and water in to a pot and stir to distribute evenly. Place on high heat and bring to a boil. When it comes to a boil, whisk the mixture to ensure everything dissolves and remove from the heat. As the brine cools, cut the pork belly lengthwise into two even pieces and then cut them widthwise to make 8 even sections. When the brine cools to room temperature, place the pork belly into a large container and pour the brine over it. Refrigerate at least 3-4 hours but no more than 8 hours.

Preheat the oven to 200° Fahrenheit. Remove the pork from the brine, discarding the brine. Rinse the pork and pat dry. Fit the pork snugly into a 4-inch-deep pan (or any large, deep baking pan). Bake at 200° 4 hours.

After 4 hours, remove the pan from the oven and let the pork cook in its fat in the pan 5-10 minutes. Transfer the pork into a clean pan. Place another pan on top of the pork and place several baking sheets on top of the pan to weight it down. Refrigerate 4-6 hours.

For the vinaigrette: Place the vinegar, honey, tarragon, basil, and mustard in a food processor and blend. While blending, slowly add the oil to the food processor until a creamy vinaigrette is formed. Set aside.

For the salad: Remove the rind from the watermelon. Cut the watermelon into 1-inch cubes and set aside.

Preheat the oven to 400°. Remove the pork form the refrigerator and cut it into 1-inch cubes. Heat a drizzle of oil in large pan. Add the cubed pork and sear the pork on the top and bottom until the edges are golden brown and crispy. Transfer to a baking sheet and bake in the oven at 400° 3-4 minutes or until the pork belly is warm in the center.

Toss the arugula with the desired amount of vinaigrette and season with the salt and pepper to taste. Evenly distribute the dressed arugula on a platter. Carefully toss the watermelon with the desired amount of vinaigrette. Remove the pork belly cubes from the oven. Place the dressed watermelon cubes and the pork cubes in a checkerboard pattern, on top of the arugula. Top with the feta and sliced peppers.

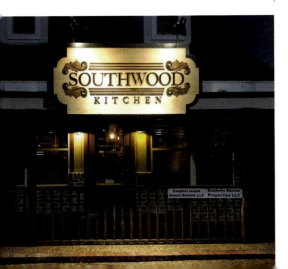

SUNSET POINTE
Fairhope

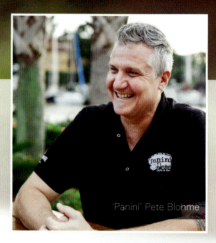

'Panini' Pete Blohme

Go for the throat! Guests have been lining up for the Gulf Snapper Throats and brilliant sunsets over Mobile Bay since Pete Blohme opened Sunset Pointe in the well-known Fly Creek Marina location in 2013. Waterfront dining among the boats and pelicans makes for the perfect snapshot of Lower Alabama. Pete is the same chef behind Panini Pete's and is the king of sandwiches and lighter-than-air beignets, which are found at his Fairhope and Mobile restaurants. Pete is also known for his support of our military, having co-founded the Messlords, a traveling culinary team that cooks for U.S. troops stationed abroad. At Sunset Pointe, Pete pays tribute to our fallen warriors with a table reserved in their honor. There is a large dining room and bar inside and a lovely outdoor patio overlooking the marina with a firepit for cooler nights.

DON'T MISS: Watch one of the unobstructed sunsets while you dine. The skies are often streaked with orange, pink, and red as the sun meets Mobile Bay. There's a daily ringing of the bell and toast to the sunset. If Pete is there, he'll lead the fun himself. Appetizer favorites include the Seared Tuna Nachos and the fried oysters served with lemon aioli. Pop's Shrimp Pasta is a dinner favorite with sautéed Gulf shrimp, fettuccine, rosemary, lemon, and a spicy tomato cream sauce. Rick Bragg's "Ode to Grouper" Sandwich, a grilled or fried fish sandwich on brioche, is named for the acclaimed Alabama author who considers it one of his Alabama cravings.

SUNSET POINTE
831 North Section Street at Fly Creek Marina | Fairhope, Alabama 36532
251-990-7766 | SunsetPointeFairhope.com

Sunset Pointe Bouillabaisse

SUNSET POINTE

1 tablespoon olive oil

8 (51/60 count) Gulf shrimp

3 ounces Gulf fish (such as redfish)

5 mussels, scrubbed and beards removed

Salt and pepper

1/2 tablespoon chopped fresh garlic

1/2 tablespoon chopped fresh shallots

1/4 cup chopped leeks

1/4 cup chopped fennel

3 ounces white wine

8 ounces fish stock

1 ounce diced red tomatoes

1 ounce diced green tomatoes

2 ounces butter

Fresh Italian parsley, chopped, for garnish

Fennel fronds, chopped, for garnish

Serves 2

Add the oil to a pan and heat to smoking hot. Quickly sauté the shrimp, fish, and mussels. Season with the salt and pepper to taste. Add the garlic and shallots and cook 2-3 minutes, taking care not to burn the garlic or brown the shallots. Add the leeks and fennel. Deglaze the pan with the white wine and cook over medium-high heat until the mixture reduces by half.

Add the fish stock and cook about 4 minutes. Add the red and green tomatoes. Finish with the butter. Garnish with the parsley and fennel fronds.

ALABAMA THEATRE | Downtown Birmingham

FISHER'S AT ORANGE BEACH MARINA | Orange Beach

Main Dishes

Braised Beef Short Rib in Red Wine Sauce, 143
COTTON ROW RESTAURANT

Seared Diver Scallops, 144
THE TRELLIS ROOM AT THE BATTLE HOUSE HOTEL

Rigatoni Carbonara, 147
ARICCIA TRATTORIA

Seared Gulf Snapper, 149
BISTRO V

Central Cedar Plank Salmon, 151
CENTRAL

Classic Shrimp and Grits, 152
CLASSIC ON NOBLE

Cast Iron Skillet Fried Chicken, 155
DYRON'S LOWCOUNTRY

Fisher's Pork Cheeks, 156
FISHER'S AT ORANGE BEACH MARINA

King Neptune's Coconut Shrimp, 159
KING NEPTUNE'S SEAFOOD RESTAURANT

Hildegard's Authentic German Chicken Schnitzel, 161
HILDEGARD'S GERMAN CUISINE

Mr. Tony's Spaghetti Sauce with Meat, 163
HUGGIN' MOLLY'S

Lobster Pot Pies, 165
OCEAN

Ricatoni's Grilled Chicken Alfredo, 167
RICATONI'S

Pork n'Greens, 169
SAW'S SOUL KITCHEN

Reggie's Original Chicken + Waffles, 173
SOUTHERN NATIONAL

Greek-Style Beef Tenderloin, 175
THE BRIGHT STAR

Elote (Authentic Mexican Street Corn) & Grilled Cilantro-Lime Shrimp, 177
THE DEPOT

Lamb Lollipops, 181
BELOW THE RADAR BREWING COMPANY

Gulf Coast Paella, 183
VOYAGERS AT PERDIDO BEACH RESORT

Wolf Bay Lodge Fried Oysters, 185
WOLF BAY LODGE

COTTON ROW RESTAURANT

Huntsville

Cotton Row features classically modern cuisine centered on seasonal and locally grown produce with a French influence and Southern flair. James and Suzan Boyce graduated from the Culinary Institute of America in Hyde Park, New York. With that came prestigious kitchen positions in New York, Arizona, and California, along with James Beard Foundation awards, Michelin stars, glamour, and celebrity. The opportunity came in 2008 to start a new restaurant group in Huntsville, and since then, Cotton Row and the Boyces have flourished. *Town & Country* magazine recently named Cotton Row the "most romantic restaurant" in Alabama—and it certainly is that. From the quiet and elegant setting to the thoughtful lighting choices to the exemplary menu and wine cellar, Cotton Row offers a perfect dining experience.

DON'T MISS: If the duck is on the menu, try it. The Braised Beef Short Rib in Red Wine Sauce, which is rich, savory, and tender, is one of my own most-craved dishes; I am thrilled Chef Boyce shared the recipe with us. The desserts are inventive, and decadent. The Peanut Butter and Jelly in Phyllo made with strawberry compote, chocolate ice cream, salty peanuts, and marshmallow fluff is D-I-V-I-N-E and found on the 100 Dishes to Eat in Alabama Before You Die list.

COTTON ROW RESTAURANT
100 South Side Square | Huntsville, Alabama 35801
256-382-9500 | CottonRowRestaurant.com

Braised Beef Short Rib in Red Wine Sauce

COTTON ROW RESTAURANT

3 pounds beef short rib, cleaned

Salt and freshly ground pepper

1/2 cup all-purpose flour

3 tablespoons olive oil

1 tablespoon sweet butter

1 small onion, cut into 1/2-inch dice

2 stalks celery, cut into 1/2-inch dice

4 garlic cloves, crushed

1/2 bottle dry red wine

1 quart veal stock (beef broth)

1 Bouquet Garni (bay leaf, thyme, rosemary, and parsley tied together with cooking twine)

Serves 6

Place the short ribs on a baking sheet and dry well with paper towels. Season both sides of the short ribs with the salt and pepper to taste. Dust the ribs completely with the flour and brush off any excess.

Heat the olive oil in a thick-bottom cast iron pot over medium heat. Place the prepared short ribs into the pot and brown evenly on both sides, about 3-4 minutes on each side. Add the butter, onion, celery, and garlic and cook an additional 2 minutes, browning the vegetables lightly.

Remove the excess grease from pot and slowly add the wine. Continue to cook slowly until the liquid is reduced by half. Add the veal stock and Bouquet Garni; bring the mixture to a simmer. Cover the pot and continue to simmer (cooking slowly) over low heat approximately 2 hours. (Or you may place the pot in the oven pre-heated to 300° Fahrenheit and cook until ribs are tender, approximately two hours.)

Remove from the stove or oven and let cool to room temperature. Once cool, carefully remove the meat from the pot and strain the liquid through a fine strainer into another pot. Return the liquid to the heat and cook until a gravy consistency is reached. Return the meat back to the thickened liquid, warm thoroughly, and serve with your favorite starch and vegetables.

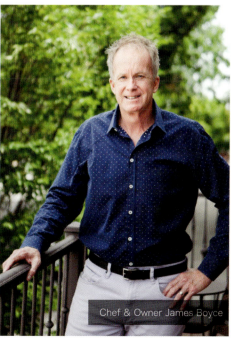

Chef & Owner James Boyce

Seared Diver Scallops
with Wild Mushroom Risotto, Sautéed Spinach, and White Truffle Oil

THE TRELLIS ROOM AT THE BATTLE HOUSE HOTEL

Risotto:

2 tablespoons olive oil

2 cloves garlic, minced

1 cup Arborio rice

4 cups chicken stock, divided

1 cup wild mushrooms

1 tablespoon Parmesan, grated

3 tablespoons unsalted butter

Salt and pepper

1 tablespoon fresh parsley, chopped

Scallops:

16 U/10 dry scallops

Salt and pepper

1 tablespoon olive oil

1 tablespoon unsalted butter

Spinach:

2 cups fresh spinach leaves

1 clove garlic, minced

Salt and pepper

Juice of 1 lemon

1 teaspoon truffle oil (optional)

Serves 4

For the risotto: Heat the olive oil in a medium-size saucepan over medium-high heat. Add the minced garlic and rice and sauté until the garlic becomes golden brown. Add 1/2 cup of the chicken stock and stir constantly with a wooden spoon. Once the stock has been absorbed, stir in another 1/2 cup of stock and continue this process until all the chicken stock is used and the rice is tender and creamy but still has a slight bite to it. Add the mushrooms and cook until tender, about 2 minutes. Stir in the cheese, butter, salt and pepper to taste, and chopped parsley.

For the scallops: Season the scallops with the salt and pepper to taste. Heat the olive oil in a saucepan over high heat. Add the scallops and sear 3 minutes. (Make sure the pan is hot before adding the scallops to obtain a good sear.) Flip the scallops and cook for an additional minute. Add the butter and baste the scallops for about 30 seconds as the butter melts. Remove the scallops to a platter; don't wipe out the pan.

For the spinach: Add the spinach, minced garlic, and salt and pepper to taste to the pan and sauté. Finish with the lemon juice.

To serve: Divide the risotto in a pasta bowls. Arrange the scallops around the risotto. Top the scallops with the sautéed spinach and drizzle with the truffle oil, if desired.

THE TRELLIS ROOM AT THE BATTLE HOUSE HOTEL
Mobile

The Trellis Room, located within the stately and perfectly restored Battle House Hotel, is the only AAA 4-Diamond restaurant in Mobile. It offers elegant but comfortable dining and the most-requested scallop dish in the state. All baked goods are made fresh daily. Make sure to gaze upwards when you enter—you'll see a Tiffany-designed stained-glass ceiling that is over 100 years old, the only one in Alabama. Sunday Brunch at the Battle House is a ritual. Try the Conecuh Sausage and Potato Hash or the Crab Cake Benedict with their signature Creole Hollandaise.

DON'T MISS: The Shrimp and Grits is an eternal favorite; guests have been known to order them multiple times during their stay. Try to score one of their incredible house-made mini Moon Pies. (Mobile is known for dropping a huge lighted mechanical moon pie on New Year's Eve, and revelers toss moon pie cookies from floats during Mardi Gras parades.) Request a seat at the chef's show-kitchen. You'll not only be entertained, you will learn some tricks of the trade for your own kitchen. Be sure to say I sent you.

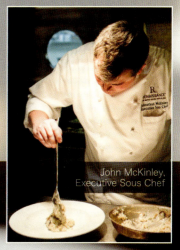

John McKinley, Executive Sous Chef

THE TRELLIS ROOM AT THE BATTLE HOUSE HOTEL
26 North Royal Street | Mobile, Alabama 36602
251-338-5373 or 251-338-5493 | Facebook.com/TrellisRoom

ARICCIA TRATTORIA
Auburn

Ariccia Trattoria is an Italian restaurant located within the lobby of The Hotel at Auburn University. Named for a town outside of Rome known for its wine, Ariccia has an extensive selection of Italian wines along with a remarkable selection of premier wines from California. Serving breakfast, lunch, and dinner 365 days a year, Executive Chef Leo Maurelli (the Alabama Restaurant Association's Chef of the Year in 2011) and his staff use fresh, seasonal ingredients and make everything on the premises. They bake the croissants and muffins from scratch each morning and crank out fresh pasta daily. Italian favorites like bruschetta, arancini, and slow-roasted porchetta are menu staples. Try the Burrata and fresh basil or the Porchetta pizza.

DON'T MISS: The Pappardelle Frutti di Mare with shrimp, scallops, octopus, clams, lump crab, garlic, white wine, and pomodoro. Brunch, served Saturdays and Sundays, is like a trip to the Italian countryside, with fresh breads for the paninos and Farm Eggs all' Amatriciana with three farm eggs, pomodoro, pancetta, and grilled bread. The desserts are crafted in house; try the Italian doughnuts (zeppole) or the coffee-liqueur-flavored tiramisu. The Piccolo bar located behind the restaurant is warm and intimate—the perfect spot to meet a client or relax after a long day.

Executive Chef Leo Maurelli

ARICCIA TRATTORIA
241 South College Street | Auburn, Alabama 36830
800-228-2876 (Reservations) or 334-821-8200 (Main)
auhcc.com/dining/ariccia-auburn-restaurant

Rigatoni Carbonara

ARICCIA TRATTORIA

Roasted Garlic Butter:

1 garlic bulb, peeled, cloves only

Extra-virgin olive oil

2 sticks butter, room temperature

Carbonara:

6-7 ounces freshly made rigatoni or 5 ounces dry pasta

4 ounces pancetta

4 ounces guanciale

2 tablespoons minced garlic

2 tablespoons diced shallots

1 ounce whey liquid (liquid from ricotta or mozzarella cheese)*

4 ounces Pecorino cheese, grated, divided

1 ounce Parmesan cheese, grated

1 ounce Roasted Garlic Butter (See recipe above.)

1 large farm egg yolk

Fresh chives, chopped, for garnish

Serves 2

For the Roasted Garlic Butter: In a small pot, add the garlic cloves and cover with the extra-virgin olive oil. Heat over medium-high and bring to a simmer. Reduce the heat and allow the garlic to cook until soft. Turn off; allow to cool completely. Reserve oil for another use. Add the cooled garlic and butter to a food processor and process until smooth. Turn out onto plastic wrap and roll into a log. Wrap and chill. Slice and use as desired.

Cook the pasta in salted water until al dente. (If using fresh pasta, cook 8-9 minutes; if using dry pasta, cook 10-12 minutes.)

In a skillet, render (cook) the pancetta and guanciale 2-3 minutes. Add the garlic and shallots and sauté until tender. Be careful not to brown them to keep the dish as light-colored as possible. Add the cooked pasta and the whey liquid. Cook over medium heat to reduce the liquid. Add 2 ounces of the Pecorino and the Parmesan. Toss. Add the Roasted Garlic Butter and toss well to coat the pasta.

To finish, add the egg yolk to the hot pasta and incorporate well. Serve with the remaining 2 ounces grated Pecorino and garnish with the chives.

*You can substitute pasta water for the whey liquid, if necessary.

BISTRO V
Vestavia Hills (Birmingham)

The 2018 winner of the Alabama Gulf Seafood Cookoff, Chef Jeremy Downey hails from Bayou la Batre, the heart of Alabama's Gulf seafood region. Chef Downey grew up cooking seafood alongside his mother, grandmother, aunts, uncles, and cousins, who were all on hand to see him compete and win the cookoff title on his first try. No stranger to competition, Chef Downey was a member of the University of Alabama's 1992 National Championship football team and today channels his love for competition and family cooking into his restaurant. Bistro V offers Southern favorites such as Gulf Shrimp and Grits with Spinach, in White Wine Cream Sauce over Stone Ground Grits. There are also European comfort food dishes such as Francisco's Paella, with fish, shrimp, chorizo, corn, sweet peppers, and saffron rice. You will always find a handmade pasta special and a risotto of the day on the menu.

DON'T MISS: The daily lunch specials, which include everything from Red Beans and Rice to Chicken Pot Pie to a fresh vegetable plate. The Bistro Cheeseburger, made patty-melt style with grilled onions, is one of Birmingham's best. The oyster, shrimp, and fish po' boys are authentic and made on Gambino's bread like they are in New Orleans. The real star of the menu is anything made with Alabama Gulf seafood, which Chef Downey brings in fresh daily.

BISTRO V
521 Montgomery Highway | Vestavia Hills, Alabama 35216
205-823-1505 | Bistro-v.com

Seared Gulf Snapper
with Heirloom Tomatoes, Chilton County Peaches, and Arugula

BISTRO V

Salt and pepper (Use freshly ground salt and pepper for best flavor.)

2 (7-8 ounce) Gulf snapper fillets

2-3 heirloom tomatoes

1 Chilton County peach

1 bunch arugula

1 teaspoon extra-virgin olive oil, plus more for skillet and garnish

Juice of 1 lemon

Lemon slices

Serves 2

Salt and pepper the snapper to taste.

Cut the tomatoes into 1-inch-thick slices. Salt and pepper each slice to taste. Peel and slice the peach.

Add the arugula to a large bowl. Add the sliced peaches and tomatoes. Dress with a drizzle of the extra-virgin oil. Add the lemon juice. Salt and pepper the salad to taste. Toss. Set aside.

Add a little bit of olive oil to a cast iron skillet and heat over medium-high. Once the pan and oil are hot, add the snapper and sear 4-5 minutes per side. Make sure the fish has a nice light brown color and is cooked through.

To serve: Place the tomatoes onto plates and arrange the peaches and arugula on top of them. Put the snapper in middle. Garnish the fish with the lemon slices and extra-virgin olive oil.

Chef & Owner Jeremy Downey

CENTRAL
Montgomery

Central is an upscale-casual restaurant in the heart of downtown Montgomery. Rated #1 in Montgomery by diners on TripAdvisor, the beautifully refurbished restaurant is housed in an 1890s warehouse with exposed brick, flickering gas lanterns, and a fast-paced open-concept kitchen, where guests can watch the chefs man the wood-fired ovens. Executive Chef Jason McGarry hails from the Lowcountry of South Carolina and brings many of that region's standard fare to the menu. Central uses local and seasonal ingredients in their updated Southern comfort food classics such as their sweet tea-brined pork chop and Fett Sow Fries, a deep-fried pork belly served with peach chutney. It is a perfect date-night spot, with low, romantic gas lamps lighting the room with a soft glow, and it is an easy place to entertain your business associates, too. There's something for everyone: Steak, seafood, chicken, pasta, or creatively cooked local veggies. I had a wonderful time at Central and am looking forward to my next visit.

DON'T MISS: Try the "Smokra"—a Carolina rice-crusted smoked okra served with the chef's Lowcountry Remoulade—or the Tuna Niçoise, which is as beautiful as it is delicious. If you get the chance, attend one of Central's exclusive wine dinners or plan your next celebration in one of their signature event spaces. The bar crafts seasonal cocktails, like "Not a Date"—an ingenious fig-infused libation with an equally clever name. Save room for Central's decadent desserts such as the homemade doughnuts with a bourbon-praline sauce and bacon-powdered sugar.

CENTRAL
129 Coosa Street | Montgomery, Alabama 36104
334-517-1155 (Dining) or 334-517-1121 (Events)
Central129Coosa.com

Central Cedar Plank Salmon
with Heirloom Tomatoes and Basil Pesto

CENTRAL

3 (12-inch) untreated cedar planks

Salmon:

1/3 cup vegetable oil

1 1/2 tablespoons rice vinegar

1 teaspoon sesame oil

1/3 cup soy sauce

1/4 cup chopped green onions

1 tablespoon grated fresh ginger

1 teaspoon minced garlic

2 (2-pound) salmon fillets, skins removed

Heirloom Tomatoes:

3 heirloom tomatoes, cut into wedges

1/4 cup olive oil

1/4 cup shaved chives

1/4 cup white balsamic vinegar

Salt and pepper

Basil Pesto:

2 cups fresh basil leaves

1/2 cup pine nuts

2 garlic cloves

1/2 cup grated Parmesan

1/2 cup olive oil

Serves 2

Note: You must soak the cedar planks in water for at least one hour before using them on the grill or they will burn. Soak them longer if you have the time.

For the Salmon: In a shallow dish, mix together the vegetable oil, rice vinegar, sesame oil, soy sauce, green onions, ginger, and garlic. Place the salmon fillets in the marinade and turn to coat. Cover and marinate 15 minutes to 1 hour.

For the Heirloom Tomatoes: Toss the tomato wedges with the olive oil, shaved chives, and balsamic vinegar. Season with the salt and pepper to taste. Cover and keep refrigerated until ready to serve.

For the Basil Pesto: Add all the ingredients to a food processor and process until smooth. Store in an airtight container until ready to serve.

To Grill the Salmon: Preheat an outdoor grill to medium heat. Place the wet planks, side by side, along the length of the grill grate. The boards are ready when they start to smoke and crackle. Place the salmon fillets on the planks; discard the marinade. Cover and grill about 20 minutes or until the salmon flakes with a fork. (The fish will continue to cook after you remove it from the grill.)

To serve: Add a swirl of Basil Pesto to the plate and top with the heirloom tomatoes; add the salmon and a bit more of the pesto, if desired.

Executive Chef Jason McGarry

Main Dishes

Classic Shrimp and Grits

CLASSIC ON NOBLE

1/2 pound bacon

1/2 pound fresh collard greens

1/2 cup chopped Roma tomatoes

1/2 cup shrimp or seafood stock

Salt and black pepper

Grits:

1 1/2 cups whole milk

1 1/2 cups heavy cream

1 cup uncooked coarse ground grits

1/4 teaspoon salt

1 tablespoon unsalted butter

1/2 cup Parmesan cheese, grated

Lemon Beurre Blanc:

2 shallots, finely chopped

1 cup white wine

1/4 cup lemon juice

1 tablespoon heavy cream

12 tablespoons cold unsalted butter, cubed

Salt

White pepper

Shrimp:

1/2 tablespoon olive oil

2 cloves garlic, minced

1/2 pound Andouille sausage

1 pound (26-30 count) large Gulf shrimp, peeled and deveined with tails left on

Fresh Italian flat-leaf parsley, chopped, for garnish

Large shards of shaved Parmesan cheese, for garnish, optional

Serves 4

Cook the bacon until crisp and drain on paper towels. Once cooled, chop and set aside. Remove and discard the hard center vein and hard stems from the collards. Chop the collards. Add to the hot bacon drippings along with the chopped tomatoes. Stir to wilt the collards; add the stock and cook until the liquid is reduced by half. Season with the salt and pepper to taste. Keep warm and set aside.

For the grits: Place the milk and cream in sauce pot and warm over medium heat. Do not let the milk come to a boil. When it is hot, whisk in the grits. Switch to a wooden spoon and stir continuously. Cook the grits according to package instructions. When the grits are fully cooked, remove from the heat and stir in the salt, butter, and Parmesan cheese. Taste and adjust the seasoning as desired. Set aside and reheat before serving.

For the Lemon Beurre Blanc: Combine the shallots, white wine, and lemon juice in a saucepan over high heat and cook, reducing to 2 tablespoons. Add the cream. Once it bubbles, reduce the heat to low. Add the cold butter, one cube at a time, whisking first on the heat and then off the heat. Continue whisking the butter into the mixture until it is fully emulsified and has reached a rich sauce consistency. Season to taste with the salt and white pepper. (You can keep the sauce warm in a Thermos until ready to serve.)

For the shrimp: Heat the olive oil in a sauté pan. Add the garlic and sausage and cook over medium-high heat about 2 minutes. Carefully add the shrimp and cook 2 minutes on each side.

To plate: Divide the grits evenly among 4 shallow bowls. Top each evenly with the collard green mixture, Lemon Beurre Blanc, shrimp, and bacon. Garnish with the parsley and the Parmesan shavings.

Note: If the Lemon Beurre Blanc starts to thicken, you can thin it with a few drops of hot water or hot white wine.

CLASSIC ON NOBLE
Anniston

When David Mashburn's employer moved its operations to Mexico, it looked like his career was ending. Instead, that event motivated David and wife Cathy to turn their successful part-time catering business into a full-time restaurant. They found a historic building in downtown Anniston and renovated it. That renovation sparked a revival of Anniston's downtown area. Classic on Noble has become an iconic Alabama restaurant destination, best known for their legendary holiday celebrations. They spend four weeks decorating for Christmas, and longtime customers make reservations for Christmas on Noble a year in advance. The lavish Sunday brunch offers everything imaginable, from carving, omelet, and waffle stations to a chocolate fountain. Classic's Shrimp and Grits have been featured in *Southern Living* and are also found on the *100 Dishes to Eat in Alabama Before You Die* list. Reservations are recommended. They only use the freshest Gulf seafood and get their signature beef from Miller Farms.

DON'T MISS: Dessert. It will be difficult, but save room for dessert, especially the White Chocolate Bread Pudding, which is a family recipe and made by David's mother. If you take the staircase upstairs, you'll find the Green Olive, an upscale dining room and bar decorated with a vintage supper-club feel. The tables near the window overlooking Noble Street are particularly romantic; it is the perfect setting for a first date, an anniversary, or a proposal.

CLASSIC ON NOBLE
1024 Noble Street | Anniston, Alabama 36201
256-237-5388 | ClassicOnNoble.com

Main Dishes | 153

DYRON'S LOWCOUNTRY
Birmingham

Executive Chef Randall Baldwin

Located on a quaint corner in one of Mountain Brook's villages, Dyron's Lowcountry and Chef Randall Baldwin have a longstanding reputation for bringing the best of South Carolina's Lowcountry coastal cuisine to Birmingham. The menu offers steaks, rich braises, and Lowcountry favorites such as gumbo. The gumbo even has a fan club; regular customers demand it, even when it is blazing hot outside. The dark roux takes 3-4 hours to cook, and it is loaded with Gulf lump crabmeat and whole shrimp. (The gumbo recipe is featured in my book *Magic City Cravings*.) Dyron's always has a good selection of oysters.; the list usually includes oysters from Alabama farmers as well as bivalves from around the country. Chef Baldwin's Cast Iron Skillet Fried Chicken has always been a favorite but recently experienced a surge in popularity when it was reported that Chef Frank Stitt's daughter, Marie, served it to guests at her wedding reception.

DON'T MISS: The authentic West Indies Salad—Dyron's is one of the few places you can find it off the coast—along with She-Crab Soup when it is in season. The ribeye is one of the best in town, and if short ribs happen to be on the menu when you visit, order them. The back porch is casual and great for watching the game with friends. Sunday brunch is a tradition. Eggs and grits share the menu with beignets, a Gulf crabmeat omelet, and pork belly. The bar program includes seasonal craft cocktails along with an excellent wine list.

DYRON'S LOWCOUNTRY
121 Oak Street | Mountain Brook, Alabama 35223
205-834-8257 | DyronsLowcountry.com

Cast Iron Skillet Fried Chicken

DYRON'S

Brine:

1 gallon water

1/4 cup kosher salt

1 cup honey

12 sprigs fresh rosemary

1 bunch fresh thyme

12 black peppercorns

12 bay leaves

6 lemons, cut in half

1 all-natural fryer chicken, cut into breasts, thighs, and legs

Dredge:

2 cups all-purpose flour

2 tablespoons garlic powder

2 tablespoons onion powder

Salt and pepper

1/2 tablespoon paprika

1 quart whole buttermilk

2 cups peanut oil

Fresh thyme for garnish

Fresh rosemary for garnish

Serves 4-6

For the brine: Combine the water, salt, honey, rosemary, thyme, peppercorns, bay leaves, and lemons and simmer 30 minutes. Strain the brine, discarding the solids, and refrigerate until completely cold. After cutting up the chicken, soak in the cold brine for 12 hours.

For the dredge: Combine the flour, garlic powder, onion powder, salt and pepper to taste, and paprika in a shallow bowl and mix together well. Place the buttermilk in another bowl.

Remove the chicken from the brine and pat dry. Lightly dust the chicken in the flour mix, making sure to shake off any excess flour from the chicken. Move the dusted chicken to soak in the buttermilk.

In a large cast iron skillet, heat the peanut oil to 325° Fahrenheit.

Once the oil has reached temperature, strain the chicken from the buttermilk and return to the flour mix. Coat well, again shaking any excess flour.

Gently lay the chicken in the skillet. Fry the chicken about 8 minutes on each side until dark golden brown and a meat thermometer registers 165°.

Transfer to a cooling rack to rest. Garnish with the thyme and rosemary.

Fisher's Pork Cheeks

FISHER'S AT ORANGE BEACH MARINA

2 tablespoons olive oil

1-1 1/2 pounds pork cheeks (Ask your butcher to cut them for you.)

Salt and pepper

1 cup celery, diced large

1 cup carrots, diced large

1 cup onion, diced large

8 cups red wine

1/2 gallon chicken stock

3 bay leaves

1 bunch fresh thyme

1 tablespoon unsalted butter

Serves 4

Preheat the oven to 350° Fahrenheit.

Heat the olive oil in a Dutch oven with a heavy bottom. Season both sides of the pork cheeks with salt and pepper and sear the pork cheeks well. Remove to a platter.

Add the celery, carrots, and onion to the Dutch oven and brown. Deglaze the pan with the red wine, scraping up all the bits from the bottom. Return the pork cheeks to the pan. Stir in the chicken stock. Add the bay leaves and thyme. Cover and cook at 350° for an hour.

Next, remove the pork cheeks to a platter. Strain the liquid, discarding the vegetables, bay leaf, and thyme. Add the liquid back to the Dutch oven and cook over medium-high heat, reducing the liquid until thickened. Finish with a tablespoon of butter and season with salt and pepper to taste.

Serve with your favorite starch and drizzle with the warm reduction.

Executive Chef Bill Briand

FISHER'S AT ORANGE BEACH MARINA

Orange Beach

Owner Johnny Fisher

From an exceptional setting at Orange Beach Marina, restaurateur Johnny Fisher and Chef Bill Briand have teamed up, scoring the perfect trifecta of hospitality, cuisine, and location complete with signature sunsets. Fisher's Upstairs and Fisher's Dockside are housed in the same space. Fisher's Upstairs offers comfortable yet sophisticated fine dining from Chef Briand. The room is prettier than your favorite Pinterest board, designed with antique cypress tables, custom chandeliers, and a pale blue color palette taken from the water below. Downstairs, Fisher's Dockside offers casual fare and a fun, family-friendly environment with the same degree of excellence you'll find upstairs. Chef Briand has been nominated for a James Beard Foundation Best Chef award for three years in a row—a first for Alabama's Gulf coast restaurants. Menu items include a fish of the day, oysters from local farms, Seared Jumbo Scallops, and Black Angus beef with seasonal sides like Sweet Corn Risotto and Tasso Creamed Kale.

DON'T MISS: Arrive early for cocktails and a sunset on the deck before dinner. The bar programs Upstairs and at Dockside feature an assortment of finely crafted cocktails such as the Saltwater Margarita with a unique saltwater foam garnish. If you're dining Dockside, the Gulf Courtboullion with Creole tomato sauce is an excellent choice. House-made desserts are worth the calories and change with the seasons. Fisher's earns kudos for their Southern Grace dinner series featuring renowned chefs Frank Stitt, Emeril Lagasse, Hugh Acheson, and many of the chefs featured in this book.

FISHER'S AT ORANGE BEACH MARINA
27075 Marina Road | Orange Beach, AL 36561
251-981-7305 | FishersObm.com

KING NEPTUNE'S SEAFOOD RESTAURANT

Gulf Shores

King Neptune's is a classic boat-to-table restaurant with a long-standing reputation of serving the freshest seafood available and of true Southern hospitality. Owners Al and Diane Sawyer treat every guest as a friend, stopping by tables to welcome the regulars and visitors alike. Al grew up on Alabama's Gulf Coast, where he learned a sincere appreciation for fresh seafood as a fisherman, salesman, chef, and restaurant owner. King Neptune's is renowned in Gulf Shores for their po'boys loaded with shrimp or oysters. Their fresh seafood platter, massive burgers, and daily specials keep the locals hooked and make it an area favorite year after year. Guests come from far and wide for the Coconut Shrimp. Al is credited for creating the recipe way back in the 70s—it is so popular, you can find it on menus all around the region.

DON'T MISS: One of the daily specials. Try the King's Seafood Casserole made with a creamy Mornay sauce or the catch of the day—right off the docks. King Neptune's is one of the best places for steamed Royal Red shrimp, prized as the crown jewel of the Gulf. The Shrimp Boat Mary is extremely popular—served in a red pepper salt-rimmed Hurricane glass with a celery, olive, and shrimp skewer. If you like oysters, King Neptune's is a great place for them. You won't go wrong with the Baked Oyster Sampler with Oysters Casino, Oysters Rockefeller, and South of the Border Baked Oysters with salsa, jalapeno, and cheese.

KING NEPTUNE'S SEAFOOD RESTAURANT
1137 Gulf Shores Parkway | Gulf Shores, Alabama 36542
251-968-5464 | KingNeptuneSeafoodRestaurant.com

King Neptune's Coconut Shrimp

KING NEPTUNE'S SEAFOOD RESTAURANT

24 (26/30) count Gulf shrimp, peeled and deveined, tail on (almost 1 pound)

Batter:

2 cups self-rising flour, plus 1 cup for breading

6 ounces Coco-López cream of coconut

1/4 cup fresh lime juice

1 egg, beaten

3/4 cup water

2 cups sweetened shredded coconut

Oil for frying (canola is recommended)

Makes 2 dozen shrimp Note: You'll need a large Dutch oven or fryer for this recipe.

Butterfly the shrimp and set aside.

For the batter: In a bowl, mix together 2 cups flour, cream of coconut, lime juice, and beaten egg. Slowly drizzle in the water, whisking until smooth.

Set up a breading station by placing the remaining 1 cup flour in a shallow dish. Hold the shrimp by the tail and dredge the shrimp into the flour and shake off the excess.

Dip the shrimp into the batter but do not submerge the tail of the shrimp. Line the shrimp neatly on a baking sheet and refrigerate for 30 minutes. When the shrimp are chilled, cover the shrimp one at a time with the shredded coconut, taking care to open the butterfly when covering with the coconut; press to make sure the coconut adheres to the shrimp.

If you are using a Dutch oven, fill it halfway with canola oil. When you are ready to fry, heat the oil in your Dutch oven or fryer to 350° Fahrenheit. Working in batches, add the shrimp a few at a time and cook 3 minutes or until golden brown. Remove to a paper towel to drain.

Tip: King Neptune's serves their Coconut Shrimp with a tangy dipping sauce. Make your own by heating 1/2 cup orange marmalade. Whisk in a squeeze of fresh lime juice, a pinch of salt, and a dash of Tabasco or more to your taste.

Chef & Owner Al Sawyer

HILDEGARD'S GERMAN CUISINE
Huntsville

HILDEGARD'S GERMAN CUISINE
2357 Whitesburg Drive Southeast | Huntsville, Alabama 35801
256-512-9776 | HildegardsGermanCuisine.com

Hildegard's Authentic German Chicken Schnitzel

HILDEGARD'S GERMAN CUISINE

4 boneless, skinless chicken breasts

1 1/2 cups all-purpose flour

2 eggs, beaten

2 cups seasoned breadcrumbs

Canola oil for frying

Lemon slices for garnish (optional)

Serves 4 Schnitzel is thin pieces of meat that are breaded and fried. The meat can vary—beef, pork, veal, etc.—to make different types of schnitzel. Schnitzel can be served plain, garnished with a lemon slice, or topped with your choice of gravy or sauce. The favorite sauce at Hildegard's is the Brown Mushroom Sauce.

Position the chicken breasts between 2 pieces of plastic wrap and use a meat mallet to pound them each to 1/4-inch thickness. Set aside.

Set up a breading station: Place each of the flour, beaten eggs, and breadcrumbs in separate shallow dishes.

One at a time, dredge the chicken breasts in the flour and shake off any excess. Dip the floured chicken in the beaten eggs and then dredge in the seasoned breadcrumbs. Set aside on a platter.

Add the canola oil to a non-stick sauté pan, filling the pan about 1/4 of the way up the sides. Gradually heat the oil to about 350° Fahrenheit. Fry the breaded chicken until golden brown, about 3-4 minutes per side. Drain the schnitzel on paper towels before serving. Garnish with the lemon slices, if desired.

Owner Amy Miller

Within months of moving to Huntsville, Amy Miller unexpectedly found herself to be the new owner of The Original Hildegard's German Cuisine, considered to be Huntsville's most authentic German restaurant for many years. Amy has a long career in the hospitality industry and is of German descent, so the move was a natural fit. Amy greets her customers with a warm smile and is passionate about Hildegard's scratch-made German cuisine. There is always a dining room full of regulars at lunchtime; I spoke with several customers who said they have been eating at Hildegard's for more than 10 years. We had a delightful time with Amy and her staff when I visited. The food was comforting and hearty; it felt like we were dining in a home rather than a restaurant. The hand-breaded schnitzels are crave-worthy—no wonder so many Hildegard's fans asked me to obtain the Chicken Schnitzel recipe. Hildegard's also has a substantial selection of German beers—order one served in a large frosted mug.

DON'T MISS: You'll want to order the Goulasch and the German potato pancakes; they have no rival. The Classic Rueben also has many fans, as do the pretzels and the Spätzle, a house-made German pasta they make from scratch. One of my personal favorites is the Geschnetzeltes, a.k.a. Hunter's Stroganoff of tender pork, mushrooms, and onions in cream gravy served over spätzle. Other scratch-made favorites include the Apple Strudel, Black Forest Cake, and German Chocolate Cake. Save room for dessert, or order one for your next special occasion.

HUGGIN' MOLLY'S
Abbeville

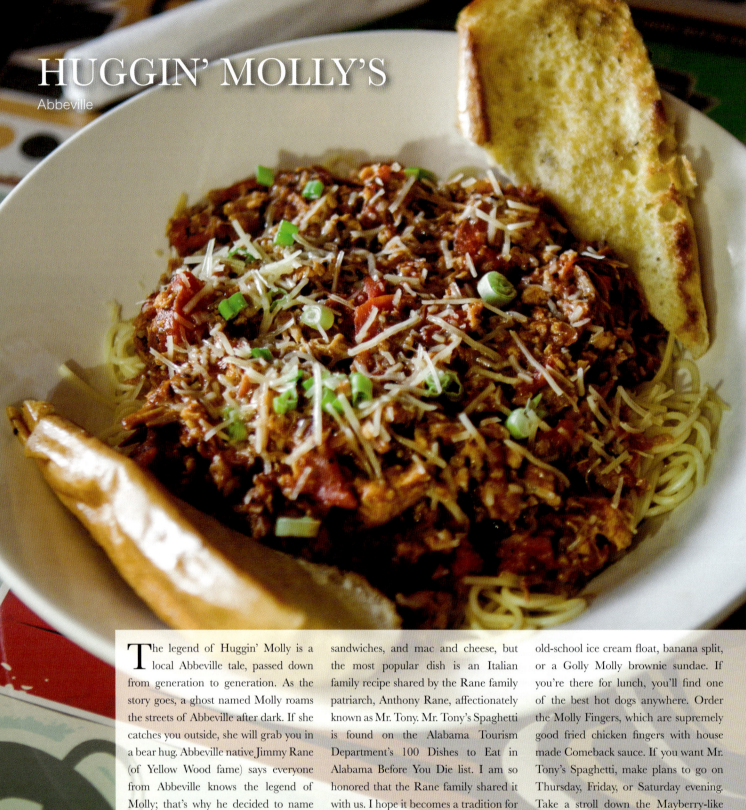

The legend of Huggin' Molly is a local Abbeville tale, passed down from generation to generation. As the story goes, a ghost named Molly roams the streets of Abbeville after dark. If she catches you outside, she will grab you in a bear hug. Abbeville native Jimmy Rane (of Yellow Wood fame) says everyone from Abbeville knows the legend of Molly; that's why he decided to name his restaurant after her. The vintage soda fountain and bar is outfitted with authentic 1950s décor and the menu is fittingly all-American with great burgers, sandwiches, and mac and cheese, but the most popular dish is an Italian family recipe shared by the Rane family patriarch, Anthony Rane, affectionately known as Mr. Tony. Mr. Tony's Spaghetti is found on the Alabama Tourism Department's 100 Dishes to Eat in Alabama Before You Die list. I am so honored that the Rane family shared it with us. I hope it becomes a tradition for family gatherings at your home.

DON'T MISS: Have dessert first! Sit at the counter and order a milkshake, old-school ice cream float, banana split, or a Golly Molly brownie sundae. If you're there for lunch, you'll find one of the best hot dogs anywhere. Order the Molly Fingers, which are supremely good fried chicken fingers with house made Comeback sauce. If you want Mr. Tony's Spaghetti, make plans to go on Thursday, Friday, or Saturday evening. Take a stroll down the Mayberry-like main street after dinner with a scoop or two of ice cream but be on the lookout for Molly!

HUGGIN' MOLLY'S
129 Kirkland Street | Abbeville, Alabama 36310
334-585-7000 | HugginMollys.com

Mr. Tony's Spaghetti Sauce with Meat

HUGGIN' MOLLY'S

Makes approximately 10 servings, depending on portion size
Recipe from "Mr. Tony" Anthony Rane, courtesy *Great Southern Wood Cookbook*

- 2 (28-ounce) cans tomato purée
- 3 1/2 cups water
- 2 pounds pork spareribs
- 1 cup cooking oil
- 2 large onions, sliced
- 2 pounds ground chuck or ground round
- 1/2 pound lean ground pork
- 1 cup sifted breadcrumbs
- 1/2 cup grated Parmesan cheese
- 1 cup milk, plus more as needed, divided
- 3 eggs
- Salt and pepper
- 2 (6-ounce) cans tomato paste
- 1/2 teaspoon granulated garlic

Combine the tomato purée and water in large stockpot and allow to come to a boil, stirring constantly to avoid scorching. Reduce the heat to a low simmer.

In a large skillet, sauté the spareribs in the oil and drop into the stockpot. Add the sliced onions to the sparerib grease in the skillet and sauté until transparent. Drop them in the stockpot.

In a large bowl, combine the ground chuck, ground pork, breadcrumbs, Parmesan, milk, eggs, and salt and pepper to taste. Mix the ingredients thoroughly (add more milk as needed to make a pliable but thick consistency) and sauté in the same skillet used for the onions. Once browned, add to the stockpot.

Combine the tomato paste with a little water until a thick purée consistency is formed. Add to the same skillet and bring to a boil, adding the garlic and salt and pepper to taste. After it comes to a boil, add to the stockpot and allow to simmer on lowest heat for 6 or more hours, stirring regularly to keep it from scorching on the bottom.

Serve the meat sauce over your favorite pasta.

OCEAN
Birmingham

Ocean has been the seafood destination in Birmingham since it opened in 2002. Chef George Reis is one of the country's premier seafood chefs and the winner of the 2015 Alabama Seafood Cook-Off. He and his team create a new menu nightly, and there is always a whole-fish entrée included—which is perfect for two people to share. (Find Chef Reis's Whole Red Snapper recipe in my book, *Magic City Cravings*.) The restaurant frequently hosts Lowcountry oyster roasts, clam bakes, and New England–style lobster bakes out on the patio; you'll feel like you've been transported to the Eastern shore. The Lobster Pot Pie has legions of fans who crave it, even when it is not on the menu. For that reason, it is on the Alabama Tourism Department's list of 100 Dishes to Eat in Alabama Before You Die.

DON'T MISS: Ocean's raw bar offers a variety of oysters, shrimp, mussels, lobster, and Alaskan king crab. Invite a few friends to meet you at the bar after work and share a few dozen oysters on the half shell. There is a nice lineup of cocktails, wines, and sparkling beverages to pair with your oyster selection. Save room for the elaborate selection of house-made desserts, such as the Caramel Lava Cake or seasonal ice cream. Chef Reis has a very cool oyster bar and pub next door to Ocean. 5 Point Public House and Oyster Bar has an incredible assortment of raw oysters and craft beers plus a mighty fine oyster stew, when in season.

Chef & Owner George Reis

OCEAN
1218 20th Street South | Birmingham, Alabama 35205
205-933-0999 | OceanBirmingham.com

Lobster Pot Pies

OCEAN

3 1/2 pounds live lobster (Retain the shells for the stock.)

Stock:

4 medium onions, diced

1 1/2 cups celery, diced

1 1/2 cups carrots, diced

10 peppercorns

5 garlic cloves

4 fresh rosemary sprigs

Filling:

2 cups unsalted butter

2 cups all-purpose flour

1/2 tablespoon olive oil

1 teaspoon minced garlic

1 teaspoon minced shallot

3 carrots, diced medium

1/2 pound okra, sliced

2 ears corn, shucked

1 1/2 ounces sherry

Topping:

3 sheets frozen puff pastry, thawed according to package instructions

1 egg beaten for egg wash, optional

Makes 6-12 individual pot pies depending on the size of the container If you want to shortcut this recipe for the sake of time, you can use store bought unsalted seafood stock and premade roux from a jar.

Bring a large pot of water to a boil. Add the live lobsters and boil for 10 minutes. Remove the lobsters from the water and immediately submerge them in an ice bath.

Remove the lobster meat from the shells. Reserve the shells for the stock. Chop the lobster meat and set aside.

For the stock: In a stock pot, cook the onions, celery, carrots, peppercorns, and garlic cloves until translucent. Add the rosemary sprigs and the lobster shells and cover completely with water. Bring to a boil and then reduce to a simmer. Simmer 1 hour. Strain and reserve the stock. Discard the vegetables, rosemary, peppercorns, and lobster shells.

For the filling: In a separate pan, make the roux. (You can use store-bought roux if you prefer.) Melt the butter over low heat. Increase the heat to medium and add the flour, a bit at a time, whisking to keep it from browning. After the flour has been incorporated, cook 3-4 minutes and remove from the heat. You want a light-colored roux for the sauce, so do not allow the roux to brown at all.

Bring the strained stock back to a boil. Add a ladle of the hot stock to the pan with the roux and whisk rapidly. Working in small batches, whisk the roux into the stock, allowing the stock to return to a simmer between each addition. Continue this process until the stock has thickened and coats the back of a spoon.

In a large sauté pan, add the olive oil and sauté the minced garlic and shallots until translucent, and then add the carrots, okra, and corn. Continue to sauté until all the vegetables start to caramelize. Deglaze the pan with the sherry and reduce until nearly dry.

Add the chopped lobster meat and 12 ounces (1 1/2 cups) of the thickened stock to the vegetable mixture and simmer 5 minutes to allow the flavors to combine. (Reserve any leftover stock for another use.)

Preheat the oven to 450° Fahrenheit.

Arrange individual heatproof ramekins on a baking sheet. Ladle the filling into the ramekins, filling each 1/2 inch from the top.

For the topping: Measure and cut the thawed puff pastry 1 inch larger on all sides than the ramekins.

Top the ramekins with the puff pastry and crimp the edges to the side of the container. Brush the egg wash on the top of the puff pastry with a pastry brush, if desired.

Bake until the puff pastry rises, and the top is golden brown.

RICATONI'S
Florence

Ricatoni's. Almost everyone had that answer when we asked for recommendations for dinner in Florence. Located in the restaurant and entertainment district in historic downtown Florence, Ricatoni's has quite a following. The pizzas are handmade in the old-world Italian way—the crust is thin with just the right amount of crisp to it. The hearty Chicken Marsala, and classic Spaghetti with Meatballs are favorites with the locals. The Smoked Duck and Sausage Pasta—penne pasta tossed in a pomodoro sauce with Italian sausage and goat cheese—is unexpected and fabulous. Ricatoni's freshly baked warm bread and the herbed olive oil they serve with it is a dish folks have requested repeatedly; it is on the Alabama Department of Tourism's list of 100 Dishes to Eat in Alabama Before You Die. Ricatoni's owner, Rick Elliott, is a Florence legend. His alter ego, Ricatoni Valentino, has become famous for his humorous television commercials promoting the restaurant.

DON'T MISS: The Veal Parmesan, a breaded veal cutlet that is lightly fried and topped with pomodoro sauce and mozzarella cheese and served with a generous portion of Ricatoni's famous fettuccine alfredo. What's not to love about that? The pizza is fantastic and everything you'd expect from a place that has one of the only authentic Italian pizza ovens in the state. Desserts are also on the "don't miss" list at Ricatoni's, especially the rich and luscious cannoli or the Tiramisu made with Italian coffee liqueur and mascarpone cheese. All desserts are made from scratch and big enough to share.

RICATONI'S
107 North Court Street | Florence, AL 35630
256-718-1002 | Ricatonis.com

Ricatoni's Grilled Chicken Alfredo

RICATONI'S

1 box fettuccine noodles, uncooked

Sautéed Mushrooms (optional):

1 tablespoon olive oil

1 tablespoon minced garlic

12 ounces fresh mushrooms, roughly chopped (any type you prefer)

Kosher salt and black pepper

1 tablespoon fresh parsley, roughly chopped, plus more for garnish

Alfredo Sauce:

1 quart heavy whipping cream

1 1/3 sticks butter

1 tablespoon kosher salt

1/2 teaspoon white pepper

2 tablespoons Romano cheese, grated, plus more for garnish

12 ounces chicken, grilled and kept warm

8 ounces green peas, optional

8 ounces Sautéed Mushrooms, optional (See recipe above.)

Serves 2-4 depending on portion size

Bring a large pot of water to a boil. Add the pasta and cook to al dente, 12-15 minutes. Set aside.

For the Sautéed Mushrooms: Heat the olive oil in a sauté pan and add the minced garlic, chopped mushrooms, and a pinch of the salt and black pepper. When the mushrooms are almost finished cooking, add the chopped parsley. Set aside. (This step may be omitted, if desired.)

For the Alfredo Sauce: In a sauce pan, combine the heavy cream, butter, salt and white pepper. Once the butter has melted, stir in the Romano cheese.

Chop the warm grilled chicken and add to the Alfredo Sauce. Fold in the peas and Sautéed Mushrooms, if desired. As the Alfredo Sauce thickens, drain the pasta and stir it into the sauce. Pour the pasta mixture into pasta bowls to serve. Garnish with the additional parsley or Romano cheese.

Do not rinse the pasta. Retain some of the pasta water and use it to thin the Alfredo Sauce a bit, if needed.

SAW'S SOUL KITCHEN
Birmingham

SAW'S SOUL KITCHEN
215 41st Street South | Birmingham, Alabama 35222
205-591-1409 | SawsBBQ.com

Pork n' Greens

SAW'S SOUL KITCHEN

Pulled Pork:

1 small (8-10 pound) bone-in pork butt (shoulder)

1/2 cup yellow mustard

1 cup Saw's Rub (you can substitute another)

Hickory wood for smoker

Turnip Greens:

4 ounces bacon, cut into 1/4-inch pieces

1 yellow onion, julienned

2 1/2 pounds turnip greens, chopped and rinsed

1 1/2 quarts water

1 tablespoon Lawry's Seasoned Salt, plus more to taste

1 cup Saw's Sauce, plus more to taste and for serving (you can substitute)

1 teaspoon freshly ground black pepper

Serves 4-5, with pork left over for another use

For the pulled pork: Coat the pork butt with a thin layer of yellow mustard on all sides. Pour the Saw's Rub into a large bowl and dip the butt on all sides, making sure there is a uniform layer of seasoning on all sides.

Smoke the seasoned pork butt, fat side up, with hickory wood at 275° Fahrenheit, for 6-8 hours until the bone starts to protrude from the butt, the fat cap has softened, and the desired color has been achieved. Remove from the smoker, wrap with heavy-duty aluminum foil, and return to the heat. Cook another 4-6 hours until the butt is soft to the touch and the bone comes out with no resistance.

Before serving the pork, unwrap from the foil. Using tongs, remove the bone and separate the meat from the remaining pieces of fat inside the butt.

For the turnip greens: In a large pot, cook the bacon until crispy; add the onions and cook until soft. Add the greens, along with the water, Lawry's, Saw's Sauce, and pepper. Bring to a boil, lower to simmer, and cook until the greens are tender, about 1 1/2 hours. Adjust the seasoning with more Lawry's and Saw's Sauce as desired.

Recipe continued on next page.

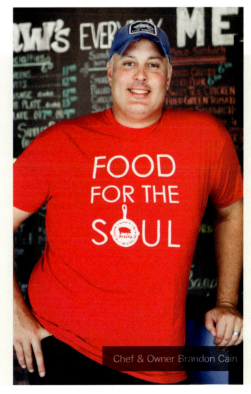
Chef & Owner Brandon Cain

Known for their award-winning barbecue, killer collard greens, great burger, and huge BBQ-stuffed 'tater—which is so remarkable that it made the Alabama Tourism Department's list of 100 Dishes to Eat in Alabama Before You Die—Saw's Soul Kitchen in Birmingham is a landmark Southern barbecue haven. Located next to Avondale Brewery, the place truly defines the term "soul kitchen"—while the place isn't fancy, but you won't find better barbecue anywhere. And there's always soul music playing. If you don't want barbecue, there's a chalkboard menu with other options such as the crazy-good smoked chicken wings and smoked sausage. You'll also find some not-so-conventional items on the menu, such as Saw's version of the Southern classic shrimp and grits. Chef Brandon Cain and business partner Mike Wilson have opened a new Saw's in Birmingham's Southside. The original Saw's is in Homewood, and Saw's Juke Joint in Crestline was opened with partner Taylor Hicks of *American Idol* fame.

DON'T MISS: It is the Pork n' Greens served over grits and topped with a nest of skinny fried onions that everyone has raved about for years, but the Sweet Tea Fried Chicken recently made a name for itself after it won the Made South Great Slider Showdown in 2018 against some steep competition. The Smoked Chicken with White BBQ Sauce Plate is a sure thing as is the cheeseburger. My newest craving at Saw's is the pork rinds. They are like puffs of porky air, and as the saying goes, you can't eat just one.

Recipe continued from previous page.

Pork n' Greens

SAW'S SOUL KITCHEN

Cheese Grits:

3 1/2 cups water

1 teaspoon kosher salt, plus more to taste

1 cup McEwen and Sons Stone Ground Grits

1 cup whole milk, plus more as needed

2 tablespoons unsalted butter

2 cups cheddar cheese, shredded

Fried Onions:

1 yellow onion, sliced as thinly as possible, preferably on slicer or Japanese mandoline

1 small can evaporated milk

1 small box Zatarain's seasoned cornmeal

Oil for frying

For the cheese grits: Bring the water and salt to a boil, and then whisk in the grits until well combined with no lumps. Stir frequently, bring to a boil, reduce the heat to a simmer, and cook until the grits are tender and most of the liquid is absorbed.

In small saucepan, heat the milk until just below boiling; slowly add it to the grits and stir to combine. Continue to cook until the liquid is absorbed into the grits. Add the butter and cheese; stir well and cook until melted and combined. Adjust the consistency as desired with extra milk or water, and add more salt as desired.

For the fried onions: In a medium bowl, soak the onion slices in the evaporated milk at least 1 minute.

Pour the cornmeal in a separate bowl, remove the onions from the milk mixture, allow the excess to drip off, and dredge into the cornmeal. Shake well to remove all the excess breading.

Deep fry in the oil at 350° for about 30-45 seconds or until crispy.

To assemble: Carefully ladle 8 ounces of the cheese grits onto each of 4 or 5 large plates and spread to form a uniform layer. Top each with 6 ounces of the well-drained turnip greens, 6 ounces of the pulled pork, and 2 ounces of Saw's Sauce, and top each evenly with the fried onions.

SAW'S SOUL KITCHEN
Birmingham

Sweet Tea Fried Chicken Sandwich

SAW'S SOUL KITCHEN
215 41st Street South | Birmingham, Alabama 35222
205-591-1409 | SawsBBQ.com

SOUTHERN NATIONAL
Mobile

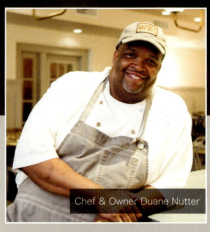
Chef & Owner Duane Nutter

Southern National arrived on the restaurant scene in Mobile with a lot of flourish and high expectation. Chefs Duane Nutter and Reggie Washington already had notoriety and quite a reputation from their stint at the much-acclaimed One Flew South restaurant at the Atlanta-Hartsfield airport. The two decided to open a new restaurant together and left Atlanta for Washington's hometown of Mobile, a city they felt was ripe for the type of restaurant they wanted to create. If they had any doubts about their decision to open in the heart of downtown Mobile, those doubts were quickly alleviated. Southern National was a hit from the day it opened. If they needed further assurance they were onto something special, they got it a few months after opening when the James Beard Foundation named Southern National as a semi-finalist for Best New Restaurant 2018.

DON'T MISS: A seat in the courtyard. With views of Dauphin Street and the Cathedral Basilica of the Immaculate Conception, you'll feel as if you've been transported straight to New Orleans. Southern National fans asked me to obtain recipes for the Chicken Schnitzel and the Pimento Cheese, and they absolutely begged me to get the recipe for Southern National's famous Reggie's Original Chicken and Waffles. When you go, try the Garlic-Rosemary Tater Tots, one of my newest Alabama cravings. Another favorite is the Pan-Roasted Duck with Duck Confit Grits. I am so glad Chefs Nutter and Washington decided to make Mobile, Alabama, their home!

SOUTHERN NATIONAL
360 Dauphin Street | Mobile, Alabama 36602
251-308-2387 | SoutherNational.com

Reggie's Original Chicken + Waffles

SOUTHERN NATIONAL

Soy-Chicken Marinade:

3 tablespoons olive oil

1/2 tablespoon grated ginger

1 teaspoon Chinese five spice

1/2 teaspoon ground coriander

1/4 teaspoon red pepper flakes

Juice from 1 lime

3 tablespoons lower-sodium soy sauce

1/4 teaspoon salt

1/4 teaspoon black pepper

1 teaspoon brown sugar

1 (4-pack) package boneless chicken thighs

Chicken Dredge:

2 cups flour

1 tablespoon cornstarch

1/4 teaspoon salt

1/4 teaspoon black pepper

1 pint buttermilk

Oil for frying

Waffles:

2 cups all-purpose flour

2 tablespoons sugar

2 teaspoons baking powder

1/2 teaspoon salt

4 ounces oil or melted unsalted butter

4 large eggs

1 1/2 cups whole milk

1/2 cup buttermilk

Shaved fresh chives for garnish, optional

Maple syrup for serving, optional

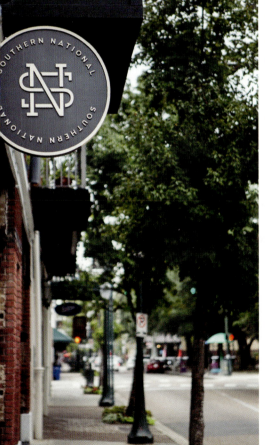

Makes approximately 6 waffles depending on the size of your waffle iron

For the Soy-Chicken Marinade: In a large bowl, whisk together the olive oil, grated ginger, Chinese five spice, ground coriander, red pepper flakes, lime juice, soy sauce, salt, pepper, and brown sugar. Pour into a 1-gallon zip-top plastic bag and set aside.

Open the 4-pack of chicken thighs and clean off the excess fat. Cut each thigh into thirds. Place the chicken in the marinade bag, seal, and marinate for at least 2 hours. (It's best to marinate overnight.)

For the chicken dredge: In a small bowl, mix together the flour, cornstarch, salt, and pepper. In another small bowl, place the buttermilk. Dip each chicken thigh piece into the buttermilk and dredge in the seasoned flour mixture. Place the dredged chicken pieces onto a baking sheet or wire rack.

To fry the chicken: Fill the fryer with the oil and heat the oil to 350° Fahrenheit. Carefully place the dredged chicken pieces into the fryer and fry until golden brown and a thermometer inserted into the thickest part of the pieces registers 160°—the chicken will carryover cook to 165°. (If you don't have a fryer at home, you can use a cast iron skillet or Dutch oven instead). Remove the fried chicken pieces to a wire rack or paper towels to drain.

For the waffles: Preheat the waffle iron and mix together the flour, sugar, baking powder, and salt in a large bowl. In a small bowl, mix together the oil, eggs, whole milk, and buttermilk. Pour the wet mixture into the dry mixture and gently whisk together, being careful not to overmix. Pour the waffle batter, in batches, onto the hot waffle iron to make about 6 waffles.

To serve: Top each waffle with 2 fried chicken pieces. Garnish with the chives and drizzle with the maple syrup, if desired.

THE BRIGHT STAR
BESSEMER

Just about everyone in Birmingham has eaten at The Bright Star. Opened in Bessemer in 1907, it's recognized as Alabama's oldest restaurant and is honored with a state-issued historical marker out front. The Bright Star has always been the place to go for fresh seafood, steaks, and special occasions. Since 1966, restaurant icons Jimmy and Nick Koikos's family has owned The Bright Star, which was named an American Classic by the James Beard Foundation in 2010. Today, Chef Andreas Anastassakis runs the family's culinary operations. The Broiled Seafood Platter is on the Alabama Tourism Department's list of 100 Dishes to Eat in Alabama Before you Die and The Bright Star brings in fresh seafood from the Gulf several times per week. Their Greek-style snapper, snapper throats, and seafood gumbo have set the standard for decades. The pies with cloud-like meringue are made just as they have been since the place opened. Lunch at The Bright Star is a big deal—call the "lunch line" (205-426-1861) to listen to the day's menu.

DON'T MISS: Greek-style snapper and the Lobster and Crabmeat Au Gratin still bring in generations of fans, but it is the famous Greek-Style Beef Tenderloin for which so many requested the recipe. It won the Alabama Cattlemen's Association award for best steak in the state in 2012 and has also won several other similar titles. The Bright Star's Seafood Gumbo has been named the best in the Southeast by *The National Restaurant News*— legions of fans order it by the gallon for special occasions.

THE BRIGHT STAR
304 19th Street North | Bessemer, Alabama 35020
205-426-1861 | TheBrightStar.com

Greek-Style Beef Tenderloin

THE BRIGHT STAR

4 (10-ounce) beef tenderloin steaks

2 cups olive oil

1/2 cup (8 tablespoons) lemon juice, divided

2 tablespoons garlic, minced, divided

2 teaspoons dried oregano, divided

Salt and pepper

6 ounces (1 1/2 sticks) butter

Serves 4

Clean the steaks, trimming away any silver skin, fat, or connective tissue. Butterfly each filet and set aside.

Add the olive oil, 6 tablespoons of the lemon juice, 1 1/2 tablespoons of the garlic, and 1 teaspoon of the oregano, along with the salt and pepper to taste, to a zip-top plastic bag or a Pyrex dish large enough to fit all the steaks. Add the steaks and marinate in the refrigerator 2-3 hours, turning occasionally. Remove from the refrigerator at least 45 minutes prior to cooking.

Place a rack closest to the broiler. Preheat the broiler. Place a large broiler pan on the rack to heat.

In a saucepan, melt the butter and add the remaining 2 tablespoons lemon juice, 1/2 tablespoon garlic, and 1 teaspoon oregano. Mix thoroughly and set aside.

Remove the steaks from the marinade, discarding the marinade. Using tongs and an oven mitt, carefully place the steaks on the hot pan and broil to the desired degree of doneness, turning only once. You will likely cook the steaks about 4 minutes per side, depending on the degree of doneness you prefer. Remove the steaks from the oven and transfer to a serving plate. Tent with foil and allow to rest 2 minutes. Remove the foil, add 3 tablespoons of the butter sauce to each steak, and serve.

Note: Use a meat thermometer for the best results: 140° Fahrenheit = medium rare, 155° Fahrenheit = medium. Keep in mind that the meat will continue to cook and increase about 5 additional degrees once you remove it from the oven.

Owners Jimmy & Nick Koikos with Chef Andreas Anastassakis

THE DEPOT
Auburn

Executive Chef & Co-Owner
Scott Simpson

A beautifully restored train depot is the setting for owner Richard Tomasello and Executive Chef and co-owner Scott Simpson's Auburn dining destination where it is all about the finest fresh seafood paired with gracious Southern hospitality. The space is gorgeous—one of the prettiest I've seen in all my travels. Reclaimed wood from the old pine train platform is fashioned into the Chef's table and the bar; the black and white floor tiles are original to the building. The menu at The Depot is varied and seafood-centric, featuring dishes from their custom wood-fired Asadaor. The Depot was the first restaurant in the state to have this open-fire cooking system. Though known for its seafood, The Depot really knows how to cook beautiful cuts of big beef and pork—the Prime Linz Farms New York Strip with Blue Cheese Butter or the Bone-in Can-Can Pork Chop with Asian BBQ Sauce are sure to satisfy the meat lover in your crowd; they are cooked to your requested temperature with adept precision.

DON'T MISS: The Gourmet Gumbo Pot—it is a great bowl of gumbo, trust me. If you've never had wood-grilled lettuce—try it! The Depot's Wood Grilled Baby Romaine with Asiago Sourdough Croutons and Green Goddess Dressing is one of my favorite salads. Leave room for one of their elegantly executed desserts. I am a fan of all of them but would walk to Auburn for the Chocolate Espresso Pots De Crème with Spiced Whipped Cream and Whiskey Caramel Sauce!

THE DEPOT
124 Mitcham Avenue | Auburn, Alabama 36830
334-521-5177 | AllAboardAuburn.com

Elote (Authentic Mexican Street Corn) and Grilled Cilantro-Lime Shrimp

THE DEPOT

Mexican Street Corn:

4 ears fresh sweet corn, in their husks

3 tablespoons unsalted butter, melted

Juice of 2 limes

1/2 cup Mexican crema (or substitute sour cream mixed with a little mayonnaise)

1/3 cup crumbled Mexican queso añejo, queso fresco, or substitute Parmesan or feta

1 tablespoon hot powdered chile

Grilled Cilantro-Lime Shrimp:

Juice and zest of 2 limes, plus lime wedges for garnish, if desired

1/2 cup olive oil

1/2 cup garlic, minced

1 teaspoon ground ancho chili powder

1 teaspoon cumin

1/2 teaspoon paprika

Salt and pepper

1/4 teaspoon red pepper flakes, or more to taste

1 cup chopped cilantro, reserve some leaves for garnish, if desired

2 dozen (16/20 count) Gulf white shrimp

Serves 8 The corn recipe and the shrimp recipe can be made independently or combined for this popular version.

For the Mexican Street Corn: About an hour before grilling, place the corn ears in husks in a deep bowl, cover with ice-cold water, and weight to keep them submerged.

For the Grilled Cilantro-Lime Shrimp: In a small bowl, whisk together the lime juice and zest, olive oil, garlic, chili powder, cumin, paprika, salt and pepper to taste, red pepper flakes, and cilantro. Pour into a large zip-top plastic bag and add the shrimp. Toss to coat and marinate 30 minutes. If you are using wooden skewers to grill the shrimp, soak them in water for at least 30 minutes.

To grill: Preheat the grill to medium-high and adjust the grill grate 4 inches above the fire. Remove the corn from the water and place it (still in the husk) on the grate. Grill 15-20 minutes, turning frequently. The outer husks will become blackened.

Recipe continued on next page.

Recipe continued from previous page.

Elote (Authentic Mexican Street Corn) and Grilled Cilantro-Lime Shrimp

THE DEPOT

While the corn is cooking, remove the shrimp from the marinade, discarding the marinade. Thread the shrimp on the skewers. Set aside.

After 15-20 minutes of cooking, remove the corn from the grill, let cool slightly, and remove and discard the husks and silk. Using a kitchen towel, break the ears in half. Brush the corn with the melted butter. Return to the grill and turn frequently until nicely browned.

In a small bowl, mix the lime juice and the crema. Set aside.

Next, place the shrimp skewers on the grill. Grill over medium heat about 2 minutes per side.

While the shrimp is cooking, remove the corn from the grill and place it on a serving platter. Brush the corn generously with the crema mixture, top it with the crumbled cheese, and sprinkle with the powdered chile.

Working quickly so the corn stays hot, remove the shrimp from the grill. Garnish with the cilantro leaves and lime wedges, if desired. Serve the shrimp with the corn.

THE DEPOT
Auburn

BELOW THE RADAR BREWING COMPANY

Huntsville

If you think breweries serve only burgers and pub food, you need to visit Below the Radar Brewing Company in downtown Huntsville. The creative, made-from-scratch menu includes seasonal specials, which are often infused with their craft beer—made right on the premises. Of course, the menu does include top-notch bar food favorites such as wings and burgers; the hot dogs have quite a following. In addition to their own brand of beer, Below the Radar also offers a vast selection of craft beers from all over the world. They have 32 rotating taps and sell 32- and 64-ounce growlers to take home. The hearty homemade lunch specials, such as Country Fried Steak with Mashed Potatoes and Shepherd's Pie, are popular with the downtown crowd. They have live music on weekends and are usually packed after work for happy hour.

DON'T MISS: Sandwich specials like the Corned Beef Brisket, Roast Beef Sandwich, and Fried Green Tomato BLT are touted by the brewery's fans on social media, and the hand-cut-and-dipped onion rings are on almost every order. Don't miss Below the Radar's seasonal brews such as Sour Peach, Marzen Oktoberfest Lager, and English Porter that are crafted in small batches for special events. Stop in to taste their latest brews with a flight; the knowledgeable servers and bartenders will help you with your selection. Desserts are made on site and change frequently. When it's offered, try the crème brûlée with seasonal berries.

BELOW THE RADAR
220 Holmes Avenue Northeast | Huntsville, AL 35801
256-469-6617 | btrbrew.com

Lamb Lollipops
with Parmesan Polenta, Wilted Garlic Spinach, and Bacon Jam

BELOW THE RADAR BREWING COMPANY

Parmesan Polenta:

Splash extra-virgin olive oil

1/2 tablespoon minced shallot

1/2 tablespoon minced garlic

3 cups water

2 cups heavy cream

2 1/2 cups polenta

1 cup Parmesan cheese

Kosher salt and white pepper

Lamb:

Lamb rack with 14-16 bones

Olive oil

Kosher salt and black pepper

Pat of unsalted butter (about 1 tablespoon)

Wilted Garlic Spinach:

1 tablespoon unsalted butter

2 cloves minced garlic

1 clove minced shallot

4 cups fresh baby spinach

Kosher salt and black pepper

Bacon Jam:

3 pounds bacon, drippings reserved

1 tablespoon unsalted butter

1 medium yellow onion, diced

1 teaspoon kosher salt

1/2 cup brown sugar

1/2 cup apple cider vinegar

3 teaspoons fresh thyme leaves, divided

2 teaspoons black pepper

1 cup water

1 cup bourbon

4 teaspoons dark balsamic vinegar

Honey

Serves 6

For the Parmesan Polenta: Add the olive oil and minced shallot to a large sauce pot. Cook until the shallots are translucent. Add the garlic and cook 45 seconds. Add the water and heavy cream and bring to a boil. Once boiling, whisk in the polenta and then stir in the Parmesan. Stir continuously until the polenta is no longer grainy. Add the salt and white pepper to taste. Set aside. (The polenta will firm up as it sits. If you make this in advance, you can loosen it before serving by stirring in a bit of hot heavy cream until you reach the desired consistency.)

For the lamb: Preheat the oven to 350° Fahrenheit. Cut the lamb rack into 14-16 bones, or have the butcher do this for you. Add enough olive oil to coat the bottom of a sauté pan and heat the oil until it smokes slightly. Season the lamb with the salt and pepper on both sides. Place the lamb in the pan in batches and sear well on each side until medium rare*, approximately 140-145° Fahrenheit on a meat thermometer.

Remove the lamb from the pan and let rest 3-5 minutes. While the meat is resting, add the butter to the pan drippings and scrape the bits off the bottom of the pan to create a quick pan sauce. Season the pan sauce with the salt and pepper to taste; set aside.

For the Wilted Garlic Spinach: Melt the butter in a sauté pan over medium-high heat. Once melted, but not browned, add the minced garlic and shallot and cook until they are translucent. Add the spinach and cook until it has wilted. Season with the salt and pepper to taste.

For the Bacon Jam: Place the bacon in a large heavy-bottomed pot and cook over medium heat until the bacon is crispy and the rendered fat is foaming, about 10 minutes. Remove the bacon to a paper towel to cool. Strain the rendered fat into a bowl, reserving 2 tablespoons (discard the rest). Once the bacon is cool, finely chop and set aside.

Return the pot to medium heat; add the reserved bacon fat and butter to the pan. Add the onion and salt and sauté until the onions are soft and translucent, about 7-10 minutes. Stir in the brown sugar, apple cider vinegar, 1 teaspoon of the thyme, and black pepper into the onion mixture; add the chopped bacon. Stir the water into the bacon mixture and cook until the jam is a brick-brown color and has a jam consistency, about 10-15 minutes. Remove from the heat and stir in the bourbon and balsamic vinegar. Add the honey to taste and the remaining 2 teaspoons thyme. Stir until shiny. You can make this in advance and keep covered in the refrigerator until ready to use.

To serve: Divide the Parmesan Polenta evenly among 6 plates. Top each evenly with the Wilted Garlic Spinach and the lamb. Drizzle with the pan sauce. Top with the Bacon Jam.

Note: Lamb chops are ideal for a dinner party. The Bacon Jam and Parmesan Polenta for this recipe can be made early in the day and reheated after you've started cooking the lamb, so it is also easy on the cook!

If a different degree of doneness is preferred, place the lamb on a pan and into the preheated oven until it reaches the desired temperature.

VOYAGERS AT PERDIDO BEACH RESORT

Orange Beach

Executive Chef Brody Olive

With panoramic Gulf views, an executive chef who is an avid Gulf fisherman and who has won multiple seafood competitions, and an award-winning wine list, Voyagers is hard to beat when it comes to fine dining on Alabama's Gulf coast. Executive Chef Brody Olive won the Southern Breeze Gulf Coast Cook-Off in 2008, Zatarain's Annual National Shrimp Festival Chef Challenge in 2009 and again in 2013, and the Alabama Seafood Cook-Off in 2017. You can bet Chef Olive knows a thing or two about elegantly prepared Gulf seafood. Voyagers's wine list spans eight countries and boasts over 130 selections, and received *Wine Spectator's* Award of Excellence for 2017. Voyagers has a special wine-dinner series with winemakers and VIP guests. Tickets are always in high demand and sell out quickly.

DON'T MISS: While many places on the Gulf offer a crab bisque, few have a lobster bisque on the menu as Voyagers does. You'll want to begin your meal with this creamy and delicious cup of heaven. The Pecan-Crusted Snapper is a dish customers order again and again. The aged ribeye might be the best steak I've ever had. Paired with a delicious root vegetable gratin, it's perfection. (Steaks at Voyagers are dry-aged a minimum of 35 days.) It seems wrong to order beef at a restaurant so renowned for its seafood, but their steak is everything. Do save room for dessert. The pastry team at Voyagers is one of the best on the coast.

VOYAGERS AT PERDIDO BEACH RESORT
27200 Perdido Beach Boulevard | Orange Beach, Alabama 36561
251-981-9811 | PerdidoBeachResort.com

Gulf Coast Paella

VOYAGERS AT PERDIDO BEACH RESORT

Charred Leek-Tomato Broth:

1 leek

4 whole tomatoes

4 tablespoons olive oil, divided

Salt and pepper

1 yellow onion, julienned

1/4 cup garlic, julienned

2 cups white wine

1 bunch fresh parsley, leaves only

2 pinches saffron

1 pound unsalted butter

2 tablespoons olive oil

1/2 pound chorizo

1 stalk celery, diced small

1 small onion, diced small

1 carrot, diced small

1 cup Two Brooks Farm sable rice (substitute, if desired)

1 cup Two Brooks Farm scarlet rice (substitute, if desired)

1 tablespoon minced garlic

3 ounces fire-roasted tomatoes (you may use canned)

5 cups shellfish stock (you may use any good quality seafood stock)

2 cups Charred Leek-Tomato Broth (See recipe at left)

1 pound large Gulf brown shrimp, peeled and deveined

1/2 pound lump crab meat, picked over for shell and cleaned

4 (3- to 4-ounce) spiny lobster tails

1 tablespoon aged sherry vinegar

1/4 cup chopped fresh parsley

1/2 cup spring peas, blanched (you can use defrosted frozen peas)

Juice of 1 lemon

Serves 4

For the Charred Leek-Tomato Broth: Cut the green from the leek and discard. Rub the leek and tomatoes with 2 tablespoons olive oil and season with salt and pepper to taste.

Preheat the grill and blister the tomatoes and leek for about 3-4 minutes per side. Set aside. (Note: You may roast the leek and tomato in the oven if you do not have a grill.)

In saucepan, sauté the onion and garlic in the remaining 2 tablespoons olive oil until translucent.

Deglaze the pan with the white wine. Roughly chop the blistered leeks and tomatoes. Add the leek, tomatoes, parsley, and saffron to the pan. Reduce the mixture by half and add the butter. Using an immersion blender, blend into a thick broth. Season with the salt and pepper to taste. Set aside. (Note: Use a regular blender if you do not have an immersion blender.)

Preheat the oven to 400° Fahrenheit.

Heat olive oil in a large cast iron pan or Dutch oven over medium-high heat. Add the chorizo and render 2-3 minutes. Add the celery, onion, and carrot. Cook an additional 5 minutes, stirring constantly. Add the rice, garlic, and fire-roasted tomatoes. Add the shellfish stock and 1 cup of the Charred Leek-Tomato Broth. Stir and bring to a simmer.

Carefully place the pan in the oven and cook at 400° 45 minutes or until the rice becomes tender.

Remove from the oven. Stir in the shrimp, crab meat, lobster tails, the remaining cup of the Charred Leek-Tomato Broth, sherry vinegar, chopped parsley, peas, and lemon juice.

Preheat the oven to broil. Move the oven rack to the lowest position.

Return the pot to the oven and cook 10-12 minutes or until the top becomes nicely toasted and crunchy.

WOLF BAY LODGE
Foley & Orange Beach

Back in the day, folks were willing to drive forever to get to Wolf Bay Lodge, known for its stuffed whole flounder, crab-stuffed shrimp, gumbo, and fried oysters. It was back then—as it is now—a family-owned-and-operated business, and while the location has changed (now there are three!) the food and the hospitality have not. Charlene Haber's parents bought Wolf Bay back in the early 70s, and Charlene worked there from the time she was old enough to hand out a menu. Mama Char, as she is lovingly called by her staff, owns and runs the place now; she has a hand in making every pot of gumbo and every plate of seafood. Lunch at Wolf Bay is popular with the locals. There is a football-field-sized (well, almost!) salad bar filled with every kind of salad you can imagine and dressings made from the family's original recipes. There is so much variety, you could go there every day of the week and have something different.

DON'T MISS: That gumbo, y'all! Wolf Bay Seafood Gumbo wins a lot of gumbo honors and competitions—and rightfully so. It is one of my favorite gumbos and puts some New Orleans gumbo to shame. Start with an order of Cha Cha's Crab Dip, Mama Char's latest creation. Served hot with bourbon sauce and fried pita points, it is a dish you will crave once you've had it. The Wolf Bay fried oysters are hand-dipped and perfectly fried. With this recipe, all you oyster fanatics can try them at home!

WOLF BAY LODGE
20801 Miflin Road | Foley, Alabama 36535
251-987-5129 | WolfBayLodge.com

26619 Perdido Beach Blvd | Orange Beach, Alabama 36561
251-965-5129 | WolfBayLodge.com

Wolf Bay Lodge Fried Oysters

WOLF BAY LODGE

Oil for frying

2 cups self-rising flour

1 tablespoon salt

1/2 tablespoon white pepper

3 eggs

1 cup water

1 cup whole milk

2 dozen raw Gulf oysters removed from their shells

Pinch sea salt, optional

Lemon wedges

Cocktail sauce

Makes 2 dozen

Heat the oil in a fryer or Dutch oven to 350° Fahrenheit.

Add the flour, salt, and white pepper to a wide, shallow dish. Use a whisk to mix well. Set aside. In a separate bowl, add the eggs and beat well. Add the water and milk and whisk together.

Add the oysters to the egg mixture and allow to soak a few minutes. Remove the oysters, one at a time, shaking off the excess egg mixture; dredge in the flour mixture. Shake off the excess flour and place immediately into the hot oil.

Cook the dredged oysters at 350° until golden brown, about 2-3 minutes depending on the size of your oysters.

Drain on paper towels and sprinkle with the salt, if desired. Serve hot with lemon wedges and your favorite cocktail sauce.

Owner Charlene Haber

GAINES RIDGE DINNER CLUB | Camden

Desserts

Fig and Goat Cheese Ice Cream, 189
BIG SPOON CREAMERY

Coconut Pecan Cake, 191
BOTTEGA, BOTTEGA CAFÉ

Chocolate Bourbon Pecan Pie, 193
COMMERCE KITCHEN

Freight House Strawberry Cake, 195
FREIGHT HOUSE

Half Moon Cookies, 197
FULL MOON BAR-B-QUE

Black Bottom Pie, 199
GAINES RIDGE DINNER CLUB

Little Savannah Buttermilk Biscuit Shortcake, 201
LITTLE SAVANNAH RESTAURANT & BAR

Martin's Sweet Potato Pie, 203
MARTIN'S RESTAURANT

Peanut Butter Texas Sheet Cake, 205
NEW MARKET BBQ

Niki's Banana Pudding, 207
NIKI'S WEST

Pie Lab Double-Crust Apple Pie, 209
PIE LAB

Lemon "Jubilee" Beignets 211
PANINI PETE'S

Southern Pecan Bread Pudding, 213
RAY'S AT THE BANK

Wildflower Crepes, 215
WILDFLOWER CAFÉ

Zack's Pear Cobbler, 217
ZACK'S FAMILY RESTAURANT

Coconut Popsicles, 219
STEEL CITY POPS

Key Lime Bread Pudding, 221
WASH HOUSE RESTAURANT

BIG SPOON CREAMERY
Birmingham

Chefs & Owners Geri-Martha and Ryan O'Hara

BIG SPOON CREAMERY
4000 3rd Avenue South | Birmingham, Alabama 35222
205-703-4712 | BigSpoonCreamery.com

Fig and Goat Cheese Ice Cream

BIG SPOON CREAMERY

Fig Swirl:

2 pints fresh figs, cleaned and halved (Big Spoon uses figs from Petals from the Past in Jemison, Alabama.)

Juice of 1 lemon

1 vanilla bean, split and seeds scraped

1/2 cup granulated sugar

Pinch of kosher salt

Goat Cheese Ice Cream Base:

6 cups whole milk

1/4 cup heavy cream (Use 35% cream, if you can find it.)

1/4 cup non-fat milk powder

3/4 cup dextrose (You can find dextrose at most grocery stores. Look for it on the sugar or baking aisle. You can substitute 3/4 cup granulated sugar in its place.)

1 cup granulated sugar

12 egg yolks

12 ounces Stone Hollow Farmstead goat cheese (You can substitute a different brand.)

Makes 2 quarts

For the Fig Swirl: Place the figs, lemon juice, vanilla bean and seeds, and sugar in a small saucepan. Bring to a simmer and cook 15 minutes. Remove and discard the vanilla bean and add the pinch of salt. Blend the mixture using an immersion blender or regular blender. Pour into a heat-proof container to cool down. Chill in refrigerator until you are ready to swirl into your ice cream.

For the Goat Cheese Ice Cream Base: Pour the milk and cream into a container with twice the capacity of the mixture. While whisking the mixture, add the milk powder. Purée the mixture with an immersion blender or regular blender.

Pour the puréed mixture into a large saucepan and heat over medium heat. Once it reaches 104° Fahrenheit, whisk in the dextrose, sugar, and egg yolks. Whisking constantly, heat to 185°. Remove from the heat.

Prepare an ice bath using ice and cold water. Submerge the bottom half of the saucepan in the ice bath and whisk a bit to cool the mixture to 40°. Place in a container and refrigerate 6-12 hours to allow the ice cream base to mature.

Add the goat cheese to the chilled ice cream base and blend with an immersion blender or regular blender. Strain.

To freeze: Pour the mixture into the ice cream freezer. When the ice cream is almost finished spinning, swirl in the chilled Fig Swirl.

Note: Big Spoon uses a commercial ice cream freezer. When using a home-model ice cream freezer, the result is often like soft serve. If you want a "scoopable" ice cream, after the ice cream finishes spinning in the machine, transfer it to a metal loaf pan lined with plastic wrap and swirl in the fig purée. Cover the surface with plastic wrap and freeze 2 hours or until firm.

If your ice cream freezer only freezes 1 quart of ice cream at a time, save the other quart of base and half of the Fig Swirl in the refrigerator until you are ready to spin it or use a second tub to spin the remaining quart.

The husband-wife chef team of Geri-Martha and Ryan O'Hara make incredible, artisanal small-batch ice cream in seasonal flavors with locally sourced ingredients. The couple spun their love of cooking and community into the best ice cream in Alabama. Big Spoon came to life in 2014 with ice cream socials in the O'Hara's driveway after church on Sunday. After that came an ice cream trike, then a truck. Fans drive to find Bessie Blue, Big Spoon's big blue ice cream truck, for sweet scoops in homemade waffle cones or the creamery's trademark ice cream "sammies," in which ice cream is packed between two house-baked gourmet cookies. Big Spoon has a brick-and-mortar location in Birmingham's Avondale neighborhood and plans to open a Homewood location at the end of 2018.

DON'T MISS: The flavors at Big Spoon change with the seasons. When summer hits, you'll find Chilton County peach, local blueberry, blackberry, or some incredible mash-up of seasonal flavors. If there is anything on the menu with buttermilk in it, get it. When fall rolls around, the caramel and coffee flavors make a comeback. Big Spoon's Coffee Almond Toffee is utterly addictive. They also sell superb sundaes, milkshakes, floats, and more, ensuring there's something sweet at Big Spoon for everyone.

BOTTEGA AND BOTTEGA CAFÉ

Birmingham

Pastry Chef Dolester Miles

Italian twin sisters Bottega and Bottega Café are in the stately Bottega Favorita building on Birmingham's Southside and are part of Frank and Pardis Stitt's restaurant group which includes Highlands Bar and Grill and Chez Fonfon. The Bottega dining room is a bit more refined than her casual sister but make no mistake—on either side you will find beautifully crafted dishes created with integrity and passion with ingredients obtained from Italian artisans and local growers.

The café has an open-concept kitchen with a Renato wood-fire oven, where the chefs fire pizzas, fish, and other specialties, including their famous Café Mac and Cheese. The dining room is romantic, refined, and a wonderful place to impress a date or celebrate a special occasion. The intimate bar is a wonderful place to dine when you're on your own; I always order the Capellini Bottega with San Marzano tomatoes, garlic, basil, and Parmigiano—it has been my go-to for more than 20 years.

DON'T MISS: The Beef Carpaccio with horseradish cream and shaved Parmigiano and the Chicken Scaloppine on the Café side have been on the menu forever for good reason. Save room for desserts created by 2018 James Beard Foundation Best Pastry Chef winner Dolester Miles, affectionately known as Mrs. Dol. Her iconic Coconut Pecan Cake is on almost every order. It is so requested that the cake is also on the menu at Highlands Bar and Grill and Chez Fonfon. We are so honored to share this celebrated recipe with you.

BOTTEGA and BOTTEGA CAFÉ
2240 Highland Avenue South | Birmingham, AL 35205
205-939-1000 | BottegaRestaurant.com

Coconut Pecan Cake

BOTTEGA and BOTTEGA CAFÉ

Cake:

1 cup (85 grams) firmly packed sweetened shredded coconut

3/4 cup (74 grams) pecan halves, toasted

2 cups (402 grams) granulated sugar, divided

2 1/4 cups (287 grams) all-purpose flour, plus more for the pans

1 tablespoon baking powder

3/4 teaspoon kosher salt

3/4 cup (170 grams) unsalted butter (1 1/2 sticks), softened, plus more for the pans

1/4 cup (60 milliliters) cream of coconut

4 large eggs

1/4 teaspoon coconut extract

1 cup plus 2 tablespoons (270 milliliters) unsweetened coconut milk

Filling:

2 large egg yolks, lightly beaten

3/4 cup sweetened condensed milk

4 tablespoons (57 grams) unsalted butter

1 tablespoon cream of coconut

1 cup (85 grams) sweetened shredded coconut

Simple Syrup:

1/2 cup (101 grams) granulated sugar

1/2 cup water

Icing:

1 cup (240 milliliters) heavy cream

1/4 cup (31 grams) confectioners' sugar

1 teaspoon coconut extract

2 cups (170 grams) sweetened shredded coconut, toasted

Serves 12 to 14

For the cake: Preheat the oven to 350° Fahrenheit. Grease 2 (9-inch) round cake pans and line the bottom of each with parchment paper. Grease the parchment paper, then dust with the flour, tapping out the excess.

Finely grind the shredded coconut in a food processor, then transfer to a bowl. Add the pecans to the food processor, along with 2 tablespoons of the sugar, and finely grind them. In a large bowl, sift together the flour, baking powder, and salt. Stir in the ground coconut and pecan mixture.

In the bowl of a mixer fitted with the paddle attachment, beat the butter, cream of coconut, and the remaining 1 7/8 cups sugar on high speed until light and fluffy, about 4 minutes. Add the eggs one at a time, mixing well after each addition and scraping down the bowl as necessary, then beat in the coconut extract.

Add the flour mixture in 3 batches, alternating with the coconut milk, starting and ending with flour mixture. Divide the batter between the pans and smooth the top of each with a spatula. Bake at 350° until the cakes are golden and a tester comes out clean, 30-35 minutes. Let the cakes cool in the pans on a wire rack for 30 minutes. Run a knife around the edge of each cake, invert onto the rack, and discard the parchment paper. Let cool completely.

Meanwhile, make the filling: Place the egg yolks in a small heatproof bowl and set aside. In a saucepan, combine the condensed milk, butter, and cream of coconut and cook over medium-low heat, stirring constantly, until hot, about 4 minutes. Whisk 1/3 of the hot milk mixture into the egg yolks. Transfer the hot egg mixture to the saucepan of hot milk mixture and whisk constantly over medium-low heat until the mixture has the consistency of pudding, about 4 minutes. Do not let the custard get too thick. Transfer to a bowl and stir in the shredded coconut. Let cool completely.

For the simple syrup: In a saucepan, heat the sugar and 1/2 cup water, stirring occasionally, until the sugar has dissolved. Remove from the heat.

Assemble the layer cake in a pan: Cut each cooled cake layer in half horizontally. Place one layer in the bottom of a 9-inch cake pan, moisten the top with 2-3 tablespoons of the simple syrup and spread 1/2 cup of the coconut filling in a thin, even layer with an offset spatula. Repeat to make 2 more layers of cake and filling, then place the last cake layer on top. Refrigerate the cake for about 1 hour. To unmold, run a spatula around the edges, invert a cake plate over the top, and flip the cake over onto the plate.

For the icing: Whip the cream with the confectioners' sugar and coconut extract until stiff peaks form. Spread on the top and sides of the cake and sprinkle with the toasted coconut. Refrigerate until ready to serve.

COMMERCE KITCHEN
Huntsville

Southern cuisine with French flair under the direction of Executive Chef James Boyce makes Commerce Kitchen one of the true gems of the Alabama restaurant landscape. Chef Boyce and his wife, Suzan, are also partners in Huntsville's renowned restaurants Cotton Row and Pane e Vino Pizzeria and Birmingham's Galley & Garden. You may recognize Chef Boyce from his cooking segments on NBC's *Today Show*, *CBS This Morning*, and from the pages of *Food & Wine* and other notable magazines. Chef Boyce and his team are passionate about their food and the ingredients they bring to the menu.

Eternal favorites include Gulf Shrimp and Falls Mill Grits and the Fried Green Tomatoes and Pimento Cheese. It is a popular lunch destination for the downtown crowd. For dinner service, the lights are lowered and the mood and menu change; look for elegant entrees like the Roasted Harissa Salmon with Asian slaw and ponzu or the pan-seared Gulf fish with Parmesan orzo, and ratatouille.

DON'T MISS: The vintage bar is a nice spot to meet friends after work. Order a craft cocktail such as the Twickenham Jewel—made with Woodford Reserve bourbon, Pama liqueur, and fresh-squeezed lemonade. Order an array of the bar bites to share; try the Old Bay Hot Crab Dip or the Cornmeal Crusted Gulf Oysters. Pair (or try the equally fanstastic fried chicken) with a glass of bubbly. The Beef Shortrib Grilled Cheese with aged Cheddar and caramelized onions is a scrumptious sandwich—I'm already craving it for next time.

COMMERCE KITCHEN
300 Franklin Street Southeast | Huntsville, Alabama 35801
256-382-6622 | TheCommerceKitchen.com

Chocolate Bourbon Pecan Pie

COMMERCE KITCHEN

1 (9-inch) packaged pie crust

3 cups pecans, toasted and roughly chopped

1 1/2 cups granulated sugar

1/4 cup honey

1/8 cup whiskey

1 teaspoon vanilla extract

1/2 stick unsalted butter, melted

3 eggs, beaten

1 cup chocolate chips

Pinch of salt

Makes 1 (9-inch) pie This is the perfect ending to dinner or a holiday meal. Add more or less whiskey as desired.

Preheat the oven to 300° Fahrenheit. Bake the pie crust for 10 minutes and set aside.

Spread the chopped pecans on a baking sheet and bake at 300° for 5-7 minutes or until lightly toasted. Allow to cool.

In a bowl, whisk together the sugar, honey, whiskey, vanilla, and melted butter. Add the eggs and stir well to completely combine. Fold in the cooled pecans, chocolate chips, and salt. Pour into the prepared crust and bake 19-21 minutes. Allow to cool at least 20 minutes before serving.

Executive Chef & Owner James Boyce

FREIGHT HOUSE
Hartselle

Between Cullman and Decatur, just off one of the state's prettiest main streets, sits one of the most unique restaurant settings in the state. The old L&N railroad freight terminal in Hartselle sat empty for many years before it was rescued by Sandra Sowder and turned into the Freight House restaurant and bakery. Many of the components of the original building were reclaimed and used to create its authentic feel, and artifacts of the period are used in the décor, including the large Empress clock found at the entrance and the player piano in the dining room. The Brick Room upstairs has the terminal's original marble-topped registration desk, a fireplace, and a view of historic downtown Hartselle. The menu is modern-Southern and offers excellent steaks and seafood. The paninis have their fair share of fans, as does the Signature Chicken Salad and Homemade Potato Chips. The bakery, however, is the star of the show, and the house-made layer cakes have reached celebrity status.

DON'T MISS: The bakery! Freight House pies and cakes are hugely popular, especially for the holidays, so order well in advance. The Orange-Pretzel Salad is a local favorite, and the homemade train-shaped sugar cookies are a tradition for the kids. The chocolate cake with peanut butter frosting is not to be missed, but it is the Strawberry Cake recipe fans asked for most. Ask for Sandra when you visit; she might just play a tune for you on the old player piano!

FREIGHT HOUSE
200 Railroad Street Southwest | Hartselle, Alabama 35640
256-773-4600 | FreightHouseHartselle.com

Freight House Strawberry Cake

FREIGHT HOUSE

Cake:

Cooking spray or oil and flour to grease pans

2 cups granulated sugar

3 1/4 cups self-rising flour

1 (3-ounce) package strawberry Jell-O gelatin

1 cup frozen sliced strawberries, thawed and juices reserved

1 1/2 cups vegetable oil

5 eggs

2 tablespoons ricotta cheese

Strawberry Frosting:

12 ounces cream cheese, room temperature

1 stick butter or margarine, room temperature

1 teaspoon strawberry extract

1 (2-pound) bag confectioners' sugar, divided

1/3 cup frozen strawberries, thawed and strained

Makes 1 (9-inch) layer cake For the 4-layer cake as shown in the photo, slice both of the layers in half before frosting.

For the cake: Preheat the oven to 350° Fahrenheit. Grease and flour 2 (9-inch) cake pans. Set aside.

In the bowl of a stand mixer fitted with the paddle attachment, mix the sugar, flour, and Jell-O. Add the thawed strawberries with juice, oil, and eggs, one at a time, while mixing on medium speed. Add the ricotta cheese and continue mixing 1 minute more.

Divide the cake batter evenly between the prepared cake pans.

Bake at 350° for 20-25 minutes or until the sides release from the pan. Remove the cakes from the oven and place on wire racks to cool 10 minutes; turn out onto the racks to cool completely. After the layers cool completely, wrap them tightly in plastic wrap and freeze 24 hours.

For the Strawberry Frosting: In the bowl of a stand mixer fitted with the paddle attachment, mix the cream cheese and butter at medium-low speed until smooth. Add the extract and half of the confectioners' sugar. Continue beating on medium-low speed while adding the thawed and strained strawberries and the remaining confectioners' sugar until the desired consistency is reached. Refrigerate the frosting until ready to use. (When ready to frost the cake layers, stir the frosting until smooth.)

To assemble: Remove the cake layers from the freezer and unwrap them. Place one layer on the bottom of a cake stand or plate; spread some of the Strawberry Frosting on top. Top the frosted layer with the second cake layer. Frost the top and sides of the cake with the remaining Strawberry Frosting as desired. Let the cake come to room temperature before serving.

Chef & Owner Sandra Sowder

FULL MOON BAR-B-QUE
15 Alabama Locations

Owners David and Joe Maluff

FULL MOON BAR-B-QUE RESTAURANT
Locations: Alabaster, Dothan, Fultondale, Homewood, Hoover, Inverness, Jasper, McCalla, Montgomery, Opelika, Pelham, Southside, Trussville, Tuscaloosa, UAB
FullMoonBbq.com

Half Moon Cookies

FULL MOON BAR-B-QUE

Cookies:

2 1/4 cups all-purpose flour, unsifted

1 teaspoon baking soda

1 teaspoon salt

1/2 pound butter, softened

3/4 cup granulated sugar

3/4 cup light brown sugar, packed

2 large eggs

1 teaspoon pure vanilla extract

3 cups semi-sweet chocolate chips

1 cup pecans, chopped

Milk Chocolate Dip:

1 (1-pound) Hershey's milk chocolate bar, chopped

Makes about 4 dozen

Preheat the oven to 375° Fahrenheit.

For the cookies: Combine the flour, baking soda, and salt in a medium bowl and set aside. Cream together the butter, granulated sugar, and brown sugar in a large bowl. Beat the eggs and vanilla into the butter mixture. Slowly add the flour mixture to the butter mixture; beat until blended. Stir in the chocolate chips and pecans.

Use a rounded teaspoon to scoop out the dough and drop onto ungreased cookie sheets.

Bake at 375° 8-10 minutes. Cool the cookies on a rack and refrigerate until cold.

For the Milk Chocolate Dip: Melt the Hershey's bar. After the cookies have been refrigerated, dip half of each cookie into the melted chocolate. Set the half-dipped cookies on cold cookie sheets until the chocolate has hardened.

Joe and David Maluff's Birmingham-based Full Moon Bar-B-Que is an Alabama barbecue institution, now found in more than a dozen locations around the state. Their carefully crafted pit barbecue is cooked low and slow over hickory, the preferred wood for authentic Alabama barbecue. While they specialize in pork, ribs, and Boston butt, it is Full Moon's beef brisket that many say is the best in Alabama. In 2013, Full Moon was named one of the top ten barbecue restaurants in the entire USA by the Huffington Post. Their famous brisket recipe is featured in my first cookbook, *Birmingham's Best Bites*. Full Moon's famous Half Moon Cookies have a cult following. If you are not a baker, order tins of these "can't-eat-just-one" cookies online; they will ship them anywhere in the country. Half Moon cookies make a great gift for homesick friends living elsewhere and are a wonderful favor for a wedding, too.

DON'T MISS: Their famous spicy-yet-sweet Chow-Chow relish. Order some to take home; it's good with pork, chicken, or veggies. Full Moon's Famous Slaw is found on the Alabama Department of Tourism's 100 Dishes to Eat in Alabama Before You Die list. They also offer a vegetable of the day, which includes Southern favorites like Fried Green Tomatoes and Squash Casserole. When dining in, you will absolutely want to try the Pork Links and Pimento Cheese Plate or the Smoked Wings with Alabama White Sauce.

Note: Menus vary by location, so the items mentioned may not be available at every location.

GAINES RIDGE DINNER CLUB
Camden

GAINES RIDGE DINNER CLUB
933 Highway 10 East | Camden, Alabama 36726
334-682-9707 | WilcoxWebworks.com/gr

Look up "steel magnolia" in the dictionary and you might find Mrs. Betty Kennedy, proprietor of Gaines Ridge Dinner Club. Mrs. Betty founded the popular dinner and holiday destination in 1985 in her childhood family home. Mrs. Betty serves Southern specialties and family recipes such as Shrimp Bisque and her famous Parker House yeast rolls. Set on a hill with a meandering drive, Gaines Ridge feels like a step back in time. Mrs. Betty's handmade quilts and table linens gives the place a homey and authentically Southern feel. Mrs. Betty's famous Black Bottom Pie is on the Alabama Tourism Department's 100 Dishes to Eat in Alabama Before You Die list, and dozens of her long-time fans recommended it to me. Gaines Ridge is also known for their steaks, and Mrs. Betty still cuts each one by hand. Holidays are special at Gaines Ridge, as the home is filled with dozens of Christmas trees and decorations. Make reservations for dates between Halloween and New Year's Eve well in advance as they fill up early. Thanksgiving at Gaines Ridge is also a tradition for many families.

DON'T MISS: In the winter, the cozy fireplace is always in use. In the spring, you can enjoy the back porch and brick patio that overlook the grounds. Order one of the signature salads with the Shrimp and Crabmeat en Casserole—it's divine and enough to share. Everything at Gaines Ridge tastes like Grandma made it—mainly because everything is made from scratch in the old-school way and because Mrs. Kennedy and much of her staff ARE grandmothers!

Black Bottom Pie

GAINES RIDGE DINNER CLUB

Crust:

1/2 stick oleo (margarine)

1 1/4 cup gingersnap cookie crumbs

Filling:

1 1/2 ounces unsweetened chocolate, chopped or broken into pieces

2 teaspoons pure vanilla extract, divided

1 (0.25-ounce) envelope unflavored gelatin

1/4 cup cold tap water

2 cups whole milk

2/3 cups granulated sugar plus another 1/2 cup, divided

2 1/2 teaspoons cornstarch

4 large eggs, separated

1/4-1/3 cup rum or bourbon

Topping:

1 cup heavy whipping cream

Chocolate shavings for garnish

Makes 8-9 Servings

Preheat the oven to 350° Fahrenheit.

For the crust: Melt the oleo and stir in the cookie crumbs. Press the mixture into a 9-inch glass pie pan. Bake at 350° 10-12 minutes. Remove and set aside to cool.

For the filling: Place the chopped chocolate and 1 teaspoon of the vanilla in a glass bowl. Set aside.

Place the gelatin in a small bowl and add the cold water. Stir and set aside.

In a saucepan, scald the milk in a double boiler over medium heat. While it is heating, in a heat-proof bowl, mix 2/3 cup of the sugar and the cornstarch together. Add the egg yolks and mix well.

Temper the egg-yolk mixture by slowly adding 1/2 cup of the scalded milk to the yolk mixture and whisking constantly. Add the remaining 1 1/2 cups scalded milk to the tempered yolk mixture and return the scalded milk–yolk mixture to the double boiler. Cook over medium heat, stirring constantly with a wooden spoon until thickened into a custard. Bring to a boil and immediately remove from the heat.

Add one cup of the hot custard to the chocolate and vanilla to melt the chocolate. Stir and set aside to cool.

Add the gelatin mixture to the remaining hot custard. Stir and cool to room temperature. (You can set the bowl in a sink or larger bowl filled with cold tap water to help cool the mixture.) When it has cooled completely, add the rum or bourbon and the remaining 1 teaspoon vanilla.

To assemble: Once the chocolate mixture has completely cooled, spread it over the cooled pie crust. Place in the refrigerator.

Beat the egg whites with an electric mixer on high speed until peaks begin to form. Slowly add 1/4 cup of the sugar while continuing to beat the whites until stiff peaks are formed. Use a large spatula to fold the egg whites into the cooled custard.

Spread the custard over the chocolate layer. Return the pie pan to the refrigerator and chill at least 4 hours or overnight.

To serve: Whip the heavy cream and remaining 1/4 cup sugar with an electric mixer until it reaches a spreadable consistency. Spread over the custard layer and garnish with chocolate shavings.

Owner Betty Gaines Kennedy

The pie cuts best when it is cold. Store it in the refrigerator to keep it well chilled.

LITTLE SAVANNAH RESTAURANT AND BAR
Birmingham

A Forest Park neighborhood institution since 2003, Little Savannah has been hosting farm-to-table dinners by Chef Clifton Holt long before it was fashionable to do so. The menu is ever changing and filled with the freshest of what is currently available, including seafood, seasonal produce, and locally sourced meats. Signature brunch dishes, such as Fried Deviled Eggs and the Holt House Breakfast Platter with its scrumptious potato hash, have made Sunday brunch at Little Savannah quite a "thing" so I'd recommend making a reservation. Instead of the typical "meat and three" plate, Chef Holt offers a value-packed "meat and five" weekday lunch special that includes Southern favorites such as Country Fried Steak or Fried Chicken paired with seasonal vegetables. Little Savannah is only moments away from downtown, and there is easy street parking. Chef Holt is a Veteran and proudly displays the American flag in front of his restaurant.

DON'T MISS: The crab cakes have quite a following, and Little Savannah's Shrimp and Grits is found on the Alabama Tourism Department's list of 100 Dishes to Eat in Alabama Before You Die. (The recipes for these dishes are in my first two cookbooks: *Birmingham's Best Bites* and *Magic City Cravings*.) Stop by for Birmingham Burger Nights on Tuesdays, where you'll find $10 burgers and drink specials. Little Savannah is a warm and cozy space so it's great for a business dinner or date night. Chef Holt often stops by the table to visit with his guests; many have been his regular customers for 15 years.

LITTLE SAVANNAH RESTAURANT AND BAR
3811 Clairmont Avenue South | Birmingham, Alabama 35222
205-591-1119 | LittleSavannah.com

Little Savannah Buttermilk Biscuit Shortcake

LITTLE SAVANNAH RESTAURANT AND BAR

2 cups White Lillly all-purpose flour

1/4 teaspoon baking soda

1 tablespoon baking powder

1 teaspoon granulated sugar

1 teaspoon kosher salt

6 tablespoons unsalted butter, cubed and chilled

1 cup whole buttermilk, well chilled

Seasonal fruit purée and fresh fruit for serving

Mascarpone, fresh whipped cream, or ice cream for serving (optional)

Makes 6-8 Biscuits

Preheat the oven to 450° Fahrenheit. Line a baking sheet with parchment paper.

Sift the flour, baking soda, baking powder, and sugar together in medium bowl. Mix in the salt. Cut in the cubed, cold butter using a pastry blender until the mixture resembles coarse cornmeal. Add the buttermilk and mix just until combined.

Working quickly, turn out the dough onto a floured surface and gently pat out the dough to about 3/4-inch thickness; do not use a rolling pin. Using a 3-inch biscuit cutter, cut the biscuits without twisting and place them—almost touching—on the prepared baking sheet. Bake at 450° 15-18 minutes or until the tops are a rich golden brown.

Serve the shortcakes warm with the fruit purée and fresh fruit. You can top with mascarpone, fresh whipping cream, or ice cream, if desired. (For this recipe, we served the shortcakes with a purée of Chilton County peaches and a bit of local honey and topped it all with fresh peaches slices and blueberries.)

Chef & Owner Clifton Holt

MARTIN'S RESTAURANT
Montgomery

Since it was established in the 1930s, Martin's has been a Montgomery standard for "meat and three" lunches, with homemade favorites like Baked Turkey with Dressing, pork chops, and chicken and dumplings. Pair those with Southern sides such as candied yams, collard greens, and fried okra and you'll understand why this Montgomery classic has so many fans. Owner Mary Ann Merritt and her team work incredibly hard to serve scratch made everything—including their fantastic pies and desserts. They greet every guest with a warm smile, making sure the hospitality and service is equal to the food. Martin's is one of the oldest restaurants in Montgomery, and their Famous Fried Chicken, served with the "pulley" bone (see box at right), in true Southern fashion, has been on the menu from the beginning. Sweet Potato Casserole is on the menu every Tuesday, and it has a huge following, especially during the holidays.

DON'T MISS: Martin's Famous Fried Chicken. Served piping hot and crunchy, it is what fried chicken ought to be. I also really like their Homemade Salmon Croquettes with lots of salmon and not too many breadcrumbs. Stop by on Sunday after church for Sunday lunch. For Thanksgiving, Martin's offers homemade cornbread dressing and giblet gravy to take home; but be certain to place your order early. Martin's proudly servers the many military men and women stationed in and around the Montgomery area. There are always tables filled with our service members who come to Martin's for a home-cooked meal away from home.

MARTIN'S RESTAURANT
1796 Carter Hill Road | Montgomery, Alabama 36106
334-265-1767 | Facebook.com/MartinsFriedChicken

Martin's Sweet Potato Pie

MARTIN'S RESTAURANT

4 cups cooked, mashed sweet potatoes

1 1/2 cups firmly packed brown sugar

1/8 teaspoon salt

3/4 cup unsalted butter, softened to room temperature

4 eggs, separated

1 tablespoon pure vanilla extract

1 (12-ounce) can evaporated milk

1 (10-inch) unbaked pie shell

Whipped cream for serving (optional)

Makes 1 (10-inch) pie

Preheat the oven to 400° Fahrenheit.

Combine the sweet potatoes, brown sugar, salt, and butter in a bowl; you can use a mixer or beat by hand. Add the egg yolks, one at a time, to the potato mixture, beating well after each addition. Add the vanilla and mix. Add the milk and mix.

In a separate bowl, beat the egg whites until they reach stiff peaks. Gently fold the egg whites into the potato mixture. Pour into the unbaked pie shell. Bake at 400° for 15 minutes. Reduce the heat to 350° and bake 30 minutes.

Remove to a cooling rack and allow to cool at least 30 minutes before slicing. Serve with a dollop of whipped cream, if desired.

For those raised above the Mason-Dixon line, the pulley bone is the y-shaped bone in the chicken's center known as the wishbone. You don't often see it served these days and Martin's has become famous as one of the few places that still serve it. Southern legend has it that two people grab a side of the pulley bone, each one making a wish before they pull it to break it apart. The wish is reported to come true for the person ending up with the larger side; however, if this legend were true, I would have married Donny Osmond in 1971.

NEW MARKET BBQ
New Market

Libby and Kelly Webb are North Alabama transplants, but they are not BBQ novices. Kelly's passion for smoking meats started when he was a teen. The Webbs purchased New Market BBQ in 2008 from its original owners, Virginia and Darrel Day, including the recipes the Day family has passed down from generation to generation. New Market offers REAL old-school pit-smoked barbecue, and their pits are built right into the building, as is the traditional method. The quaint and cozy front porch adds to the family feel of the place—it feels like your grandma's house. The unique Smoked Mac n' Cheese made the Alabama Tourism Department's list of 100 Dishes To Eat in Alabama Before You Die, and the beef brisket and homemade banana pudding help make New Market, and the city for which it's named, a BBQ destination worth the drive from anywhere.

DON'T MISS: The brisket. Not many Alabama barbecue joints serve brisket; most serve only pulled pork. New Market serves Texas-style brisket, dry rubbed and smoked with pecan and cherry wood, rather than hickory, which is the Alabama-barbecue style. New Market's brisket is fall-apart tender and succulent. The Smoked Mac n' Cheese is made with a scratch-made cheese sauce flavored with the restaurant's own barbecue rub. It's then baked in the pit for its super-smoky flavor. Don't leave without dessert. All desserts are made from Mrs. Day's recipes and they include seasonal favorites such as Pumpkin Cake and traditional favorites such as Pecan Pie.

NEW MARKET BBQ
5601 Winchester Road | New Market, Alabama 35761
256-379-5525 | NewMarketBbq.com

Peanut Butter Texas Sheet Cake

NEW MARKET BBQ

Baking spray with flour

2 sticks unsalted butter

1 cup water

1/2 cup creamy peanut butter

2 cups granulated sugar

2 cups all-purpose flour, sifted

1 teaspoon salt

1 teaspoon baking soda

1/2 cup whole buttermilk

2 eggs

1 teaspoon vanilla

Frosting:

1 stick butter or margarine

1/4 cup 100% cocoa

1/4 cup creamy peanut butter

1/2 cup milk

3 1/2 cups confectioners' sugar, sifted

1 teaspoon vanilla

Nuts for topping (optional)

Serves 15

For the cake: Preheat the oven to 350° Fahrenheit for a 13- x 9-inch baking pan or 375° Fahrenheit for a 17- x 11-inch baking pan. Grease the pan with the baking spray with flour. Set aside.

Heat the butter, water, and peanut butter in a large saucepan over medium heat; stir constantly until melted.

Remove from the heat and use a whisk to stir in the sugar, flour, salt, and baking soda until smooth.

Add the buttermilk, eggs, and vanilla and continue whisking until smooth.

Pour the batter into the prepared pan and bake until a wooden pick inserted in the center comes out clean, about 30 minutes if using the 13- x 9-inch pan and 15-18 minutes if using the 17- x 11-inch pan.

Start making the frosting as soon as the cake comes out of the oven.

For the frosting: Melt the butter in a large saucepan over medium heat and whisk in the cocoa until smooth. Add the peanut butter and whisk until melted. Add the milk and bring to a boil. Remove from the heat and stir in the confectioners' sugar and vanilla. Whisk until smooth.

Spread the frosting evenly over the warm cake. Top with the nuts, if desired.

Owners Libby and Kelly Webb

New Market BBQ Smoked Mac-n-Cheese

Pete and Teddy Hontzas are the second-generation owners at the helm of their family's renowned restaurant, which has been a Birmingham landmark since it opened in 1957. The pair have proudly maintained the quality, service, and heritage set forth by their beloved father, Gus Hontzas. Niki's West has one of the longest steam tables anywhere, always filled with fresh vegetables and classics such as Baked Chicken and Dressing, Fried Pork Chops, and Country Fried Steak. There are always lots of salads on the menu; the Beet Salad and 7-Layer Salad are local favorites. The yeast rolls and the desserts are all made on the premises. The warm Banana Pudding is by far the most popular dessert, followed by the Chocolate Cream Pie and the Egg Custard Pie. Niki's West is massive with multiple dining rooms, making it the perfect spot to take your family for a special occasion.

DON'T MISS: The hand-cut steaks, seafood, and traditional Greek dishes that are found on the a la carte menu. My favorite dishes are the Broiled Center-Cut Pork Chops with Baked Apples and the Fresh Hamburger Steak with Onions—both remind me of my mother's cooking, as does the Banana Pudding, served warm from the steam table. Order breakfast from the menu and they will bring you their giant iced cinnamon rolls, which are made fresh daily, just as they have been for the past 60 years.

NIKI'S WEST
233 Finley Avenue West | Birmingham, Alabama 35204
205-252-5751 | NikisWest.com

Niki's Banana Pudding

NIKI'S WEST

Pudding:

1 3/4 cups granulated sugar

3/4 cup all-purpose flour

2 3/4 cups milk

4 egg yolks (Save the whites for the meringue.)

2 tablespoons vanilla extract

1 (11-ounce) box Nilla® Wafers

3 ripe bananas, cut into 1/4-inch-thick slices (approximately 3 cups)

Meringue:

4 egg whites

1/4 cup granulated sugar

1/8 tablespoon vanilla extract

Serves 10-12 depending on portion size

Preheat the oven to 400° Fahrenheit.

For the pudding: Whisk together the sugar and flour in a medium-size heavy saucepan. Gradually whisk in the milk until blended. Cook over medium heat, whisking constantly, 5 minutes or until thickened.

In a separate bowl, whisk the egg yolks until thick and pale. Gradually whisk about 1/4 of the hot milk mixture into the yolks. Add the tempered yolk mixture to the remaining hot milk mixture, whisking constantly. Pour into a clean saucepan. Cook over low heat, whisking constantly, 5 minutes or until thickened. Remove from the heat. Stir in the vanilla.

Toss together the vanilla wafers and banana slices and spread over the bottom of an 11- x 7-inch baking dish. Top with the warm pudding.

For the meringue: Beat the egg whites at high speed with an electric mixer until foamy. Gradually add the sugar, 1 tablespoon at a time, beating until stiff peaks form and the sugar dissolves, about 2-4 minutes. Beat in the vanilla with the last tablespoon of the sugar. Spread the meringue over the warm pudding, making sure to seal the meringue at the edges of the dish.

Bake the meringue-topped pudding at 400° for 8 minutes or until golden brown. Let stand 30 minutes before serving. Serve warm.

Owner Teddy Hontzas

PIE LAB
Greensboro

Chefs Seaborn and Kelley Whatley have a quaint little pie shop in Greensboro, Alabama. Saying that is almost the equivalent of saying Muscle Shoals has a nice little recording studio. Just as fans flock to Muscle Shoals for the music, pie seekers from around the world trek to Greensboro, Alabama, for the perfect slice of pie. Chocolate–Peanut Butter Fudge, Chocolate Chess, Buttermilk, Peach-Bourbon, Brown Sugar–Buttermilk, Key Lime Icebox, and many other Southern-heritage pies are rolled out by hand each week. I have eaten lots of Pie Lab pie, purchased at the Pepper Place market in Birmingham. (You must arrive at the market early because Pie Lab sells out quickly. If it is tomato season, well, you better just camp out in a tent in the parking lot to score one of their prized Tomato Pies.) *Southern Living*, *Garden & Gun*, *Food & Wine* and other publications have named Pie Lab to their "Best of" lists. Take a trip to Greensboro and taste why.

DON'T MISS: Besides pie, Pie Lab serves breakfast and lunch. The menu changes daily and offers specials such as meatloaf or chicken and dumplings with turnip greens and cornbread. The way I look at it is this: If you order a salad, you have saved your calories for pie. Nothing is better than Pie Lab's Apple Pie—except, perhaps, Apple Pie served warm with a scoop of vanilla ice cream. Quoting the famed author Jane Austen, "Good apple pies are a considerable part of our domestic happiness."

PIE LAB
1317 Main Street | Greensboro, Alabama 36744
334-624-3899 | ThePieLab.com

Pie Lab Double-Crust Apple Pie

PIE LAB

1 large egg yolk

1 tablespoon heavy cream

2 tablespoons fresh lemon juice

1/4 cup raw cane sugar, plus extra for sprinkling

1/4 cup all-purpose flour

1/8 teaspoon ground cinnamon

1/4 teaspoon ground nutmeg

1/4 teaspoon kosher salt

3 pounds Empire apples, peeled and sliced

1 tablespoon unsalted butter

1/2 cup toasted pecans

2 (9-inch) pie crusts (Use store-bought or make your own.)

Heavy cream, whipped, or whole-cranberry sauce for garnish, optional

Makes 1 (9-inch) pie (6-8 slices)

Preheat the oven to 350° Fahrenheit.

In a small bowl, whisk together the egg yolk and cream for the egg wash. Set aside.

Mix the lemon juice, sugar, flour, cinnamon, nutmeg, and salt in a large bowl. Add the apple slices and toss to coat. Dot with the butter. Fold in the pecans.

Place 1 of the pie crusts in a 9-inch pie dish. Add the apple filling. Top with the remaining pie crust and crimp the edges to seal, discarding any excess dough. Brush the top crust with the egg wash. Sprinkle with the extra cane sugar and cut several small slits to ventilate.

Bake at 350° 35-45 minutes or until the crust is golden brown. Serve warm with a generous drizzle of the whipped heavy cream and a dollop of the cranberry sauce, if desired.

Chef & Owner Seaborn Whatley

PANINI PETE'S
Fairhope and Mobile

Chef & Owner 'Panini' Pete Bohme

I've been a fan of Panini Pete's since 2006. When in Fairhope, I plan my day around getting to the French Quarter for a Mozzarella and Tomato panini. Everybody knows chef Pete Blohme, or "Panini" Pete, as he is better known. If you haven't seen him riding his Segway around the French Quarter in downtown Fairhope, you've certainly seen him hanging out on Food Network with one of his favorite guys, Guy Fieri. Panini Pete has been featured on several Food Network shows: *Diners, Drive-Ins and Dives*; *Guy's Grocery Games*; *Guy's Big Bite*; and *The Great Food Truck Race*. Panini Pete's paninis, burgers, and hot dogs are all on point. Everything is made from scratch. The mozzarella, aioli, remoulade, and other sauces are all made in house and the turkey and roast beef are roasted daily. Pete says his proudest accomplishment is co-founding the Messlords—a group of traveling chefs who cook delicious meals for U.S. troops on military ships and bases around the world.

DON'T MISS: Pete's Famous Muffaletta Panino, made with Italian meats and cheeses and an olive salad on rustic Italian bread, is different than its Crescent City counterpart but equally fantastic. As good as the sandwiches are, it might be the beignets that have folks lined up out the door. Pete's light, golden-brown puffs of delicious fried dough are generously sprinkled with powdered sugar and served with lemon wedges. It is the lemon that makes the beignets indescribably delicious. They are my weakness and one of my top Alabama cravings.

PANINI PETE'S
42 1/2 South Section Street | Fairhope, Alabama 36532
251-929-0122 | PaniniPetes.com

102 Dauphin Street | Mobile, Alabama 36602
251-405-0031 | PaniniPetes.com

Lemon "Jubilee" Beignets

PANINI PETE'S

1 cup self-rising flour

4 eggs

1/2 tablespoon vanilla

1 cup water

1/2 tablespoon granulated sugar

1/2 teaspoon kosher salt

1/4 pound unsalted butter

Oil for fryer (Canola is preferred)

Confectioners' sugar

Fresh lemon wedges

Makes approximately 24 depending on size

Place a sifter in a medium bowl. Measure the flour and then sift it into the bowl. Set aside.

In a separate bowl, whisk the eggs until blended and add the vanilla. Set aside.

Bring the water, sugar, salt, and butter to a boil in a saucepan. Remove from the heat. Add the sifted flour, all at once, and stir with a whisk to combine and form a dough.

Add the egg mixture to the dough in 3 stages, blending well with a wooden spoon between each stage.

Fill a fryer or Dutch oven with the oil and heat to 360° Fahrenheit. Using a 1-ounce scoop, scoop the dough into balls, and place the balls into the fryer basket. Submerge the basket into the hot oil. (If you are using a Dutch oven, carefully drop the dough into the hot oil. Do not overcrowd or you will lower the oil temperature.)

Cook about 8 minutes and then release the beignets from the fryer basket into the hot oil. Move the beignets around the fryer or Dutch oven using tongs or a slotted spoon and fry until golden brown and the insides are done.

Strain the fried beignets and transfer them to a bowl. Immediately sprinkle the hot beignets with the confectioners' sugar. Serve with lemon wedges.

RAY'S AT THE BANK
Florence

Owner Katrina Hudson

Relatively new to Florence, Ray's at the Bank is in the old bank building in the emerging restaurant and entertainment district on Huntsville Road. Owner Katrina Hudson features family recipes, sophisticated Southern cooking, smoked meats, and local entertainment from top musicians. Her father, Ray, is her business partner, and you can find his Firehouse Chili recipe on page 133. They have a large smoker on the premises that turns out competition-worthy barbecue. Guests raved to me about the pulled pork, ribs, and chicken, but it is the brisket that seems to have the most loyal fans. Lunch at Ray's features soups, salads, and sandwiches. Don't skip the Cornbread Salad, a local favorite. The dinner menu often features fresh Gulf seafood and prime cuts of beef. The menu and the atmosphere are casually elegant; you can get dressed up or go somewhat casual—both are appropriate. The Prime Rib is always popular and so are the Gulf seafood specials. I had this bread pudding years ago at another of Katrina's restaurants. I was so pleased to find it on the menu at Ray's! It is certainly one of my personal Alabama cravings.

DON'T MISS: Catch one of the special-menu nights or attend one of Ray's wine dinners, where the menu and wine pairings are created around a featured vineyard. The soups are made fresh daily as are the desserts. For lunch, try the Salad Trio or the barbecued chicken. The Lava Cake and Crème Brûlée are quite good.

RAY'S AT THE BANK
1411 Huntsville Road | Florence, Alabama 35630
256-275-7716 | Facebook.com/RaysAtTheBank

Southern Pecan Bread Pudding

RAY'S AT THE BANK

4 croissants

1/2 package silver dollar rolls

4 (6-inch) baguettes

11 eggs

4 cups granulated sugar

1 1/2 tablespoons vanilla extract

4 cups whole milk

Topping:

8 ounces unsalted butter, softened, plus more to butter the dish

1 pound light brown sugar

2 cups chopped pecans

Salted Caramel Sauce: (optional; you can use store bought.)

2 cups granulated sugar

6 ounces unsalted butter, at room temperature, cut into small cubes

1 cup heavy cream, at room temperature

1 tablespoon fleur de sel (salt)

Vanilla ice cream for serving

Whipped cream for garnish

Serves 6-8 This recipe requires that you allow the bread to soak in the custard overnight before assembly.

Preheat the oven to 200° Fahrenheit.

Cut the croissants, rolls, and baguettes into small cubes. Lightly toast them at 200° about 15 minutes or until lightly browned. Set aside and allow to cool.

In a large bowl, combine the eggs, sugar, and vanilla. Whisk together to blend well. Add the milk and whisk. Add the toasted bread. Cover and refrigerate overnight.

For the topping: In a food processor, combine the butter, sugar, and pecans and pulse until coarse and crumbly.

To assemble: Preheat the oven to 325°.

Pour the bread-and-custard mixture into a buttered 13- x 9- x 2-inch baking dish. Crumble the topping mixture over the top. Bake at 325° 1 hour or until the top is puffed and brown and the custard is set.

For the Salted Caramel Sauce: Meanwhile, melt the sugar over medium heat in large saucepan. When the sugar is a light amber color, add the butter and whisk vigorously until the butter has melted. Remove the pan from the heat and pour in the cream while whisking. Continue whisking until the cream is incorporated. Stir in the fleur de sel. Cool completely; store in the refrigerator. Before serving, heat the sauce slightly in the microwave so it can be drizzled. Makes 2 cups.

To serve: Serve the bread pudding with a scoop of the vanilla ice cream. Drizzle with the warm caramel sauce and garnish with the whipped cream.

WILDFLOWER CAFÉ
Mentone

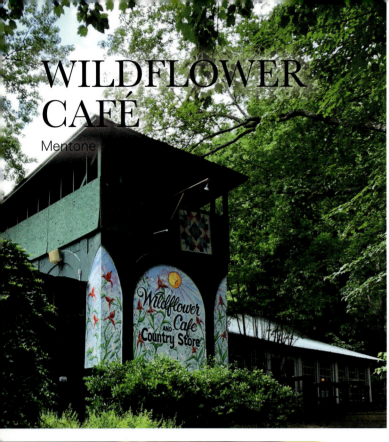

Laura Catherine Moon, a self-proclaimed hippie chick who grew up in Birmingham, left her home behind to see the world. Upon arriving on the West Coast, she became fascinated with the heathy-eating culture for which California is known. Moon, as she is appropriately known, began to learn about edible and medicinal plants and decided to come home to Alabama to hone her craft. She landed in Mentone, where she grew herbs and vegetables to study and sell to local businesses. One of her customers was Margaret Baker, the original owner of Wildflower Café. Moon eventually became a partner in the café, and it is now known for her organic recipes and gourmet café fare. The menu offers specials ranging from sushi to Mexican, with vegan, vegetarian, and gluten-free options available. Wildflower Café has won numerous awards and was named Best Café in Alabama in an *Alabama* magazine readers' poll.

DON'T MISS: The Tomato Pie is Wildflower Café's most popular dish and is highly applauded by locals and the flocks of tourists who come to the mountain town of Mentone each year. It is found on the Alabama Tourism Department's list of 100 Dishes to Eat in Alabama Before You Die. The recipe is just "not gettable," so I requested the Wildflower Crêpes recipe instead. (Which happens to be my favorite.) It is totally worth a weekend to visit Mentone when the trees are blooming in the spring or the leaves are turning in the fall. If you go, please tell Moon I sent you!

WILDFLOWER CAFÉ
6007 AL-117 | Mentone, Alabama 35984
256-634-0066 | MentoneWildflower.com

Wildflower Crêpes

WILDFLOWER CAFE

Strawberry Topping:

1 pint fresh strawberries

1/3 cup sugar in the raw

Sweet Cream Cheese Filling:

2 pounds cream cheese, room temperature

1 cups confectioners' sugar

3/4 tablespoon pure vanilla extract

Whipped Cream:

1 1/2 cups cold heavy whipping cream

3 tablespoons sugar

1/2 tablespoon pure vanilla extract

Crêpes:

8 eggs

4 cups unbleached flour

2 cups cool water

2 cups heavy cream

1/4 pound unsalted butter

Pinch of sea salt

Chef & Owner Laura Catherine Moon

Makes 8-12 filled crêpes

You can top these crêpes with your favorite sweet topping. Strawberry and chocolate toppings are favorites at Wildflower Café but a warm crepe with Nutella or Dulce de Leche topped with ice cream is also a winner.

Place a mixing bowl (taken from a stand mixer fitted with a whisk attachment) in the freezer for at least 30 minutes.

For the Strawberry Topping: Wash and hull the strawberries. Chop into small pieces and place in a saucepan. Add the sugar and cook over medium to medium-high heat, stirring occasionally. As juice begins to form, continue to stir and mash the berries with a spoon to create more juice. Cook until the juice thickens, about 15 minutes. Remove from the heat. Set the mixture aside to cool completely.

(Alternate method: Thaw frozen sweetened strawberries, reserving their juice. Place the juice and thawed berries in a blender and purée. Store in the refrigerator until ready to use.)

For the Sweet Cream Cheese Filling: Place the cream cheese, confectioners' sugar, and vanilla in a blender and blend thoroughly until smooth. Place the filling in a piping bag or a zip-top plastic bag with a corner cut to about the diameter of a nickel. Set aside.

For the Whipped Cream: After 30 minutes, remove the mixing bowl from the freezer and attach to the stand mixer fitted with the whisk attachment. Add the whipping cream, sugar, and vanilla and whisk on high speed until peaks form, about 45-90 seconds. Chill until ready to use.

For the Crêpes: Place the eggs, flour, water, cream, butter, and salt in a large bowl and mix well.

Heat a 9-inch skillet or a crêpe pan coated with non-stick cooking spray. Pour 1/4 cup of the crêpe batter into the pan and, rolling the pan, spread the batter thinly over the surface. (Note: It takes a bit of practice. You might mess up the first one.) Cook until the batter is stiff and easy to flip. (To test, gently lift the edge with a spatula to see if it can be flipped without falling apart.) Flip and cook about 30-45 seconds on the other side. Place the first crêpe on wax paper and repeat the procedure with the remaining batter. (The crêpes can be stacked directly on each other if you plan to fill them while they are still hot. If you plan to fill them after they have cooled, or if you plan to freeze them, place wax paper between each crêpe to keep them from sticking. With practice, you could cook 3 crêpes in separate pans at the same time.)

To assemble: Spread the Sweet Cream Cheese Filling onto the crêpes as desired and roll them up. Place the cooled Strawberry Topping in a squeeze bottle with a cap, or use a spoon, and drizzle the topping over the crêpes. Garnish as desired with the chilled Whipped Cream.

ZACK'S FAMILY RESTAURANT
Dothan

A little ditty about Zach and Dianne, two Dothan kids makin' the best fried chick-en... Okay, the singing portion of the show is over, but if you are looking for great fried chicken, you found it. Zack's is a "meat and three" home-cooking restaurant with a reputation for doing Southern food right. The menu rotates, so there are different meats, veggies, and desserts every day. One thing does not change: the fried chicken. It is on the menu every day. People line up like they're at Disney World for this chicken. It's so good it is served at wedding receptions. The side dishes can hold their own with the chicken. The cornbread and fried green tomatoes are on the Alabama Tourism Department's list of 100 Dishes to Eat in Alabama Before You Die. Owners Dianne and Zack Whaley greet every customer like an old friend; you'll see them working the floor to make sure guests have everything they need. For around ten dollars, you get a meat, three sides, dessert, bread, and a drink. And the food is homemade!

DON'T MISS: The Sunday Pot Roast has almost as many fans as the chicken. Chicken and Dumplings is called a vegetable at Zack's, and I'm perfectly okay with that! As far as sides go, Zack's is one of the few places with old-school stewed okra and tomatoes and those tiny butterbeans like my mom used to make. Make sure to try the desserts; there are about six each day. Don't skip the Banana Pudding or their famous Pear Cobbler!

Owners Dianne & Zack Whaley

ZACK'S FAMILY RESTAURANT
1495 Headland Avenue | Dothan, Alabama 36303
334-673-9225 | ZacksFamilyRestaurant.com

Zack's Famous Pear Cobbler

ZACK'S FAMILY RESTAURANT

1 medium can pears, chopped and can juice reserved

1 package Duncan Hines Butter Golden cake mix

1 stick butter, melted

Vanilla ice cream

Serves 8

Preheat the oven to 350° Fahrenheit.

Pour the chopped pears and can juice into a 13- x 9-inch baking dish. Spread the cake mix over the pears and juice. Drizzle the melted butter over the cake mix.

Bake at 350° until golden brown, about 35-45 minutes.

Remove the baked cobber from the oven and serve hot with a scoop of the ice cream.

STEEL CITY POPS
Alabama Chain: 6 Alabama Locations

Alabama popsicle king Jim Watkins has proven that popsicles are not just for kids, and the lines out of the door at any of their six Alabama locations proves it. Jim and the pop makers at Steel City Pops make luxury popsicles from all-natural and local ingredients using fresh fruits, seasonal ingredients, and the very best milk he can find. (Steel City Pops can also be found in Kentucky, Georgia and Texas. The Birmingham-born chain has grown quickly since it opened in 2012; there 23 locations and more to come. You'll see their Pop carts popping up everywhere; I was so pleased to see a familiar Steel City Pops cart at Joanna and Chip Gaines' Magnolia Market Silos in Waco, Texas! The pop flavors are inventive so be adventurous when you order; they'll replace it if you don't like your choice. Seasonal flavors like Toasted Marshmallow, Pumpkin, and Cinnamon Apple are highly anticipated.

DON'T MISS: The Buttermilk Popsicle. It has a cult following that spans generations. Try the Hibiscus or the Strawberry Lemonade if you like a fruity pop or go with a creamy classic like Chocolate or Coffee. If you like bold flavor, the Rhubarb may be your jam. You can even customize your pop; dip, dredge, drizzle, or dust your pop in extra flavor with chocolate, cocoa powder, coconut, or other toppings. **Tip:** In the winter, dunk a yummy Toasted Marshmallow pop into dark hot chocolate. In the summer, add a Lime pop to your margarita!

STEEL CITY POPS
Homewood, Highway 280/Greystone,
The Summit, Auburn, Huntsville, Tuscaloosa
SteelCityPops.com

Coconut Popsicles

STEEL CITY POPS

- 2 cups organic cane sugar
- 2 cups water
- 2 cups coconut milk
- 1/2 cup unsweetened organic coconut
- 1 cup heavy cream
- Dash kosher salt
- 1/4 cup unsweetened coconut, toasted

Makes 6-8 regular-sized popsicles

Combine organic cane sugar and water in a saucepan. Stir. Bring to a boil and immediately remove from the heat. Stir to ensure sugar is dissolved and allow to cool completely.

In a saucepan bring coconut milk, coconut, and heavy cream to a simmer for 10 minutes. Remove from heat, add salt, and let mixture sit in the refrigerator overnight until coconut flavor is infused into cream.

Strain off the raw coconut from the creamy mixture and add simple syrup. Stir in toasted coconut. Place in molds and freeze for at least 8 hours until firm. Unmold and enjoy.

Owner Jim Watkins

WASH HOUSE RESTAURANT
Fairhope

The Wash House Restaurant is a tradition for folks on the eastern shore of Mobile Bay, and it has been the area's go-to spot for special occasions for decades. Proposals, birthdays, anniversaries, rehearsal dinners, and wedding receptions are all celebrated at the Wash House. While known for special occasions, the Wash House is also just a Fairhope neighborhood restaurant and bar. It has a homey feel to it—even though it is a fine-dining restaurant with a stellar wine list. The rustic lodge-style décor has a romantic glow from hundreds of tiny white lights strung throughout the space, and the main dining room has a brick fireplace. I eat at the Wash House often. Sometimes, I will sit at the bar with friends for a glass of wine and the classic Wedge Salad with Green Goddess dressing. For dinner, I always struggle to choose between the Sweet Tea–Brined Pork Chop with Gouda Grits and the Seared Scallops. The pork chop usually wins.

DON'T MISS: Since the Wash House is in the heart of Alabama's seafood country, they pride themselves on perfectly prepared seafood. The specials are a safe bet, and The Wash House bar, a favorite gathering spot for locals, makes a mean martini. While known for their seafood and steaks, the desserts have a lot of fans. This Key Lime Bread Pudding makes a lot of "best of" lists; it was one of my most-requested recipes for the book.

WASH HOUSE RESTAURANT
17111 Scenic Highway 98 | Fairhope, Alabama 36532
251-928-4838 | WashHouseRestaurant.com

Key Lime Bread Pudding

WASH HOUSE RESTAURANT

5 (4-inch) yeast rolls (Use day-old bread, not fresh bread.)

Crumb Topping:

1/2 cup sugar

1 cup graham cracker crumbs

1/4 pound butter, melted

Egg Bath:

8-10 eggs

1 pint half-and-half

1 teaspoon vanilla extract

1 cup confectioners' sugar

Glaze:

12 egg yolks

3 (14-ounce) cans sweetened condensed milk

3/4 cup Key lime juice

Serves 6 depending on portion size

Preheat the oven to 425° Fahrenheit.

Cut the rolls into top and bottom halves about 1-inch thick, depending upon the size of the rolls.

For the crumb topping: Mix the sugar and crumbs in a bowl. Add the melted butter and stir until thoroughly combined. Set aside.

For the egg bath: Whisk the eggs, half-and-half, vanilla, and confectioners' sugar thoroughly in a bowl until sugar dissolves.

Soak the bread in the egg bath until saturated; at least 1 hour. Place the soaked bread on a greased baking sheet and bake at 425° 6-10 minutes, until lightly brown. Remove from the oven and scrape between the bread and the pan with a spatula to prevent sticking. Set aside.

Adjust the oven temperature to 375°.

For the glaze: Beat the egg yolks then whisk the egg yolks and condensed milk thoroughly in a bowl. Slowly wisk in the Key lime juice last.

To assemble: Line a greased 9-inch square greased sheet pan with the cooked bread. Pour condensed the milk-egg mixture over the cooked bread and sprinkle the crumb topping evenly over the top.

Bake the bread pudding at 375° for 12 minutes. Remove and allow to cool. Chill before serving so the bread pudding is easier to plate.

Desserts | 221

Leaving a legacy...

I would bet that when Mrs. Virginia Cobb opened her restaurant in 1948, she had no idea just how popular it would become. Birmingham residents flocked to her Cobb Lane Restaurant where they celebrated life's special occasions with Chicken Divan, homemade yeast rolls, Chicken Supreme, and her famous Chocolate Roulage. Even though Mrs. Cobb passed away in 1987, thirty years later, I frequently hear people reminisce about a dish they still crave from Cobb Lane.

Folks from Mobile still talk about Michael's Midtown Café, Constantine's, Trudy's Tiny Diny, and Gulas' Restaurant. Huntsville still misses the prime rib at The Fogcutter and the famous pretzel salad from Victoria's Café. The Tuscaloosa folks want Ireland's and those buttery Steak and Biskits back. Everyone in the state seems to have a fond memory of a trip to Birmingham and lunch at Britling's or Joy Young. Judge Roy Bean's in Daphne had that chicken sandwich with shube sauce, great music, and that famous goat.

Some of these timeless recipes have made their way into our kitchens over the years and have become part of the family. Even though the restaurants are gone, the recipes continue to influence new generations. I make a version of Mrs. Cobb's roulage (recipe on page 224) for my family every Christmas Eve. I hope my nieces will continue that tradition when they have their own families.

Mrs. Cobb left an indelible mark on Birmingham's food culture that remains to this day, as did so many others from cities all around Alabama. Including these "gone but not forgotten" recipes in my books helps preserve their legacy and takes those of us who remember these special places back to the good old days.

Martie

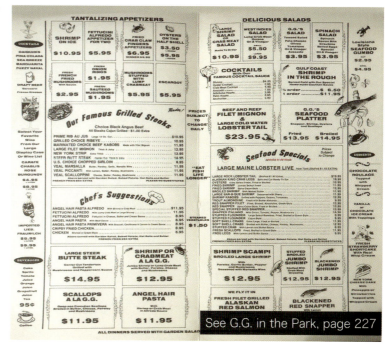

See G.G. in the Park, page 227

Gone But Not Forgotten | 223

GONE BUT NOT FORGOTTEN

Chocolate Roulage

COBB LANE RESTAURANT, BIRMINGHAM | 1948-2009

Chocolate Roulage was likely the most popular item on the menu at Mrs. Cobb's restaurant and is still a Birmingham favorite for holidays and special occasions. Cobb Lane was popular for birthdays; I even had my bridesmaid luncheon there and I feel sure we had Chocolate Roulage for dessert. Chicken Supreme, Chicken Divan, She-Crab Soup and the homemade yeast rolls were other favorites. You went to Cobb Lane for the food but also for the quaint back alley setting with tree-lined cobbled streets. It was vintage even way back then. I hated to see it go. This is my roulage recipe; I make it for my nieces every Christmas. It is not difficult, I made one in 30 minutes on *Food Network Star*.

- 1-2 tablespoons unsalted butter, softened, for greasing baking sheet
- 5 egg yolks
- 1 cup granulated sugar
- 3 ounces bittersweet chocolate, chopped
- 3 ounces semi-sweet chocolate, chopped
- 1 teaspoon vanilla
- 1 tablespoon espresso or strong, black coffee, room temperature
- 5 egg whites
- 1 cup cocoa powder
- 2 cups heavy cream
- 2 teaspoons confectioners' sugar
- 1 teaspoon vanilla extract

Makes 1 Roulage, about 8-10 slices

Preheat oven to 325° Fahrenheit.

Butter a rimmed jelly roll pan or baking sheet and line it with parchment paper. Butter the top of the parchment paper as well, especially the corners.

Fit a stand mixer with whisk attachment, beat the egg yolks and sugar on medium speed until fluffy and the sugar is not gritty, about 10 minutes. While the eggs are beating, put chocolate in a heatproof bowl and melt over a double boiler. When the chocolate is melted, remove from heat and let it cool a bit. (You may sit the bowl in some cool water for a minute, if necessary.)

Incorporate the egg mixture into chocolate by adding a little at a time to temper the mixture, so you don't cook the eggs. Add vanilla and espresso.

In a clean mixer bowl fitted with a whisk attachment, beat the egg whites until stiff peaks form. Incorporate 1/4 of egg whites into the chocolate mixture; gently folding until no white streaks remain. Carefully fold in the remaining whites into the chocolate, taking care not to deflate the whites but making sure not to have any white streaks in the batter.

Spread batter in the prepared pan and bake at 325° for 10 to 12 minutes. Remove from the oven and spread a damp tea towel or several damp paper towels over the top of the cake and let it sit for 20-30 minutes or until cool to the touch.

In a clean bowl, with whisk attachment, whip the cream, confectioners' sugar, and vanilla on medium speed until stiff peaks form.

Carefully turn the cake out onto clean parchment paper making sure to have 4-5 inches of excess paper at the end to help you roll the cake. Using a fine sieve or sifter, sprinkle 1/2 cup cocoa powder over the top of the cake. Use an offset spatula or butter knife to spread the whipped cream mixture over the top, leaving 1/4 inch on each side. Using the edge of the parchment paper, carefully roll the cake creating a jellyroll effect; tuck and roll as you go, peeling back the paper along the way. Put the rolled cake, seam side down on a platter, cover with plastic wrap, and chill 2 hours before serving. You might even put the cake in the freezer for an hour before serving so that it is easy to slice. Before serving, lightly dust the cake with cocoa powder. Carefully slice the cake with a serrated knife and place on chilled plates. Garnish with a light dusting of cocoa powder and fresh berries.

Drop Biscuits

COTTON PATCH, Eutaw | 1937-2008

Until it closed in 2008, the Cotton Patch was an Alabama institution. There have been various owners and a variety of incarnations since Cotton Patch opened in 1937 but the timeless traditions remained through to the end. The old building was destroyed by fire in 1975, but former owner Bradley Brown rebuilt, just down the road from the original restaurant, reopening in 1977. Long communal tables were always filled to capacity for the fried chicken, hand-cut steaks, angel biscuits, catfish, onion rings, and pickled watermelon rind. There is always chatter about Cotton Patch reopening here or there but until then, we have the biscuits, stuffed with butter and apple jelly, to comfort us.

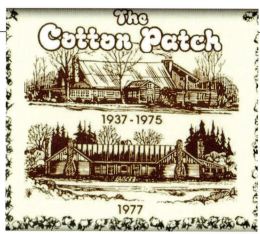

2 1/2 cups self-rising flour

1/4 teaspoon sugar

1 1/4 cups chilled buttermilk

1/2 cup butter, plus 2 tablespoons melted

Makes 18 biscuits

Preheat oven to 475° Fahrenheit. Line a baking sheet with parchment paper. You'll need a 2" ice cream scoop to drop the biscuits. If you don't have an ice cream scoop, you can use two large tablespoons to scoop the dough.

Whisk the flour and the sugar together in a large bowl.

Stir the buttermilk and 1/2 cup melted butter together in a small bowl. (The butter will clump but that is normal.) Stir the buttermilk mixture into the flour mixture until the dough pulls away from the sides of the bowl.

Scoop the dough and drop onto the prepared baking sheet about 1" apart. Bake for 12 minutes or until golden brown. Brush with 2 Tbsp. melted butter and serve.

Chocolate Gravy

Traditional buttermilk biscuits with chocolate gravy.... yes. Chocolate. Gravy. This old-school Southern treat isn't seen too much anymore. Back in the day, many farm families would make a skillet chocolate sauce or 'gravy' and turn their leftover breakfast biscuits into a sweet treat or dessert. Popular in North Alabama farming communities, you did not see it further South than Clanton. Restaurants used to offer biscuits and chocolate gravy but I've been hard pressed to find one that does. You can use your own biscuit recipe, or canned or frozen biscuits if you must. The key is to make sure the biscuits are nice and warm before you spoon over the chocolate gravy.

1 cup sugar

Pinch kosher salt

3 tablespoons cocoa powder

2 tablespoons all purpose flour

1 tablespoon unsalted butter

1 ½ cups whole milk

Makes 2 cups

Sift the sugar, salt, cocoa powder and flour together. Put butter in a cast iron skillet. Over medium-low heat, add the flour mixture and cook like you would a roux, stirring until it becomes light brown and you've cooked off some of the raw flour taste.

Whisk in the milk, a little at a time, whisking each addition until smooth. Keep whisking until there are no lumps. Turn up the heat to medium heat, stirring continually until it thickens.

Serve over hot biscuits which have been split in half and buttered.

Alabama Cravings: Gone But Not Forgotten

Dale's Steakhouse Apple Turnovers

DALE'S STEAKHOUSE, DALE'S CELLAR, DALE'S HIDEAWAY
Florence, Birmingham, Montgomery, Decatur, Huntsville | Opened in 1946
Most Dale's restaurants closed in the early 1980's. The Florence location closed in 2012.

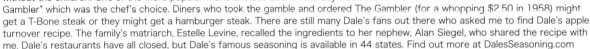

If you are from Alabama, you know Dale's. The illustrious Dale's brand began in 1946 as Dale's Cellar Restaurant in Birmingham. Either you grew up eating at one of the many Dale's restaurants around the state, or you used the mega-popular Dale's Seasoning to marinate steaks before grilling them at home. Or both.

It was a very big deal to go out to dinner at Dale's. Steaks, of course, were considered the best in town. It was a place you would go for a special occasion or a night out of the house without the children. One of the more popular menu choices back in the day was called "The Gambler" which was the chef's choice. Diners who took the gamble and ordered The Gambler (for a whopping $2.50 in 1958) might get a T-Bone steak or they might get a hamburger steak. There are still many Dale's fans out there who asked me to find Dale's apple turnover recipe. The family's matriarch, Estelle Levine, recalled the ingredients to her nephew, Alan Siegel, who shared the recipe with me. Dale's restaurants have all closed, but Dale's famous seasoning is available in 44 states. Find out more at DalesSeasoning.com

---

1 box puff pastry, thaw to package directions

3-4 large apples (Honeycrisp work well)

Juice from 1/2 lemon

3 tablespoons granulated sugar, plus more for sprinkling

1/2 cup water

2 tablespoons all-purpose flour, plus more for rolling

1/8 teaspoon ground allspice

1/2 teaspoon ground cinnamon

Pinch of ground cloves

1/4 teaspoon salt

3 tablespoons unsalted butter, melted and cooled

1 cup confectioners' sugar

1/4 teaspoon vanilla extract

2-3 tablespoons water

1 egg, beaten

Makes 8 turnovers

Remove the puff pastry from the freezer and allow to thaw at package directions. Set oven for recommended temperature for baking, likely 400° Fahrenheit. Prepare a baking sheet with parchment paper.

Peel apples; core, and dice. Toss with lemon juice. Place in a saucepan with the sugar and water. Allow to sit for 15 minutes. Stir to coat the apples and turn heat on to medium high. Cook apples until slightly softened and sugar is dissolved, about 5 minutes. Remove from heat and stir in flour, allspice, cinnamon, cloves, and salt. Allow to cool completely. The mixture should be thick.

Sprinkle flour on the work surface. Unfold 1 pastry sheet on the work surface. Use a rolling pin to roll the pastry sheet into a 12-inch square. Cut into 4 (5-inch) circles. Repeat with the remaining pastry sheet.

Spoon about 1/4 cup apple mixture in the center of each pastry. Brush the edges of the pastries with the beaten egg. Fold the pastry over the filling and press the edges to seal. Crimp the edges with a fork. Cut 3 slits in the top of each filled pastry. Use a pastry brush to brush the outside of the pastry with the egg mixture. Sprinkle with additional sugar. Place onto a baking sheet.

Bake for 20 minutes or until the pastries are golden brown. Remove from oven and allow to cool for 5 minutes on a cooling rack.

While the turnovers are baking, make the glaze. Add the melted and cooled butter to a bowl with the confectioners' sugar. Add the vanilla. Using a rubber spatula, add the water, a little at a time, stirring as you go. The glaze should be thin enough to drizzle but not runny. You may need to add a bit more water to achieve the consistency you desire. If you get the glaze too runny, whisk in a bit more confectioners sugar.

Place the cooling rack over the baking sheet with the parchment. Using a spoon, drizzle the glaze back and forth over the still warm turnovers.

Stuffed Lobster a la G.G.

GG IN THE PARK SEAFOOD, STEAK, AND LOBSTER HOUSE, Birmingham | 1969-1988

GG in the Park was a fine dining restaurant in Birmingham's Forest Park neighborhood known for steaks and seafood, specifically live Maine lobster. G.G.'s, as most of the locals called it, was one of the first places in the state to have a lobster tank. Owned by Frank and Joseph Brocato, it was the place to go for prom, homecoming, and other special occasions when I was a kid—sort of Birmingham's version of New York's Tavern on the Green. Stuffed Red Snapper, Veal Marsala, Prime Rib au Jus, and Soft Shell Crab were just a few of the favorites from their varied and extensive menu. Frank's daughter, Mary Ester, provided me with the photo of her father, and this recipe.

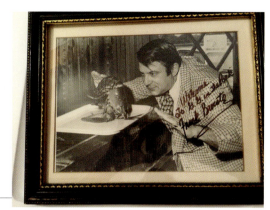

1 (2 1/2 pound) live Maine lobster

Stuffing:

1/2 cup crabmeat

1/2 cup breadcrumbs

1/2 cup fresh mushrooms, sliced

Salt and pepper to taste

Lemon, drawn butter, and paprika, to serve

Makes 2 servings

Preheat oven to 400° Fahrenheit.

Plunge the lobster head first into an 18-quart stock pot of salted, boiling water. Cover and simmer for 10 minutes. Cut lengthwise and split. Remove the vein and sac. Rinse under cold water. Then reheat for 3 minutes in the hot water. Drain and stuff.

For the stuffing: Combine all ingredients and bake at 400° for 15 minutes. Stuff into the lobster. Serve with lemon and drawn butter. Garnish with paprika.

Trout Amandine

ELITE CAFÉ, Montgomery | 1911-1990

Gump will tell you that none compares to the Trout Almandine at Elite Café. Known as the Elite and pronounced E-leet by locals, the celebrated restaurant was not just a Montgomery landmark, it was a way of life and the center of the social scene in Montgomery. Politicians, celebrities, and locals mixed and mingled; it is said Hank Williams' last performance was there in 1952. Browned butter is the key to the flavor. Watch the almonds carefully because they will burn in the blink of an eye. Once you can smell them, they are done.

1 cup all-purpose flour

1/2 teaspoon Greek oregano

1/2 teaspoon dried thyme

1/4 teaspoon dried rosemary

1 cup whole milk

6-8 trout filets, skin removed

Salt and pepper to taste

1 stick (1/2 cup) unsalted butter, divided

1/2 cup sliced almonds

Juice of 1 lemon, plus a lemon wedge for garnish

Makes 4 servings

On a plate or shallow dish, mix the flour, Greek oregano, thyme, and rosemary together. Put the milk in a separate shallow bowl.

Season the fish with salt and pepper. Dip it into the milk and shake to remove the excess. Dredge in the seasoned flour and again shake to remove the excess.

Melt half the butter (4 tablespoons) in a large sauté pan on medium-high heat. Cook the fish filets until they are golden brown. Flip and cook the other side and remove to a warm a platter in the oven. Set aside.

Add the remaining butter to the same pan. Brown the butter slowly by swirling the pan over the heat until the butter smells nutty and turns light brown. This is a slow process; cooking the butter too fast will usually result in burned butter. The butter will foam during cooking, which is what you want. Once the butter begins to turn pale brown, lower the heat and add the almonds, continuing to swirl the pan while stirring occasionally. Once the almonds are brown, add the lemon juice and season with salt and pepper to taste. Spoon the hot butter and almonds over the fish and serve while the sauce is still foamy.

GONE BUT NOT FORGOTTEN

Michael's Red Beans and Rice

MICHAEL'S MIDTOWN CAFE, Mobile | 1996-2013

Of all the restaurants which have come and gone in Mobile over the years, folks wax poetic about Chef Michael Ray Ivy and Michael's Midtown Café. The restaurant was a hit almost immediately despite its modest gas station beginnings. The inventive menus changed daily and featured what was seasonal and locally grown. In fact, Michael's was a farm-to-table restaurant before it was trendy. Chef Ivy did Southern food his own way; keeping texture intact and introducing flavors that were unique to Mobile at the time. Michael's Red Beans and Rice were a downtown Mobile staple on Mondays. Recipe courtesy David Holloway.

- 2 pounds China Doll dry red beans (kidneys)
- 6 cups ham or beef stock
- 3 large onions, chopped
- 2 tablespoons powdered garlic
- 4 tablespoons ground chili (mild) or Hungarian paprika
- 1/2 cup olive oil
- 1/2 pound butter
- 2 tablespoons salt or to taste
- 4 pounds smoked sausage

Makes 8 servings

Soak the beans overnight. Strain and discard water. In a large pot or Dutch oven, sauté the onions in olive oil until they start to caramelize or turn dark.

In a large pot, add the beans and cover with water to about one inch above the beans.

Add remaining ingredients and cook at low temperature for 3-4 hours until they reach the consistency you like. Serve with baked smoked sausage.

Holiday Cranberry Bread

ST. JAMES HOTEL, Selma | 1837-2017

The St. James Hotel was quite the showplace in its time. Opened in 1837 as The Brantley, The St. James is in downtown Selma's historic district. This hotel once offered beautiful views of the Alabama River and Edmund Pettus Bridge. It is the only surviving riverfront Antebellum hotel in the Southeast. Once upon a time, there were grand balls, afternoon tea service, and holiday celebrations. This Cranberry Bread was one of the hotel's enduring recipes and was always on the menu from Thanksgiving through Christmas. The hotel came upon hard times and is currently boarded up, hoping for a new life as a Grande dame once again.

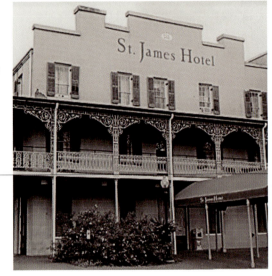

- 2 cups all-purpose flour
- 1/2 teaspoon salt
- 1/2 teaspoon baking soda
- 1 cup granulated sugar
- 1 1/2 teaspoons baking powder
- 1 orange for juice and grated skin
- 1 egg, beaten
- 2 tablespoons melted shortening
- 1 cup fresh cranberries
- 1/2 cup broken walnut pieces

Makes 1 loaf

This bread is perfect for Christmas breakfast. Sliced and toasted, with a bit of butter and orange marmalade, it's lovely with a cup of tea. This bread freezes well and slices better frozen. Use the sweetest oranges available, like Valencia.

Preheat oven to 325° Fahrenheit. Grease and a loaf pan with shortening. Set aside.

Sift dry ingredients together in a large bowl. Put the juice and grated rind of the orange into a measuring cup, add enough boiling water to make 3/4 cup and add to the dry ingredients. Add the egg and the melted shortening and mix enough just to moisten the flour mixture. Fold in the cranberries and the walnut pieces. Bake in the prepared pan for 45-50 minutes. Allow to cool for 10 minutes in the pan before turning out.

Veal Parmigiana

CARNAGGIO'S ITALIAN RESTAURANT, Midfield | 1954-2007

Loyal Carnaggio's customers still say there was no better Veal Parmesan in Alabama than the one found at Carnaggio's in Midfield. Toney and Vince Carnaggio featured their own Italian family recipes like Baked Lasagna, Ravioli, and pizza, all made from scratch. Birmingham area families celebrated their life's events at Carnaggio's and still reminisce about the family atmosphere and the food that tasted like a vacation in an Italian village.

- 1/3 cup melted butter
- 3/4 teaspoon salt
- 1/8 teaspoon pepper
- 1 cup finely crushed corn flakes
- 1/2 cup grated Parmesan cheese
- 2 pounds veal cutlets or veal steaks
- 2 eggs, slightly beaten
- 2 (8-ounce) cans tomato sauce
- 2 teaspoons oregano
- 1/4 teaspoon onion salt
- 1/2 teaspoon sugar
- 6 (3-inch) squares sliced mozzarella cheese

Makes 6 servings

Pour the butter into a 13 x 9 inch baking dish. Combine the salt, pepper, corn flake crumbs, and Parmesan cheese.

Cut the veal cutlets into 6 pieces, dip into the eggs, then dip into the crumb mixture. Place in the dish with in the melted butter.

Bake at 400° Fahrenheit for 20 minutes or until tender.

Mix tomato sauce, oregano, onion salt, and sugar in a saucepan and heat to boiling point. Pour around the veal and top each piece of veal with a slice of the mozzarella cheese. Return to the oven and bake for 3 minutes or until cheese melts.

Moo Goo Gai Pan

JOY YOUNG, Birmingham | 1919-1988

From 1919 to somewhere around 1988, Birmingham had a love affair with Joy Young, the first Chinese restaurant in Alabama. Located across the street from the original Tutwiler Hotel on 20th Street North, the restaurant was upscale and elegant with two dining levels plus private dining booths where many couples got engaged to be married. Joy Young was also known at one time for the best fried chicken in Birmingham, as the owners embraced both their Cantonese roots and Deep South location. I have heard hundreds of stories about dining at Joy Young—it was truly a memorable experience. My own parents went to Joy Young on special occasions. The egg rolls are the enduring favorite and people still talk about them. The other favorite was the Egg Foo Young—you can find that recipe in my book *Magic City Cravings*.

- 2 6-ounces boneless, skinless chicken breasts
- 1/2 cup peanut oil
- 2 cups bok choy, sliced
- 1/2 cup water chestnuts, sliced
- 1 1/2 cups fresh pea pods
- 1/2 cup celery, sliced
- 1 cup bamboo shoots
- 1 1/2 cups sliced mushrooms
- Soy sauce to taste

Makes 2 servings

Cut the chicken breasts into strips. Stir fry the chicken in the peanut oil in a wok or large skillet and cook until done and white throughout. Add the bok choy, water chestnuts, pea pods, celery, bamboo shoots, and mushrooms to the wok and stir fry until done. Add soy sauce to taste. Serve with rice, if desired.

INDEX

1847 Cocktail, 38

A

ACRE, 32, 52
ALABAMA CHANIN
 (The Factory Café), 105
ALABAMA GOVERNOR'S MANSION, 21
ARICCIA TRATTORIA, 146

Alabama Bushwacker, 37
Apple Turnovers, 226

AMARETTO
Alabama Bushwacker, 37

APPLES
Apple Turnovers, 226
Pie Lab Double Crust Apple Pie, 209

ARUGULA
Pork Belly and Watermelon Salad, 135
Seared Gulf Snapper, 149

B

BATTLE HOUSE, THE, 145
BAUMHOWER'S VICTORY GRILLE, 54
BAYLEY'S SEAFOOD RESTAURANT, 107
BELLE CHEVRE CHEESE SHOP
 AND TASTING ROOM, 56
BELOW THE RADAR BREWING COMPANY, 180
BIG BOB GIBSON BAR-B-Q, 76
BIG SPOON CREAMERY, 188
BISTRO V, 148
BOTTEGA & BOTTEGA CAFÉ, 190
BRICK & TIN, 108
BUZZCATZ COFFEE & SWEETS, 78

Baby Blue Salad, 117
Bam Bam Gulf Shrimp, 55
Bayley's Famous West Indies Salad, 106
Belle Chevre Goat Cheese Fondue, 57
Big Bob Gibson Original Alabama
 White Sauce, 77
Black Bottom Pie, 199
Braised Beef Short Rib, 143
Brussels and Kale Salad, 131
Butternut Squash Soup, 109

BACON
Brussels and Kale Salad, 131
Chicken Fried Bacon with Sawmill Gravy, 53
Classic Shrimp and Grits, 152
Crab-Stuffed Bacon-Wrapped Shrimp, 61
Curry's Southern BLT, 113
Hot and Hot Tomato Salad, 119
Lamb Lollipops, 181
Mobile Bay Stew, 115
Pork n'Greens, 169

BANANAS
Niki's Banana Pudding, 207

BARBECUE
Championship Bar-B-Q Rib Rub, 85
Pork n'Greens, 169

BASIL
Central Cedar Plank Salmon, 151
Hot and Hot Tomato Salad, 119

BAY LEAVES
Fisher's Pork Cheeks, 156
The Noble South Pickled Shrimp, 73

BEANS
Michael's Red Beans and Rice, 228 (closed)
Ray's Firehouse Chili, 133

BEEF (See also: Beef, Ground)
Braised Beef Short Rib, 143
Greek-Style Beef Tenderloin, 175

BEEF, GROUND
Mr. Tony's Spaghetti Sauce with Meat, 163
Ray's Firehouse Chili, 133

BELL PEPPERS
Lucy Buffett's Famous Seafood Gumbo, 125
LuLu's L.A. (Lower Alabama) Caviar, 127
Mobile Bay Stew, 115
SpringHouse Pimento Cheese, 65

BITTERS
Call Me Old-Fashioned, 33

BLACKBERRIES
Fresh Fruit Mojito, 47

BLUE CHEESE
Baby Blue Salad, 117

BOURBON
1847 Cocktail, 38
Black Bottom Pie, 199
Call Me Old-Fashioned, 33
Lane Cake, 21

BREAD
Key Lime Bread Pudding, 221
Southern Pecan Bread Pudding, 213

BREADCRUMBS
Hildegard's Authentic German Chicken
 Schnitzel, 161
Mr. Tony's Spaghetti Sauce with Meat, 163
Not Your Mama's Macaroni & Cheese (
 The Original), 87
Veal Parmigiana, 229

BROWN SUGAR
Championship Bar-B-Q Rib Rub, 85
Martin's Sweet Potato Pie, 203
Half Moon Cookies, 197
Pork Belly and Watermelon Salad, 135

BRUSSELS SPROUTS
Brussels and Kale Salad, 131

BUTTERMILK
Bam Bam Gulf Shrimp, 55
Butternut Squash Soup, 109
Cast Iron Skillet Fried Chicken, 155
Chicken Fried Bacon with Sawmill Gravy, 53
Ezell's Fish Camp's Famous Hush Puppies, 81
Fried Green Tomatoes, 83
Little Savannah Buttermilk Biscuit Shortcake, 201
Pimento Cheese Biscuits, 79
Reggie's Original Chicken + Waffles, 173

BUTTERNUT SQUASH
Butternut Squash Soup, 109

C

CARNAGGIO'S ITALIAN RESTAURANT, 229 (closed)
CENTRAL, 150
CHAMPY'S FAMOUS FRIED CHICKEN, 110
CHEZ FONFON, 48
CLASSIC ON NOBLE, 153
COBB LANE, 224 (closed)
COMMERCE KITCHEN, 192
COTTON PATCH, 225 (closed)
COTTON ROW RESTAURANT, 142
CRAZY HORSE, 58
CURRY'S ON JOHNSTON STREET, 112

Call Me Old-Fashioned, 33
Cast Iron Skillet Fried Chicken, 155
Central Cedar Plank Salmon, 151
Championship Bar-B-Q Rib Rub, 85
Champy's Shoals Homemade Chicken Stew, 111
Chicken Fried Bacon with Sawmill Gravy, 53
Chocolate Gravy, 225
Chocolate Roulage, 224
Chocolate Bourbon Pecan Pie, 193
Classic Shrimp and Grits, 152
Coconut Pecan Cake, 191
Coconut Popsicles, 219
Crab-Stuffed Bacon-Wrapped Shrimp, 61
Curry's Southern BLT, 113

CABBAGE
Jim 'N Nick's Coleslaw, 85

CARROTS
Fisher's Pork Cheeks, 156
Gulf Coast Paella, 183
Jim 'N Nick's Coleslaw, 85

CHEDDAR CHEESE
Heirloom Tomato Pie, 71

Melt Mac-N-Cheese Sandwich, 129
Not Your Mama's Macaroni & Cheese (The Original), 87
Pork n'Greens, 169
Vintage Mac and Cheese, 93

CHEESE (See also: Cheddar, Cream Cheese, Feta, Goat Cheese, Gouda, Mozzarella, Pecorino, Ricotta, Romano)
Baby Blue Salad, 117
Melt Mac-N-Cheese Sandwich, 129
Not Your Mama's Macaroni & Cheese (The Original), 87
Rigatoni Carbonara, 147
Shrimp Isabel, 59
SpringHouse Pimento Cheese, 65
Vintage Mac and Cheese, 93

CHERRIES
Call Me Old-Fashioned, 33

CHICKEN
Cast Iron Skillet Fried Chicken, 155
Champy's Shoals Homemade Chicken Stew, 111
Hildegard's Authentic German Chicken Schnitzel, 161
Moo Goo Gai Pan, 229
Reggie's Original Chicken + Waffles, 173
Ricatoni's Grilled Chicken Alfredo, 167

CHIVES
Belle Chevre Goat Cheese Fondue, 57
Gram Perkins' Egg Salad, 104
Hot and Hot Tomato Salad, 119
Rigatoni Carbonara, 147

CHOCOLATE
Black Bottom Pie, 199
Chocolate Bourbon Pecan Pie, 193
Chocolate Roulage, 224
Half Moon Cookies, 197
Peanut Butter Texas Sheet Cake, 205

CILANTRO
Brussels and Kale Salad, 131
Elote (Authentic Mexican Street Corn) & Grilled Cilantro-Lime Shrimp, 177

COCOA
Chocolate Gravy, 225
Chocolate Roulage, 224
Peanut Butter Texas Sheet Cake, 205

COCONUT
Coconut Pecan Cake, 191
Coconut Popsicles, 219
King Neptune's Coconut Shrimp, 159
Lane Cake, 21

COLLARD GREENS
Classic Shrimp and Grits, 152

CORN
Champy's Shoals Homemade Chicken Stew, 111
Elote (Authentic Mexican Street Corn) & Grilled Cilantro-Lime Shrimp, 177
Ezell's Fish Camp's Famous Hush Puppies, 81
Hot and Hot Tomato Salad, 119
Playa Gulf Ceviche, 69

CORNMEAL
Ezell's Fish Camp's Famous Hush Puppies, 81

CRAB
Bayley's Famous West Indies Salad, 106
Crab-Stuffed Bacon-Wrapped Shrimp, 61
Ed's Famous Crab Bisque, 123
Gulf Coast Paella, 183
Lucy Buffett's Famous Seafood Gumbo, 125
Mobile Bay Stew, 115
Stuffed Lobster a la G.G., 227

CRANBERRIES
Holiday Cranberry Bread, 228

CREAM (Half & Half, Heavy Cream, or Whipping)
Belle Chevre Goat Cheese Fondue, 57
Butternut Squash Soup, 109
Classic Shrimp and Grits, 152
Coconut Pecan Cake, 191
Coconut Popsicles, 219
Ed's Famous Crab Bisque, 123
Key Lime Bread Pudding, 221
Not Your Mama's Macaroni & Cheese (The Original), 87
Ricatoni's Grilled Chicken Alfredo, 167
Vintage Mac 'n Cheese, 93
Wildflower Crepes, 215

CREAM CHEESE
Ed's Famous Crab Bisque, 123
Freight House Strawberry Cake, 195
Wildflower Crepes, 215

CRÈME FRAICHE
Butternut Squash Soup, 109

CUCUMBER
Shrimp Isabel, 59
Tomato Salad with Cucumbers, Basil, and Lady Pea Vinaigrette, 102

D

DALE'S STEAKHOUSE, 226 (closed)
DAUPHIN'S and DAUPHIN'S BAR 424, 34, 114
DYRON'S LOWCOUNTRY, 154

Drop Biscuits, Cotton Patch, 225

INDEX

E
ED'S SEAFOOD SHED, 122
ELITE CAFÉ, 227 (closed)
EZELL'S FISH CAMP, 80

Ed's Famous Crab Bisque, 123
Elote (Authentic Mexican Street Corn)
 & Grilled Cilantro-Lime Shrimp, 177
Ezell's Fish Camp's Famous Hush
 Puppies, 81

EGGS
Ezell's Fish Camp's Famous Hush Puppies, 81
Gram Perkins' Egg Salad, 104
Key Lime Bread Pudding, 221
Lemon "Jubilee" Beignets, 211
Odette Red Curry Deviled Eggs, 89
Rigatoni Carbonara, 147
Wildflower Crepes, 215

F
**FISHER'S AT ORANGE BEACH
 MARINA,** 157
**FLORA-BAMA LOUNGE, PACKAGE
 & OYSTER BAR,** 36
FREIGHT HOUSE, 194
FULL MOON BAR-B-QUE, 196

Fig and Goat Cheese Ice Cream, 189
Fisher's Pork Cheeks, 156
Freight House Strawberry Cake, 195
French Blonde, 49
Fresh Fruit Mojito, 47
Fried Green Tomatoes, 83

FETA
Pork Belly and Watermelon Salad, 135

FIGS
Fig and Goat Cheese Ice Cream, 189

FLOUNDER
Mobile Bay Stew, 115

G
GAINES RIDGE DINNER CLUB, 198
G.G. IN THE PARK, 227 (closed)
GRAND HOTEL GOLF RESORT & SPA, 38
GUIDO'S, 60

Gram Perkins' Egg Salad, 104
Greek-Style Beef Tenderloin, 175
Gulf Coast Paella, 183

GARLIC
Rigatoni Carbonara, 147
Seared Diver Scallops, 144

GIN
French Blonde, 49

GINGER
Skylar Brown, 43

GRITS
Classic Shrimp and Grits, 152
Pork n'Greens, 169

GOAT CHEESE
Belle Chevre Goat Cheese Fondue, 57
Fig and Goat Cheese Ice Cream, 189

GOUDA
Not Your Mama's Macaroni & Cheese
 (The Original), 87
Vintage Mac and Cheese, 93

GRAPEFRUIT
French Blonde, 49

GREEK YOGURT
Shrimp Isabel, 59

GUANCIALE
Rigatoni Carbonara, 147

H
HIGHLANDS BAR AND GRILL, 100
HILDEGARD'S GERMAN CUISINE, 160
HOMEWOOD GOURMET, 116
HOT AND HOT FISH CLUB, 118
HUGGIN' MOLLY'S, 162
**HUNT'S SEAFOOD RESTAURANT
 AND OYSTER BAR,** 62

Half Moon Cookies, 197
Heirloom Tomato Pie, 71
Hildegard's Authentic German
 Chicken Schnitzel, 161
Holiday Cranberry Bread, 228
Homemade Peach Ice Cream, 16
Hot and Hot Tomato Salad, 119
Hunt's Oysters Supreme, 63

HAM
Call Me Old-Fashioned, 33
Hot and Hot Tomato Salad, 119

HONEY
1847 Cocktail, 38
Baby Blue Salad, 117
Chocolate Bourbon Pecan Pie, 193
Pork Belly and Watermelon Salad, 135

I
IRONDALE CAFÉ, 82

ICE CREAM
Alabama Bushwacker, 37
Homemade Peach Ice Cream, 16

J
JIM 'N NICK'S BAR-B-Q, 84
JOHN'S CITY DINER, 86
JOY YOUNG, 229 (closed)

Jim 'N Nick's Coleslaw, 85

K

KING NEPTUNE'S SEAFOOD RESTAURANT, 158

Key Lime Bread Pudding, 221
King Neptune's Coconut Shrimp, 159

KALE

Brussels and Kale Salad, 131

L

LITTLE SAVANNAH RESTAURANT & BAR, 200
LULU'S GULF SHORES, 124, 126

Lamb Lollipops, 181
Lane Cake, 21
Lavida Royale, 41
Lemon "Jubilee" Beignets, 211
Little Savannah Buttermilk Biscuit Shortcake, 201
Lobster Pot Pies, 165
Lucy Buffett's Famous Seafood Gumbo, 125
LuLu's L.A. (Lower Alabama) Caviar, 127

LAMB

Lamb Lollipops, 181

LEEKS

Gulf Coast Paella, 183

LEMON

Classic Shrimp and Grits, 152
Greek-Style Beef Tenderloin, 175
Hunt's Oysters Supreme, 63
Lemon "Jubilee" Beignets, 211
The Noble South Pickled Shrimp, 73
Thyme Out Martini, 35

LETTUCE

Baby Blue Salad, 117

LIME

Key Lime Bread Pudding, 221
Fresh Fruit Mojito, 47

LOBSTER

Lobster Pot Pies, 165
Gulf Coast Paella, 183
Stuffed Lobster a la G.G., 227

M

MARTIN'S RESTAURANT, 202
MELT, 128
MICHAEL'S MIDTOWN CAFÉ, 228 (closed)

Martin's Sweet Potato Pie, 203
Melt Mac-N-Cheese Sandwich, 129
Michael's Red Beans and Rice, 228
Mobile Bay Stew, 115
Moo Goo Gai Pan, 229
Mr. Tony's Spaghetti Sauce with Meat, 163

MACARONI, ELBOW

Vintage Mac 'n Cheese, 93

MAPLE SYRUP

Chicken Fried Bacon with Sawmill Gravy, 53
Reggie's Original Chicken + Waffles, 173

MAYONNAISE

Big Bob Gibson Original Alabama White Sauce, 77
Gram Perkins' Egg Salad, 104
Jim 'N Nick's Coleslaw, 85
Odette Red Curry Deviled Eggs, 89

MILK (Including Condensed, Evaporated)

Butternut Squash Soup, 109
Chicken Fried Bacon with Sawmill Gravy, 53
Classic Shrimp and Grits, 152
Coconut Pecan Cake, 191
Fig and Goat Cheese Ice Cream, 189
Key Lime Bread Pudding, 221
Martin's Sweet Potato Pie, 203
Melt Mac-N-Cheese Sandwich, 129
Niki's Banana Pudding, 207
Not Your Mama's Macaroni & Cheese (The Original), 87
Waysider Biscuit Gravy, 95
Wolf Bay Lodge Fried Oysters, 185

MINT

1847 Cocktail, 38
Brussels and Kale Salad, 131
Fresh Fruit Mojito, 47
Shrimp Isabel, 59

MOZZARELLA

Melt Mac-N-Cheese Sandwich, 129
Veal Parmigiana, 229

MUSHROOMS

Moo Goo Gai Pan, 229
Ricatoni's Grilled Chicken Alfredo, 167
Seared Diver Scallops, 144

MUSSELS

Sunset Pointe Bouillabaisse, 137

MUSTARD, (Dijon, Yellow)

Baby Blue Salad, 117
Pork Belly and Watermelon Salad, 135
Pork n'Greens, 169

N

NEW MARKET BBQ, 204
NIKI'S WEST, 206

Niki's Banana Pudding, 207
Not Your Mama's Macaroni & Cheese (The Original), 87

NILLA WAFERS

Niki's Banana Pudding, 207

O

OCEAN, 164
ODETTE, 88

Odette Red Curry Deviled Eggs, 89

OKRA

Hot and Hot Tomato Salad, 119
Lucy Buffett's Famous Seafood Gumbo, 125

OLIVES

Shrimp Isabel, 59

ONIONS

Top O' The River's Famous Pickled Onions, 91

ORANGES

Baby Blue Salad, 117

OYSTERS

Hunt's Oysters Supreme, 63
Mobile Bay Stew, 115
Wolf Bay Lodge Fried Oysters, 185

P

PANINI PETE'S, 210
PIE LAB, 208
PLAYA, 68
POST OFFICE PIES, 130

Peanut Butter Texas Sheet Cake, 205
Pie Lab Double-Crust Apple Pie, 209
Pimento Cheese Biscuits, 79
Playa Gulf Ceviche, 69
Pork Belly and Watermelon Salad, 135
Pork n'Greens, 169

PANCETTA

Rigatoni Carbonara, 147

PARMESAN CHEESE

Classic Shrimp and Grits, 152
Hunt's Oysters Supreme, 63
Lamb Lollipops, 181
Melt Mac-N-Cheese Sandwich, 129
Not Your Mama's Macaroni & Cheese (The Original), 87
Rigatoni Carbonara, 147

PASTA

Melt Mac-N-Cheese Sandwich, 129
Not Your Mama's Macaroni & Cheese (The Original), 87
Ricatoni's Grilled Chicken Alfredo, 167
Rigatoni Carbonara, 147
Vintage Mac and Cheese, 93

INDEX

PEACHES
Homemade Peach Ice Cream, 16
Seared Gulf Snapper, 149

PEANUT BUTTER
Peanut Butter Texas Sheet Cake, 205

PEANUTS
SpringHouse Famous Boiled Peanuts, 67

PEARS
Zack's Famous Pear Cobbler, 217

PEAS (Black-Eyed, Field, Green, Lady, or Spring)
Gulf Coast Paella, 183
Hot and Hot Tomato Salad, 119
LuLu's L.A. (Lower Alabama) Caviar, 127
Ricatoni's Grilled Chicken Alfredo, 167
Tomato Salad with Cucumbers, Basil, and Lady Pea Vinaigrette, 102

PECANS
Baby Blue Salad, 117
Chicken Fried Bacon with Sawmill Gravy, 53
Chocolate Bourbon Pecan Pie, 193
Coconut Pecan Cake, 191
Half Moon Cookies, 197
Lane Cake, 21
Pie Lab Double Crust Apple Pie, 209
Southern Pecan Bread Pudding, 213

PECORINO CHEESE
Rigatoni Carbonara, 147

PICKLES
Gram Perkins' Egg Salad, 104

PIMENTO
Pimento Cheese Biscuits, 79
SpringHouse Pimento Cheese, 65

PINEAPPLE
Shark Attack, 45

POLENTA
Lamb Lollipops, 181

POMEGRANATE JUICE/POMEGRANATE LIQUEUR
Lavida Royale, 41

PORK (See also: BACON, HAM, PANCETTA, PROSCIUTTO, SAUSAGE)
Fisher's Pork Cheeks, 156
Mr. Tony's Spaghetti Sauce with Meat, 163
Pork Belly and Watermelon Salad, 135
Pork n'Greens, 169

POTATOES (See also: SWEET POTATOES)
Champy's Shoals Homemade Chicken Stew, 111
Mobile Bay Stew, 115

PROSCIUTTO
Not Your Mama's Macaroni and Cheese (The Original), 87

PUFF PASTRY
Lobster Pot Pies, 165

R

RAY'S AT THE BANK, 132, 212
RICATONI'S, 166

Ray's Firehouse Chili, 133
Reggie's Original Chicken + Waffles, 173
Ricatoni's Grilled Chicken Alfredo, 167
Rigatoni Carbonara, 147

RAISINS
Lane Cake, 21

RED CURRY PASTE
Odette Red Curry Deviled Eggs, 89

RICE
Gulf Coast Paella, 183
Lucy Buffett's Famous Seafood Gumbo, 125
Michael's Red Beans and Rice, 228
Seared Diver Scallops, 144

ROLLS
Key Lime Bread Pudding, 221
Southern Pecan Bread Pudding, 213

ROMANO CHEESE
Ricatoni's Grilled Chicken Alfredo, 167

RUM
Alabama Bushwacker, 37
Fresh Fruit Mojito, 47
Shark Attack, 45

S

SAW'S SOUL KITCHEN, 168
SOUTHERN NATIONAL, 172
SOUTHWOOD KITCHEN, 134
SPRINGHOUSE, 64, 66
ST. JAMES HOTEL, 228 (closed)
STEEL CITY POPS, 218
SUNSET POINTE, 40, 136

Seared Diver Scallops, 144
Seared Gulf Snapper, 149
Shark Attack, 45
Shrimp Isabel, 59
Skylar Brown, 43
Southern Pecan Bread Pudding, 213
SpringHouse Famous Boiled Peanuts, 67
SpringHouse Pimento Cheese, 65
Stuffed Lobster a la G.G., 227
Sunset Pointe Bouillabaisse, 137

SALMON
Central Cedar Plank Salmon, 151

SAUSAGE (Andouille, Chorizo, Conecuh, or Pork)
Classic Shrimp and Grits, 152
Gulf Coast Paella, 183
Mobile Bay Stew, 115

234 | Alabama Cravings

Waysider Biscuit Gravy, 95

SCALLOPS
Seared Diver Scallops, 144

SEAFOOD (See also: Crab, Salmon, Oysters, Trout, Scallop, Shrimp, Snapper)
Sunset Pointe Bouillabaisse, 137

SHERRY
Lobster Pot Pies, 165

SHRIMP
Bam Bam Gulf Shrimp, 55
Classic Shrimp and Grits, 152
Crab-Stuffed Bacon-Wrapped Shrimp, 61
Elote (Authentic Mexican Street Corn) & Grilled Cilantro-Lime Shrimp, 177
Gulf Coast Paella, 183
King Neptune's Coconut Shrimp, 159
Lucy Buffett's Famous Seafood Gumbo, 125
Mobile Bay Stew, 115
Shrimp Isabel, 59
Sunset Pointe Bouillabaisse, 137
The Noble South Pickled Shrimp, 73

SNAPPER
Playa Gulf Ceviche, 69
Seared Gulf Snapper, 149

SPINACH
Lamb Lollipops, 181
Seared Diver Scallops, 144

SOY SAUCE
Reggie's Original Chicken + Waffles, 173

SQUASH (See also: Butternut Squash)
Butternut Squash Soup, 109

STRAWBERRIES
Baby Blue Salad, 117
Freight House Strawberry Cake, 195
Wildflower Crepes, 215

SWEET POTATOES
Martin's Sweet Potato Pie, 203

T

THE ATOMIC BAR AND LOUNGE, 42
THE BRIGHT STAR, 174
THE DEPOT, 176
THE FACTORY CAFÉ AT ALABAMA CHANIN, 105
THE GULF, 46
THE HANGOUT, 44
THE HOUND, 70
THE NOBLE SOUTH, 72
THE TRELLIS ROOM AT THE BATTLE HOUSE HOTEL, 145
THE WAYSIDER, 94
TOP O' THE RIVER, 90

The Noble South Pickled Shrimp, 73

Thyme Out Martini, 35
Tomato Salad with Cucumbers, Basil, and Lady Pea Vinaigrette, 102
Top O' The River's Famous Pickled Onions, 91
Trout Almandine, 227

TEQUILA
Lavida Royale, 41

THYME
Thyme Out Martini, 35

TOMATOES (see: Tomatoes, Green)
Central Cedar Plank Salmon, 151
Champy's Shoals Homemade Chicken Stew, 111
Ezell's Fish Camp's Famous Hush Puppies, 81
Gulf Coast Paella, 183
Heirloom Tomato Pie, 71
Hot and Hot Tomato Salad, 119
Lucy Buffett's Famous Seafood Gumbo, 125
LuLu's L.A. (Lower Alabama) Caviar, 127
Mr. Tony's Spaghetti Sauce with Meat, 163
Ray's Firehouse Chili, 133
Seared Gulf Snapper, 149
Tomato Salad with Cucumbers, Basil, and Lady Pea Vinaigrette, 102

TOMATOES, GREEN
Curry's Southern BLT, 113
Fried Green Tomatoes, 83
Sunset Pointe Bouillabaisse, 137

TROUT
Trout Almandine, 227

TURNIP GREENS
Pork n' Greens, 169

TRUFFLE OIL
Seared Diver Scallops, 144

V

VINTAGE YEAR, 92
VOYAGER'S AT PERDIDO BEACH RESORT, 182

Veal Parmigiana, 229
Vintage Mac and Cheese, 93

VANILLA
Fig and Goat Cheese Ice Cream, 189
Half Moon Cookies, 197
Lemon "Jubilee" Beignets, 211

VINEGAR (See: Vinegar, Balsamic, Rice, Sherry)
Bayley's Famous West Indies Salad, 106
Big Bob Gibson Original Alabama White Sauce, 77
Jim 'N Nick's Coleslaw, 85
Pork Belly and Watermelon Salad, 135

Top O' The River's Famous Pickled Onions, 91

VINEGAR, BALSAMIC
Hot and Hot Tomato Salad, 119
LuLu's L.A. (Lower Alabama) Caviar, 127

VINEGAR, RICE
Odette Red Curry Deviled Eggs, 89

VINEGAR, SHERRY
Gulf Coast Paella, 183
Tomato Salad with Cucumbers, Basil, and Lady Pea Vinaigrette, 102

VODKA
Thyme Out Martini, 35
Skylar Brown, 43

W

WASH HOUSE RESTAURANT, 220
WILDFLOWER CAFÉ, 214
WOLF BAY LODGE, 184

Waysider Biscuit Gravy, 95
Wildflower Crepes, 215
Wolf Bay Fried Oysters, 185

WATERMELON
Pork Belly and Watermelon Salad, 135

WHISKEY
Call Me Old-Fashioned, 33
Chocolate Bourbon Pecan Pie, 193

WINE (Red)
Braised Beef Short Rib, 143
Fisher's Pork Cheeks, 156

Z

ZACK'S FAMILY RESTAURANT, 216

Zack's Famous Pear Cobbler, 217

CONTRIBUTORS

MOESIA (MO) DAVIS | Photographer
Moesia is an Alabama native. She fell in love with photography at a young age and has had a camera by her side ever since. "Mo" has styled hundreds of food photos in her career and shot much of *Birmingham's Best Bites* as a photographer for Arden Photography. Mo shoots weddings around the country and many of Birmingham's social occasions and charity events.

ANN GRIFFIN | Production Assistant & Index Editor
Ann Griffin retired from *Southern Living* and Southern Progress Corporation after 24 years working in various capacities, the last being Photo Services Director for *Southern Living Magazine*. How can you work at *Southern Living* and not gain a keen appreciation for all things food? Her indexing skills and love of good food made working on *Alabama Cravings* a lot of fun.

TERRI JACKSON | Graphic Designer
Terri Jackson is best known for making things happen. It doesn't take long for her to turn ideas into reality. Her interests are wide and deep, and with more than 29 years experience in graphic design, she's got an eye for detail. Her career includes art direction at the Space and Rocket Center, running a successful freelance business, ownership of The Nesting Place, a retail gift store that was in Cahaba Heights, and is currently working full time at Cahaba Media Group as the Creative Director.

JOSH MILLER | Editor
Born in Birmingham, Alabama, Josh Miller has been obsessed with food after he started reading newspaper restaurant reviews when he was 9 years old. Fast-forward 30 years, and he's still wide-eyed when it comes to talking about food. The former editor of *Taste of the South* magazine and founding editor of *Southern Cast Iron* magazine, Josh has a storied love of good food. Whether he's trying out the coolest new ethnic restaurant or re-visiting his favorite local dive, he loves sharing his experiences with others so they can revel in the same deliciousness. When he's not helping Martie on her latest project, Josh can likely be found in the kitchen, cooking up something delicious, and probably making a big ole mess.

CAROLINE WARD SAYRE | Artist
Caroline W. Sayre is an artist/illustrator based in Miami Beach, Florida. Born and raised in Montgomery, Alabama, her work constantly references her Southern upbringing and heritage. Contact her at Caroline_W_Sayre@yahoo.com

ARDEN WARD UPTON | Photographer
Arden Photography specializes in celebrations, portrait, commercial, and editorial photography. Food photography has long been her specialty. Her collection of equestrian inspired prints can be seen in art galleries across the country. An equestrienne, Arden recently won her first horse showing riding for Windwood Equestrian, the Birmingham area horse farm and wedding venue she owns and manages with her husband, William.